The Dangerous World of Tommy Atkins

A Novice's Guide to Land Warfare

By

Patrick Benham-Crosswell

Copyright Statement

Acknowledgements

Writing a book is not quite the lonely solo effort one might think. I have received great support from many people in the protracted production of this book.

The inspiration to write this book came entirely from my two sons and their incessant questions. Once I had started writing they metamorphosed into my chief taskmasters, constantly demanding to know when it would be finished and when it would be published. The inevitable result of this was that they became proof readers and my test audience through the various drafts. They bore this (unpaid) burden stoically and waged war on my unfortunate addiction to the soft comma. They also ruthlessly identified clumsy prose and imprecise wording. As the reader you should be as grateful for their efforts as I am.

The knowledge for this book came from my time serving in and working for the British Army. I learnt a huge amount about soldiering and life from the many men and women whom I had the privilege to command, serve with and be commanded by. They shaped my life and we usually had great fun. We also played our small part in winning The Cold War and ending the troubles in Northern Ireland. They are far too numerous to list, and it would be invidious to mention one without mentioning them all. I thank them, profoundly.

Turning the typescript into a published book took more time than I imagined and was a quite tortuous process. Again, many helped – you know who you are and I thank you sincerely.

Dedication

For Fred and Tom

CONTENTS

Chapter 1 About This Book

Since the mid-18th century the universal nickname of the British soldier has been Tommy Atkins. Although its origin is obscure, by 1815 the name Private Tommy Atkins was used as a sample name in War Office lessons on military record keeping[1]. Throughout the subsequent quarter of a millennium Tommy's real namesakes have been killing and dying at the behest of the British monarch, government and (at least by implication) people. While the technology has changed and the locations vary the fundamental privations, bloodshed, pain and suffering of Tommy's life remain more or less constant. The name was immortalised in Rudyard Kipling's poem *"Tommy"* of 1892 and gained wide understanding after the mass conscription of the First World War.

National Service (as conscription was called in the UK) finished in 1960, the USA abolished the draft in 1973 and the last French conscripts finished their service in 2001. The military experience of the British public has therefore diminished from nearly 100% of males in 1945 to a small minority today; the result is a population with little or no direct experience of soldiering. An optimist would interpret this as a sign of a happy and peaceful society. However, the reality is that we are more frequently at war than at any time in the last fifty years and the last decade has been particularly hostile. 179 British soldiers died in Iraq; so far 446 have died in Afghanistan[2]. Over 2,200 soldiers have been seriously wounded – many in a "life-changing way."[3]

While direct experience of soldiering is diminished, modern media mean it is almost impossible not to be aware of warfare and some of its consequences. As Kipling shrewdly observed, the British people

---

[1] In the worked examples Private Thomas Atkins was in fact in the 6th Troop, 6th Dragoons, and therefore a cavalryman not an infantryman. Notwithstanding this, common usage over the past century has made Tommy an infantryman. Some British regiments refer to their private soldiers as "the Toms."

[2] As at 5 November 2013.

[3] The current euphemism for multiple amputees.

are deeply (guiltily?) fond of Tommy Atkins in times of war. Recently there has been public outrage at ineffective equipment (largely now fixed) and the treatment of the wounded – the extraordinary support given to Help for Heroes being one obvious indication. Similarly, there have been a number of excellent documentaries on training soldiers, leaders and combat in Afghanistan. These have been supported by personal memoirs, general histories and countless newspaper articles.

Unfortunately though, much of what you the reader, think you know of warfare comes from fiction. The fundamental problem faced by the makers of war films is that soldiering is 99% boredom and 1% terror – which is no way to produce a compelling plot. Reality is not as visually exciting as Hollywood (for example most explosions don't produce big yellow fireballs and lots of dark smoke) and is a good deal more gruesome – blast tends to rip bodies apart rather than toss them intact through the air. If anything, computer games have made the misconceptions worse. Combat is not an entertaining recreation, it's dead serious[4].

What is missing therefore is a general understanding of the actual mechanics of land warfare. Without this it is hard for the average member of the public to put observations, quotations, news footage and comments into the appropriate context.

This book is intended to provide the information needed for such a context. Bluntly, it will help you understand the inevitable consequences of a political decision to use military force, foremost of which is that some mother's son will kill another mother's son[5]. It explains how land warfare works, and why. As we shall see, some outcomes are dictated by geography, some by technology, others by biology and some by psychology. The outcome of any military action is therefore fundamentally uncertain – military history is littered with examples of the brave few defeating more numerous

---

[4] Why the President of the United States felt compelled to personally watch the demise of Osama Bin Laden is an open question. Clearly he was not directing operations, so the view was not operationally necessary. He had already given the orders, so it was not politically necessary. Executive voyeurism?

[5] It is also possible that some mother's daughter will end up killing some mother's daughter. We will look at the women in the armed forces later.

(or better equipped, or both) opponents. We will consider how soldiers are trained, and how courage is developed. These factors (which apply to all combatants on all sides) place constraints on what an armed force can achieve. Unfortunately they are often overlooked in the formulation of a politician's geo-political ambitions. The result is that wars are seldom, if ever, competed on schedule and never by Christmas! The price paid by victor, loser and non-combatants is usually higher than anticipated.

It is very rare for a country to start a war in the expectation of losing it. Similarly, few commanders choose to engage an enemy if they do not anticipate victory. While there is ample room for debate on the definition of winning, and there are occasions when countries are invaded with little warning or when military units are overrun before they could fight or withdraw, the outcome of combat is fundamentally uncertain – even to undisputed experts like Napoleon who somehow contrived to lose the battle of Waterloo.

Humankind is not good at history, even recent history. The First World War became known as the "war to end all wars" while it was still being fought, even though it patently was not; the Russian Civil War - between the White Russians and the Bolshevik Red Russians - kicked off in 1917 (with some 40,000 British servicemen involved). The phrase is still used, even though there has been a war somewhere every year since. The collective British understanding of how the First World War was conducted is flawed. Those who subscribe to what is sometimes termed the *"Oh! What a Lovely War"* school of thought are invited to read *"Mud Blood and Poppycock"* by Gordon Corrigan. Its compelling, evidence-based debunking of popular mythology will astonish.

The military, it seems, is little better at learning form history. During most of the 30 years of the "Ulster Troubles"[6] over 10,000 regular troops (plus another 10,000 or so part timers of the Ulster Defence Regiment and 11,000 members of the Royal Ulster Constabulary) were needed to secure the English speaking and broadly pro-British province from the activity of fewer than 2,000 IRA terrorists, who

---

[6] The Ulster Troubles were never officially a war, as that would have meant granting terrorists the rights of prisoners of war. The distinction is more political than military.

were increasingly competent but never fanatical. The initial deployment to Afghanistan involved substantially fewer troops, tasked to secure the generally anti-British (or any other foreigner), Pashtu-speaking population of an area larger than Ulster against the actions of fanatical, suicide-bombing Taleban. The Generals who briefed ministers to develop policy and then executed that deployment and most of their staffs had all served in the Ulster troubles. It is astonishing that anyone, including soldiers, politicians and commentators, is surprised or disappointed that there has not been a general outbreak of peace in Afghanistan after a mere decade.

Similarly dropping bombs on some of Gadhafi's weaponry did not cause him to spontaneously surrender any more than bombing Germany from 1940-45 made Hitler give up. Even after Gadhafi's weaponry was destroyed the rebels took a very long time to secure his downfall, in spite of dominant air-power. They have yet to produce a stable regime. Like marriage, war should neither be enterprised nor taken in hand, unadvisedly, lightly, or wanto

Many of the examples in this book come from the British Army, because that is the one I know best. However the general principles apply to battlefields, not nationalities, and thus are directly transferable to other armies. If one is going to select an army to study then the British Army is always a worthy candidate. For a start, the British Army has also been in existence for longer than any other army in the world, (its history starts with the restoration of King Charles II in 1660[7]). Thus the British Army (and many of its constituent Regiments) has more continuous history than most of the world's countries, or indeed systems of government.

Moreover, by virtue of creating, policing and ultimately surrendering the largest empire that the world has ever seen, the British Army's regiments have fought (and Tommies have died) all over the globe

---

[7] Being the British Army, this date is not undisputed. Most famously, the Coldstream Guards trace their history back to General Monck's Regiment, which was part of the Parliamentarian Army that fought (and won) against the forces of King Charles I in the English Civil War. However, since 1660 they have been second in order of precedence to the Grenadier Guards. They still harbour the grudge – as evidenced by their Regimental Motto *Nulli Secundus* or Second To None.

in all sorts of terrain. Wherever Tommy Atkins is sent to fight today, it is probably that one of his forebears fought there, or close by. This is particularly true of Afghanistan – the British Army had fought three Afghan wars by 1919 (plus countless skirmishes on the North West Frontier) before the current one.

One of the interesting effects of the British Army's unique[8] approach to organisation has been the Regimental System. This has been much misunderstood by the public and, regrettably, within some parts of the Ministry of Defence. One of the areas that we shall investigate is whether it makes a difference to Tommy that he is part of an institution with a separate and clear identity, or whether he would fight as well as part of a more anonymous (but bureaucratically more efficient) organisation.

The Invasion of Iraq has produced some unpleasant stories – particularly about maltreatment of detainees, torture and "extraordinary rendition". We'll look at how prisoners of war and non-combatants are treated. But we will do it from the context of Tommy at the time, rather than the ivory tower of a courtroom or a late night TV discussion after the fact. While there is and can be no defence of torture, it is simplistic and ill-advised only to condemn and punish, rather than to consider the wider picture in the hope of being better able to prevent repetition in similar circumstances in a future conflict. We'll return to this in later chapters.

We won't look at "extraordinary rendition" because that happens in the twilight world of intelligence and (possibly) special forces[9]. While that may or may not involve soldiers, it is not Tommy's world. The overwhelming majority of soldiers are not, have never been and will never be in Special Forces. Some of them could be and any of them could seek selection, but the Special Forces' recruitment process is arduous in the extreme. When special forces fight, they face the same broad problems of Tommy - the ground, the

---

[8] Many would say "quaint." Management consultants might be less charitable.

[9] The best known Special Forces are organisations such as the SAS, the American Delta Force or the Russian Spetznaz. They recruit from those already serving in the Army. There are other special forces groups (including in the UK) which are much less well known, and content to stay that way.

constraints of their weaponry and the enemy. Where they fight is, usually, at some distance from the traditional battlefield. Quite often the decision to deploy them is taken at the highest political levels, and in secret. However, the processes involved in clearing a house (and their consequences) are pretty much the same whether it is Tommy and his pals or Dave from the SAS actually doing the fighting. Dave is fitter, more experienced, a better shot and may have more specialist equipment, but the mechanics are the same – enter the room (possibly by blasting through a wall and often preceded by grenades), kill the bad guys, secure the area and move on. Simple on paper - not quite so straightforward in practice, as we shall see.

Before we can start you are going to have to lose some preconceptions. Recently there have been some excellent television documentaries on soldiering[10]. While these programmes give an unflinching view of what it is like to become and be a soldier (or marine, or officer) they can only provide snapshots. While these can be (and are) edited to produce a reasonable portrait of a small group of soldiers, they do not produce a complete context.

Similarly, the combat footage broadcast on TV news channels is filmed from the isolated viewpoint of the cameraman. As well as restrictions that may be in place on what is filmed by an embedded reporter for reasons of security, the fact is that standing up in a fire fight is very dangerous and filming from the bottom of a ditch can't provide wider understanding. As the late, great Professor Richard Holmes used to point out, if a photograph contains lots of soldiers standing up and running about in combat it has almost certainly been posed. In close combat you survive on your belly, and so are rarely seen by anyone.

This book has been written to fill this gap. It seeks to explain how all the various parts of the military machine work together to help Tommy kill Her Majesty's enemies. It will cover approximately the syllabus taught to Officer Cadets at Sandhurst, although you will be

---

[10] *Commando – On The Front Line* being one of the best, not least because of the total commitment of the presenter, which resulted in him being awarded his green beret as he had passed the Commando tests. The cameramen must have worked pretty hard as well.

relieved to hear that endurance runs, log races and boot polishing are not part of the reader experience. By the end you will understand the context of most of what you will see on the news, and a little bit more. Be warned though; it is one thing to read about it in the comfort of your home. It is quite another thing to actually do it on a cold wet night when you have not slept for over 24 hours. Please don't become an armchair officer cadet!

The military has jargon like a stray dog has fleas. I have tried to eschew it, but old habits die hard. Where avoidance has been impossible, I have opted for the most comprehensible version rather than the pedantically correct current ones. As this is not a military textbook the selection of clarity over precision does not undermine the validity of the message. Be warned, therefore, that quoting terms from this book to military pedants may make you a laughing stock.

If at any stage reading this book you form the opinion that Tommy is superhuman or, indeed subhuman, I have failed, as you are wrong. He is just an ordinary member of the population trained and motivated to do the extraordinary things that he does. Soldiers are as diverse as the population – with a wide range of strengths and weaknesses. Soldiering is by no means easy, but the overwhelming majority of the readers of this book could become or could have been a soldier if they wanted to enough – as their grandfathers and great grandfathers probably did in one of the world wars. Motivation is at the heart of soldiering, and as a result of our journey you will also gain understanding as to why soldiers went "over the top" in World War One.

Finally, this book is not about how wars get started or how they are won; that is the realm of military history. It is based upon the bleak assumption that there will always be wars, and the British will be involved in many of them. As British servicemen have died on operations every year since 1939[11] (except possibly 1968) this assumption seems reasonable. They die in your name and at your expense. This book explains precisely what it is that soldiers do, why they do it and how and why they kill and get killed. It is written in the hope that the next time a government is tempted to embark

---

[11] Plenty died before 1939 as well.

upon war the electorate asks politicians precise, relevant questions and demands decent answers before Parliament votes to "cry havoc and let slip the dogs of war" as Shakespeare put it. Or, as Tommy would say, "the smelly stuff hits the fan."

A modern battlefield is an incredibly complicated place. The technology involved is astonishing and much of it is at the absolute cutting edge, although some weapons (like the bayonet) would have been familiar to Ug the Caveman. Radios, computers, GPS receivers and thermal imagers abound. Aircraft, helicopters and satellites are all routinely employed in finding and killing the enemy. Bullets, bombs and missiles deliver death at varying distances, and the bayonet kills at close range. The air is full of radio signals, radar pulses and laser beams. Massive vehicles drive about, consuming thousands of gallons of fuel and oil. Roads are rendered impassable by mines; bridges are variously demolished and rebuilt. Trucks deliver men, food, fuel ammunition and all the other items needed to feed the military machine. And at the centre of it all is Tommy Atkins, tired, in mortal peril and frightened, trying to impose his nation's will through applying order to the chaos of battle.

Before we get carried away by the technology or the theories of command and leadership, we're going to have to start with the basics. At the risk of stating the obvious, land warfare is about ground, and who controls it. Whether the issue at dispute is the occupation of Kuwait, who runs Europe, the taxation of tea or who controls the policing of the Bogside in Londonderry, the key military question is who owns and controls the ground.

We'll start there.

Chapter 2 Tommy's World; Ground

Exploiting ground to our advantage is a fundamental military skill, so before we can look at weapons and tactics we need to understand ground as Tommy and his enemies see it. Ground is the chessboard on which our battles will take place, where and how our weapons will be used and where young men and women will kill and die.

Actually chessboards are pretty simple – it may be better to think of ground as a pack of cards. Depending upon the game you are playing, the queen of clubs can be valuable (as it is in bridge and poker), of no greater significance (as in snap) or potentially decisive (as in Old Maid). In the same way depending upon what you want to achieve, a geographical feature such as a hill can be of varying use and significance. Like a card sharp who can calculate the probabilities of the next card being the ace of spades and then apply this knowledge to perform better in the game, a soldier looks for bits of ground that will help him in his battle. And like the poker player whose four aces are beaten by an improbable straight flush, a professional soldier is always at risk of being killed by a lucky amateur.

The other reason for starting with ground is that you know all about it – you just don't look at it like a soldier does. So let's go for a walk in the country and look at it through Tommy's eyes. Imagine we've taken a bus out of town and are now at a country bus stop, halfway up a hill in the middle of rural England. As we look round and breathe in the fresh air the first thing that we notice is that we cannot actually see the entire ground surface. Trees yes, crops yes, hedges yes, but all the surface of the earth ground, no. Tommy tells you that the ground that you can't see is known as "dead ground." It is of fundamental importance.

DEAD GROUND, FORWARD AND REVERSE SLOPES

Dead Ground is the ground that you can't see. The drawing below shoes you looking at a house in plan and horizontal views.

In the horizontal view it is obvious that you and see nothing behind the house or through the tree trunk, which I have cross hatched. Less obviously, you can see nothing by the river due to the shape of its bank. Rivers are almost always a source of dead ground, and Tommy spends much of his time getting wet – no doubt taking comfort from the fact that skin is waterproof (but not bullet proof).

The area shaded grey in Figure2.1 shows where you cannot see the surface of the earth, primarily due to the fence. While you could see anyone walking upright, you wouldn't see anyone crawling.

Figure 2.1 Dead Ground

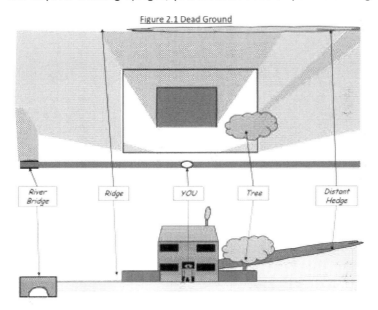

The fundamental point about dead ground is that we can't see into it from where we are. To Tommy that means that it might be full of enemy intent on killing him. Even if one of his colleagues can see behind the house and tells him that there are enemy there, Tommy can't shoot at them[12]. Of course it's not all bad news for Tommy – if he can't see the enemy they can't see him – so they can't shoot him either! Dead ground offers him a haven from the bullets of Her Majesty's enemies.

---

[12] There are ways round this, which we will come back to in the chapter on indirect fire.

It should therefore be obvious that soldiers like being in dead ground as it increases their life expectancy. However this state of ignorance has its downside, which is that the equally blissfully Ignorant enemy may come over the hill at any time. If Tommy wants to be safe and have peace of mind he therefore has to be in the dead ground, with a friend looking over other side of the hill, as shown below.

Figure 2.2 Using Ground – Forward and Reverse Slopes

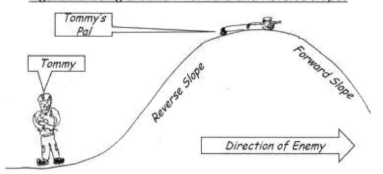

There is a bit of jargon that needs mastering; the side of the hill facing the enemy is known as a "forward slope." The side facing away from him is a "reverse slope." If Tommy finds himself on a forward slope he knows it means that the enemy can see him, and therefore shoot at him accurately. Worse than that, Tommy has nowhere to hide from the enemy's bullets. Forward slopes are best avoided. If they have to be crossed then it needs to be done at speed, or under cover of smoke (more about that later).

If Tommy is on the reverse slope, and in the dead ground, then he is safe. Of course, at some stage we're going to have to get at the enemy and take some risks, but we'll get to that in another chapter. If you remember that most of the time a soldier wants to be on the reverse slope and in dead ground you're well on the way to becoming a Rommel or Wellington[13].

---

[13] Wellington was a master at using reverse slopes, most famously at Waterloo where much of his infantry (and most of his cavalry) remained out of sight of the French, and therefore protected from Napoleon's cannons, until it was needed. At the end of the battle, when the Imperial Guard advanced over the crest they were surprised and dismayed to find

Unfortunately it is not quite as simple as that. Tommy's pal has a delicate balance to consider. Clearly if he stands on the ridge he'll be seen, so he'll be on his belly. As the Figure 2.3 below shows, the shape of the ground limits how far he can see, which in turn means that he can't see all the way into the dead ground. Of course he could crawl a little further forward, but that puts him on the forward slope, further into the enemy's side of the hill and in more danger. Tommy's peace of mind is at the expense of increased risk to his friend.

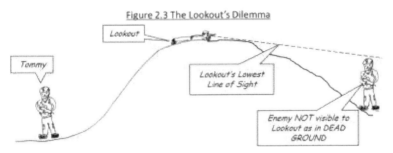

Figure 2.3 The Lookout's Dilemma

There is one other major point to consider about dead ground, which is what sort of enemy Tommy is worrying about. A man on his feet is about 1.8m high; if he lies down he's less than 50cm high. If Tommy's enemy is in a tank then it's about 3m high, possibly with a 2m high radio antenna on top of that. This changes the distance, or range, at which the enemy can be seen significantly, and reduces the effect of dead ground. While there are plenty of folds in the ground a couple of feet deep, in which a man can hide, there are many fewer deep enough to hide a four metre high tank[14]. The point to understand is that the same piece of ground will have a different significance with different sorts of enemy, and indeed types of weapon. This is exactly the point about the queen of clubs – whose worth depends upon the actual game that is being played. Unfortunately in Tommy's world it is not always obvious what game

---

ranks of Tommy's forebears there, pouring musket volleys into them. Job done, battle won.

[14] Military bluffers (including many who should know better) will often refer to open ground as "good tank country." Use of this phrase is a sure indicator that the speaker knows nothing of tank warfare. Good ground for advancing with tanks is completely different for good ground for defending with tanks.

is being played, or even who is playing. More than one game can be running simultaneously – but they all put Tommy in mortal peril.

Back to our walk. Now we have understood the concept of dead ground we will see it everywhere. As we stroll across a meadow we can probably see little folds where a man on his belly could get very close to us. If we lie down, we'll see that there are many, many more places that we can't see as our line of sight can be obstructed by a mole hill. Imagine for a moment that we actually are soldiers advancing towards an enemy. Every time we get up we enter an advanced state of paranoia where every bush and building could conceal our nemesis. Every time we lie down we know we're safer, or we think we are. Persuading men to get up and advance is why soldiering requires leadership as well as command, and we'll get to that in a later chapter.

Before we get too comfortable on our belly we had better just consider what we mean by "cover".

COVER

There are two sorts of cover that concern us here – cover from view and cover from fire. If Tommy is behind cover from fire, like in a ditch or behind a substantial wall then, even if the enemy knows where he is and shoots at him, the projectile will be stopped. All dead ground is cover from fire. However, if Tommy is only in cover from view, like behind a bush, and the dastardly enemy shoots at the bush, it won't stop the projectile. Tommy's family will be getting an unwelcome telegram.

It is also worth noting that the effectiveness of cover from fire depends largely on what sort of weapon is shooting at Tommy. A wooden door will probably stop a 9mm pistol bullet[15]. However a 5.56mm rifle bullet would penetrate. A .50" round would go through the wall or the door, and a 120 mm tank round could knock the whole house down. Obtaining the best protection from ground therefore requires Tommy to know about his enemy's weapons.

What we have learnt so far is that dead ground is the best place to be, or failing that at least in cover from view. At Tommy's

---

[15] Do not try this at home!

suggestion, we move into some woods, rather than cross open ground.

WOODS, HEDGES AND VEGETATION

The first thing that we notice in the woods is that it's darker – unsurprising as the leaves block out the light. This is significant – the less light that there is falling on us, the less gets reflected towards the enemy and the harder it is for him to see us. And better than that, the leaves overhead also make it harder for pesky enemy jets and satellites to see us. You won't be surprised to hear that Tommy spends much of his life in woods, and almost all stores and vehicles hide in them (unless they can find a nice building).

There are some problems with living in the woods. Firstly, if the trees are too close together, vehicles can get stuck. Tanks find woods particularly tricky terrain as the trees often prevent them from being able to traverse their turrets by getting in the way of their gun barrels. This makes the tank impotent and vulnerable. Secondly woods are very, very easy to get lost in – particularly at night when they can be very dark. GPS reduces this problem, but disorientation remains a threat. For example, the trees block lines of sight, so if Tommy is fighting in woods and drops to his belly he runs an increased risk of losing sight his pals. This is not good, as soldiering is a team game. Finally, if the enemy starts firing artillery shells at the wood the trees might start to fall over. This will block routes out – certainly for vehicles. Pictures of First World War battlefields, such as Delville Wood, show the effect of protracted artillery on trees.

Fortunately the enemy isn't playing today, so we wander out of the woods, back into the sunlight. As we go downhill across the meadow, glancing suspiciously at every bush and shadow while enjoying the sun and birdsong, we notice that the ground is getting softer and our socks are wet. There must be a stream up ahead, but before we worry about that we're squelching along in mud up to our ankles. While this is a little depressing for us it is highly significant to Tommy.

GROUND HARDNESS

While getting wet feet is never good, and can lead to conditions like trench foot, ground softness has other militarily significant effects. The first one is that it can change the way in which weapons perform.

As we'll see in the chapter on artillery, lobbing high explosive shells at the opposition is a common military pastime. If these have been set to detonate when they hit something hard but hit unusually soft ground they will detonate beneath the surface rather than on it. This dramatically reduces their effectiveness, as the blast is absorbed and dissipated by the ground and shrapnel (bits of shell case) is almost entirely stopped[16]. The shell is thus unlikely to cause the anticipated level of damage over such a wide area. The inverse is also true; if the shell lands on something hard, like concrete or rock, it is actually even more lethal as splinters of rock and stones will add to the fragments. We'll go into the details of how and why later, but poor Tommy will be worrying about this too.

As Tommy is an infantryman he has one other interest in ground hardness, which is how easy it is to dig. One particular tactic of infantry is to create their own dead ground by digging a hole[17] and fighting from that. Clearly it is easier to dig in clay than on rock, which translates into how long it will take Tommy to get safer. Generally the softer the ground is, the less time it will take to dig in. (Of course, if it's too wet Tommy may find himself standing in a pond of his own creation – uncomfortable at best – and he may need to shore up the sides with corrugated iron)

Tommy has a pal called Rupert who goes to war in a tank. Soft ground is a serious problem for Rupert; if it is too soft the tank will sink in, becoming bogged and unable to move. While it is likely that another tank will be able to pull it out, until it does Rupert's tank is

---

[16] In the First World War artillery shells fired in the (rocky) mountains on the Italian front caused 70 times more casualties per shell fired than those fired on the (muddy) Somme.

[17] Also known as a trench, shell scrape or fox hole. A shell scrape is less deep, and Tommy fights lying down. A trench is deep enough for Tommy to fight standing up. When he is not fighting the added depth improves the protection.

an easy target. Rupert will also be late arriving at wherever he was supposed to be, which will put whoever was relying upon his punctuality – which in the Army is pretty much everyone - at increased risk until he sorts it out. And of course, hitching up the tow ropes will mean that Rupert has to get out of his nice, safe armoured box and expose himself to fire that would otherwise have bounced off the armour plate. Getting bogged is a cardinal sin for tank soldiers.

RIVERS, CANALS, DITCHES AND BRIDGES

Returning to our walk, we find a path by the river bank and squelch along it while our feet dry out. Tommy is quite happy with this, as we're in dead ground. However we're beginning to realise what an obstacle a river can be. This one is not particularly deep (1 to 2 metres) or wide (8 metres) but the bottom is soft. Vehicles can't cross it, as they'll get bogged in the soft bottom even if they make it through the marsh on the approach. Infantrymen would have to wade, swim, or use a boat. On this fine summer afternoon the prospect of a swim might be attractive – but we would not want to do it in the winter. As Tommy explains to us, it doesn't take much of a river to be a serious obstacle to military movement. As he says this, we round a corner and see a road bridge. If rivers are substantial obstacles then bridges are hugely valuable.

Consider how many Hollywood movies, broadly based on fact, include bridges in their title. "A Bridge Too Far" is the story of how the allies tried to secure a series of crossings, ultimately over the Rhine at Arnhem, into Germany. "The Bridge at Remagen" tells of how Patton's 3rd Army managed to capture an intact crossing over the Rhine later in World War 2, while "The Bridges of Toko Ri" tell of the huge efforts the US Air Force and Navy put into destroying bridges on a supply route in the Korean War. These battles all make good drama as crossing rivers is a major military preoccupation, and the stakes are high.

As we shall see in later chapters, most armies have the ability to build bridges quickly. All we need to know for now is that rivers are almost invariably significant ground to a soldier. They don't have to be that big – armoured vehicles can be stopped by a stream if the ditch is wide and deep. Again, knowledge of the enemy's equipment capabilities is essential to making the most of the ground.

A possible solution to getting vehicles across a river is to design them to be able to float, or wade deeply. There are, inevitably, trade-offs that this causes which we will discuss in the chapter on tanks. No current Western tanks have significant swimming abilities – they need bridges or ferries. Russian tanks are a little different[18].

One special sort of river is a canal, which can usually be considered as a deep, steep-sided river with firm banks and no current. Canals give soldiers opportunities to transform ground from what would otherwise be passable land into a boggy morass simply by bursting the banks. For relatively little effort, a couple of earthmovers and some explosive, many square kilometres of land can turned into impassable lakes by emptying the canal – which remains a formidable anti-tank ditch.

We're getting ahead of ourselves, so back to our walk. We get to the bridge, climb up the embankment and find a pavement. We take it, and start heading for home along the side of the road, causing Tommy another panic attack.

ROADS, TRACKS, PATHS (AND RAILWAY LINES)

If we want to get from A to B, the quickest and easiest way is along a road. Generally the surface is smooth, dry and load-bearing. You can probably identify the problems that Tommy sees, chief of which is that road builders rarely construct roads exclusively in dead ground. Moreover, using the road is predictable, so if there is enemy about they will have arranged some unpleasant surprises. A road surface is hard – so if the enemy's surprise involves explosives

---

[18] The current generation of Russian tanks evolved from the T-72 series, designed in The Cold War. The Russian (or Soviet, as they then were) challenge was to get their army from the Iron Curtain to the Channel coast as quickly as possible. There are a large number of large rivers between Russia and the English Channel. The Soviets made the reasonable assumption that most of the bridges would be destroyed. They therefore designed all their tanks to be able to deep wade, and a range of specialist vehicles to be able to identify suitable tank routes on the river beds. This is a prime demonstration of how fundamental ground is to both tactics and weapon design.

and shrapnel it will be particularly unpleasant. If the road is on an embankment or in a cutting, Tommy (or particularly Rupert in his tank) may be stuck in a killing area[19], which is not conducive to health and happiness.

Of course, for moving large amounts of supplies a long way out of contact from the enemy, roads are essential. However in a counter-insurgency war sending stuff by road is dangerous; for a terrorist or insurgent setting up a roadside bomb is one of the easiest and surest ways of killing Tommy and his pals, and preventing them from dominating the ground.

We know this is true as many of the casualties in Afghanistan are as a result of roadside bombs. No one in the British Army should have been surprised by this, as they had the same problem in Northern Ireland during the height of the troubles[20] when bases such as Crossmaglen in South Armagh were only safely approachable by helicopter because of the IRA's widespread use of roadside bombs. However, if you can't or won't walk across country, don't have enough helicopters or want to move stuff that is too heavy for them to lift, you're stuck with using a road. It is an undeniable fact that the money saved by restricting helicopter availability is being paid for, over and over, in Tommy's blood and limbs in Afghanistan.

Generally if there is a suspicion that the enemy may be in the area, Tommy will avoid even a footpath as being too obvious and too open. In the same way, he will not use a gate but cut through a hedge, wall or fence. As you can imagine, this slows movement down and significantly increases the effort involved. Tommy regards sweat and time invested in staying alive as excellent value;[21]

---

[19] A killing area is a place into which lots of weapons can be brought to bear to kill you. Avoid them.

[20] The "Troubles" in Northern Ireland lasted from the deployment of British Troops in 1969 to the signing of the Good Friday Agreement in 1998. During this time the British Army supported the Royal Ulster Constabulary in the defeat of Terrorism. The terrorists themselves wend under a variety of names, broadly split into republicans, who wanted Northern Ireland to leave the UK and join Eire, and the Loyalists, who wanted to maintain the status quo.

[21] There is a military adage (one of many) "Sweat saves blood."

however there is always pressure to move fast.[22]   Maintaining a balance between speed and safety is another of Tommy's routine worries.

One particular terrain where paths become a problem is primary jungle, where there are very few paths and those that exist assume the equivalent importance (although not the traffic levels) of a motorway. Tommy will avoid these like the plague, preferring to laboriously cut his own path with a machete. This, of course, raises interesting questions about what to do when the path that Tommy has cut crosses another path cut by someone else. Jungle warfare is an extreme case of soldiering, and one that we will not consider in detail.

Returning to our walk, we are getting close to home and starting to rejoin the urban jungle. This is another extreme environment, and one that we do need to consider as many conflicts involve urban areas.

VILLAGES, TOWNS AND CITIES

By now you will have guessed how Tommy thinks about urban terrain. For a start there are substantial amounts of dead ground. When we were walking in the countryside we could see for miles – the average distance that you can see in open ground in North West Europe is about 1,300 metres. In a town this distance is much reduced, more so once you keep to the dead ground. Typically, it's less than 300 metres and closer to 5 metres if you are fighting inside a building. Urban combat is often described as a "three block war", the implication being that most participants only know about the building that they have come from, the one they are in and the next one down the street.

Tommy points out that most of the buildings offer excellent cover from view and fire. He is very nervous about glass – which adds significantly to the shrapnel effects of things like hand grenades. As most of the surfaces and walls are hard we can see that the urban

---

[22] It is a simple tenet of soldiering that whoever is leading an advance will never be moving fast enough to satisfy his commander – who is, of course, following sound in the knowledge that there is someone between him and the enemy.

environment is one in which explosive has the potential to be devastating. A grenade thrown into a room will have murderous effect – whether this is a good thing or not depends, of course, on whether you are throwing the grenade or on the receiving end.

There are some other worries. Generally buildings are not designed to have a war fought through them; too much explosive and the building will collapse, which will not be healthy for the occupants – including Tommy. Pictures of Stalingrad and Berlin from WW2, or more recently Beirut and Grozny, show the devastation that modern warfare wreaks on cities.

Tommy's war also becomes three dimensional – when he moves into a building he has to clear it from top to bottom, which can be a long and arduous process. Sewers, drains and underground railways and tunnels become covered approaches, creating the permanent risk of enemy emerging almost anywhere. The added dimension of height also worries Rupert – his tank has lots of thick armour on the front and sides, but it is relatively thin on top. There are also limits on how high he can elevate his gun. The normal infrastructure of cities also caused problems – gas mains catch fire, water mains rupture and cause flooding. Rats bite and spread disease. Worst of all are the inhabitants, who are caught up in the fighting.

In open countryside generally people are few and far between, and have room to keep out of the way of the war. In a village, town or city they are everywhere and inevitably become entwined in combat. Being a Brit, Tommy is compassionate and does not want to kill women and children – but how can he know if there are non-combatants in a room also occupied by an enemy sniper who is trying to kill him? His unenviable choice is throw a grenade and accept the risk that he might have killed a mother and her young children, or don't and risk dying. It is hardly surprising that post-traumatic stress disorder is so rife.

Furthermore, non-combatants may not be neutral – they may well sympathise with the enemy. This a particular concern in peacekeeping operations. Again, this is the subject for a later chapter, but it's hard to win hearts and minds if Tommy is forced to deploy all the firepower at his disposal in the non-combatants' back yard.

WEATHER

As the news regularly shows, weather can have a profound effect upon ground. Heavy rain fills rivers, floods plains and turns hard ground into bogs. Snow turns everything white (tricky for Tommy's camouflage) and, if accompanied by frost can turn impassable bogs and lakes into firm ground – at least on the surface, until someone starts lobbing artillery shells about. All of this impacts on Tommy as he has to reconsider his assessment of ground.

It also has a more direct effect, which is that Tommy gets wet and cold. Hypothermia is a constant risk for soldiers, particularly if they are dug in infantry standing in a trench. A heavy rainstorm turns a trench into a pond, soaking the inhabitants and their equipment. A cold wet soldier is far less observant and alert than a dry one. While some of the effects of rain can be mitigated by decent waterproof clothing (the inventor of Gore-Tex should, in the opinion of most soldiers, be beatified[23]), protracted damp causes other problems. These include gun sights misting up, both outside and in. The latter means that the sight requires desiccation[24] before Tommy can use it again.

Inevitably pens don't work, making it hard to write the orders in anything other than pencil. Unfortunately the paper turns soggy, which makes it hard to write on (even in pencil). Generally, electronics stop performing as advertised (although most pieces of military equipment are designed to cope with poor weather the ability of damp to penetrate "weather-proof" seals is astonishing). The moisture in the air reduces visibility, which means that the enemy can get closer without being seen and destroyed and low clouds make it hard for aircraft to attack ground targets.

A prolonged heat spell is no less hassle. At the basic level Tommy now runs the risk of dehydration and heat exhaustion, which means that he needs to carry more (heavy) water. Dry ground converts to dust, particularly when a tracked vehicle drives over it. This dust

---

[23] Inevitably, the British Army took an inordinately long time to actually issue Gore Tex to its soldiers. Poorly paid private soldiers invested in purchasing their own, at a cost of several days' pay.

[24] Desiccation is a process that removes water vapour – in this case from the spaces between the many lenses and mirrors that make a gun sight.

can be seen for miles and at the same time is hard to see through. In extreme heat engines and electronics will overheat, denying Tommy their use.

Wind alters the trajectory of projectiles, which we will cover in the next chapter. It also creates wind chill and dust storms. The former brings Tommy closer to hypothermia, the latter blinds him. Wind also moves smoke about which is infuriating if one is trying to build a smoke screen. Strong winds blow trees down, which makes getting though woods harder and more demanding.

One other point to consider about wind is that it varies in strength and direction depending on where you are. Of course, as anyone who has watched a winter soccer or rugby match knows, trees, ridges and buildings all act as windbreaks. In a town streets act as wind tunnels. The wind also changes strength and direction as you rise above the earth's surface. This doesn't affect you or Tommy much, but snipers, pilots and artillerymen have to consider it.

SEASONS

While seasonal change is not a problem during a battle, it can play merry hell with planning. One obvious seasonal effect is that deciduous foliage falls from trees. What may have been impenetrable cover from view behind a hedge or wood in the spring will change into an open position, protected only by a few tree trunks and twigs by the winter. Similarly, an open field in February may well contain six foot high maize by September.

Of course, the weather will change too. Perhaps the most dramatic example is from World War 2, on the Russian steppes. While the Germans were perfectly able to cope in the summer, the transformation from summer to winter massively reduced the German's ability to fight, or even survive. The extreme cold often stopped artillery guns from firing as the oil in their recoil system became too thick. The thaw turned roads into rivers of mud, preventing fuel and ammunition from getting to the panzers. A panzer with no fuel or ammunition is less use that a chocolate fireguard.

Some metals change their properties at around zero degrees. It is rumoured that when Napoleon's armies encountered the Russian winter the tin from which their buttons were made changed form, becoming brittle and broke[25]. It's bad enough to be wading through snowdrifts fighting a desperate battle against marauding Cossacks without your trousers falling down!

While plastic and Velcro may have solved the trouser problem, modern weapons are required to work anywhere, any time. This means operating in a temperature range of about -50°C to +50°C. Modern weapons are complex and contain a multiplicity of different materials, all of which expand and contract by differing amounts as temperatures change. The complex engineering required to make them perform in all conditions is not cheap.

CLIMATE

The effects of climate on Tommy are really an aggregation of protracted weather extremes. For all armies, fighting out of their home climate is an added challenge. The problems can be mitigated, but only by those who appreciate that the problems occur from the ground level up. In the Iraq wars, where temperature inside tank turrets regularly exceeded 60°C the crews must have blessed the accountant who, as a cost-saving measure, cancelled air conditioning for the Challenger tank.

High altitudes cause problems, mostly through the thin air playing hell with aircraft performance and, to a lesser extent, ballistics. Soldiers also need time to acclimatise to thinner air with less oxygen in it. Arctic warfare is almost a separate occupation. Effectively it is a protracted survival test against the elements, with combat only being sensible when the weather is sufficiently benign – broadly when it is warmer than -40C. Tropical jungle manages to combine some of the worst problems of heat with the penetrating power of moisture. As with all climates, the key to success is well thought through equipment and procedures, timing and acclimatisation. And remember, Tommy is not in these places as a tourist – he is there to fight an enemy who probably is used to the conditions.

So as we finally walk up the steps into our house after our stroll, we understand that soldiers see the world differently. Their

---

[25] Tin changes from its malleable β form to the brittle α form at 10°C, although the process takes time so the debagging would not be immediate.

understanding of ground is a matter of life and death. It constrains where they can go in safety, how they can use their weapons and how long they will live. We have also seen that the ground changes how weapons work, so now is a good time to consider Tommy's weaponry.

Chapter 3 Tommy's Tools; Direct Fire Weapons

The history of human society is interwoven with the development of weapons. Once Ug the Caveman realised that a spear or rock made hunting food easier it did not take him long to realise that anything that could kill a mammoth could also kill *homo sapiens;* the evolution of weapon and counter weapon has continued ever since.

Before considering Tommy's weaponry we had better consider what he requires from his weapon. Tommy wants it to remove the enemy from the fight, preventing him threatening the health and wellbeing of Tommy and his pals. Whether this is achieved through killing the enemy, incapacitating him or suppressing him is immaterial. The important point is that the enemy no longer poses a threat.[26] So let us consider the human being as a target.

Essentially the body is a complicated machine comprising a number of vital organs connected by blood vessels, held in shape by a skeleton and kept entire by skin. To incapacitate it we need to stop one or more of the vital organs working. There are a number of ways in that Tommy can do this. Option one is to bash it, so that either the organ ruptures or the skeleton can't support it. Ug the caveman did this with clubs; Tommy uses blast. An overpressure of about 15 pounds per square inch (under half the pressure of a car tyre) will rupture lungs, and a body that can't breathe is not viable. Blast may also rip off limbs, as we have seen all too often from Iraq and Afghanistan, which while not necessarily lethal incapacitate.

Another approach is to knock a hole in the body. At the least this will cause fluids to leak – and we may hit and damage a vital organ. Ug did this with a sharpened stick; Tommy does this with bullets, bayonets and shrapnel.

---

[26] There is a debate that occasionally rages about whether it is necessary to kill, and in some situations "less than lethal weapons" have a useful role. We will touch on this in a later chapter; at the moment Tommy's aim remains to remove the enemy from the battle.

Setting the enemy's body on fire will damage it. Ug wasn't too good at this; although once civilisation[27] got as far as vats of burning oil fire became commonplace, particularly in sieges. Nowadays Tommy uses napalm[28] and white phosphorous.

Alternatively we could poison it – effectively either by polluting the air enough to destroy lungs, (achieved by mustard gas and phosgene), or by introducing toxins into the body that make the nervous system go into spasm eventually leading to heart failure. Nerve gases like Sarin and Toban work like this. Alternatively we could infect it with a virus or bacteria. This was common enough in mediaeval times, where rotting carcasses were catapulted into besieged cities. Biological warfare is more sophisticated now, but (arguably) seldom used[29]. Finally we could irradiate it – through using an atomic bomb. Using atomic bombs and chemical weapons is, thankfully, uncommon[30] and has wider consequences. Nuclear, biological and chemical weapons are covered in Appendix Three; we'll start on the rest here.

We have looked at the weapon effects – what happens at the enemy end. But the whole process starts at Tommy's end where the weapon itself is. Think back to the last chapter and dead ground – the part of the land surface that Tommy can't see. There are two

---

[27] It may not be flattering to humankind, but advanced weapons are a feature of an advanced civilisations – less advanced civilisations lack the infrastructure (tangible and intangible) to produce advanced weapons, or indeed healthcare. If they're fortunate enough to sit on mineral reserves they can of course buy them, and if they pledge allegiance to an ideology they may be given them.

[28] Napalm stands for **na**phthenic acid and **palm**itic acid, which was the original formulation. More recent versions (from our more advanced and sophisticated civilisation) use different ingredients but the effect is the same. This advance enabled a spin doctor to deny that US forces were using Napalm in operations in Iraq and Afghanistan. While he may have appreciated the difference those on the receiving end won't have noticed.

[29] The argument stems from debate about where the barrier between chemical and biologic weapons is. Toxins, a chemical secreted by a biological organism are a grey area. Most accept that the Al Qaeda anthrax attacks in the US post the 911 attacks was the last

[30] Although when Saddam was in charge of Iraq the Kurds suffered several chemical weapon induced massacres.

ways in which Tommy can become aware of the enemy – either he can see them directly himself or one of his colleagues can see the enemy, but Tommy can't. In the first case Tommy can engage[31] the enemy directly, hence the term "direct fire," which we'll look at now. Indirect fire (which is the engagement of an enemy that can't be seen from the weapon's location) will be covered in Chapter 5.

Direct fire weapons are the ones that you are most familiar with – you see them in movies all the time and you may well have fired one yourself – pistols, rifles and some machine-guns. They all kill by using a bullet to knock a hole in an enemy. The tricky bit is getting the bullet to hit the target, but before we move on to that lets just consider how firearms work. As this is not a book about weapons I have simplified it a bit, and put more detail in Appendix One.

Figure 3.1 below shows a round of ammunition in the breech of a gun, ready to fire. With very few exceptions[32] all modern direct fire guns have pretty much the same arrangement. The round consists of three parts; a bullet or projectile, a cartridge case containing propellant (usually cordite) and a primer which is there to ignite the propellant. The bullet has a soft copper drive band to engage in the rifling (all gun barrels are rifled nowadays) and provide a seal.

---

[31] "Engage" in a military sense means "start killing (or incapacitating)."
[32] Inevitably, the British Challenger tank gun is one.

Figure 3.1 – A Round in the Breech of a Gun

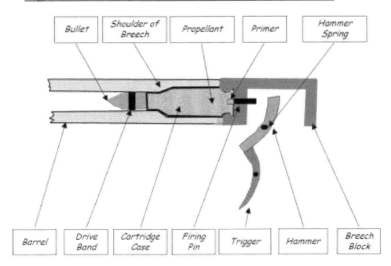

The cartridge is held tight against the shoulders of the breech by the breech block, which is locked in position, unless the weapon is a pistol or simple sub machine gun, in which case the breech is held in position by a spring. The hammer is cocked, held against the hammer spring's pressure by the trigger.

When Tommy reckons that his weapon is pointing at the target he squeezes the trigger, thereby releasing tension in the hammer spring, which forces the hammer to hit the firing pin. The pin strikes the primer, which ignites the propellant which starts to burn. As the propellant burns it creates gas, increasing its volume substantially. This generates an increase in pressure, which starts to accelerate the bullet down the barrel. It also forces the cartridge case into the chamber, providing a seal[33] and preventing the gas escaping into Tommy's face. Newton's Third Law[34] then kicks in – as well as the bullet accelerating down the barrel the propellant makes the rifle accelerate into Tommy shoulder. This is an effect know as jump. It is important as the bullet is still in the barrel and therefore jump affects where the bullet will end up.

---

[33] This seal between the cartridge case and the barrel wall is known as "obturation" – a delicious word and a great term for military bluffers.

[34] For every action there is an equal and opposite reaction.

Assuming that Tommy holds the weapon the same every shot, the jump will be the same[35] every shot. He can therefore adjust the weapon's sights to cancel out the effect. This process is known as zeroing, and it is fundamental to hitting targets, thereby killing the enemy and staying alive. Of course, Tommy's shoulder and build is unique to him. This means that a weapon zeroed to Tommy will not be accurate for Dick or Harry. Moreover, soldiers fire guns from all sorts of positions, standing, sitting, lying etc. The jump error changes for every position. Generally soldiers zero "prone", as they are safest on their belly and that is the most stable firing position. Firing from other positions will be less accurate, as jump is different to what it was when the weapon was zeroed. This problem can only be overcome by Tommy spending hours and hours on the range, practising shooting until he knows the variation in aiming points for different positions.

Jump is the reason that firing from the hip is unlikely to be accurate, as Tommy is then relying upon his strength to contain jump – even if he managed to line the barrel up with the target in the first place. Jump one of the reasons why accuracy with a pistol is rare – significant strength and practice is required to be accurate at just ten metres. For most soldiers in most roles pistols simply aren't worth the effort.

Back to Tommy's rifle; it has been a busy hundredth of a second or so and the bullet leaves the barrel at its maximum speed. This is known as muzzle velocity[36]. From here on in there are three forces acting on the bullet, namely gravity, friction with the air (also known as aerodynamic drag) and something called gyroscopic precession[37]. Tommy is left holding a tube with a stream of high pressure gas coming out of it. This is a bit like holding onto a water hosepipe some distance from the end – the pipe flails about all over the place. The effects of recoil are similar to and greater than jump, and this is

---

[35] With a magazine fed weapon it will not be identical, as the number of bullets in the magazine will vary thereby altering the mass of the weapon and its moment of inertia. No one said this was going to be simple!

[36] Muzzle velocity is actually the speed of the projectile measured 1m from the end of the barrel

[37] Another great term for military bluffers – more information in appendix one.

when you can see muzzles moving and smoke coming out. The important bit is that all this movement does not affect the bullet, which is long gone. It will affect Tommy, who will experience kick. In general terms, the larger the bullet the more propellant, and therefore the more kick. If the weapon is firing on automatic then the next bullet will be fired at whatever the weapon is pointing at when the loading process is complete, which is unlikely to be the same point that Tommy aimed the first bullet at. Firing accurately on automatic requires significant strength and training. For the moment we'll assume Tommy is firing single shots.

While Tommy is experiencing the recoil he is watching the target to see if he hit or missed, known as "observing the fall of shot". If Tommy missed, he should be able to see the fall of shot and therefore correct his aim for the next shot. This is all fine and dandy on a rifle range – but when the enemy has the potential to shoot back calm observation of the fall of shot requires resolution and courage. However if Tommy wants to hit the target it is unavoidable.

SUPPRESSION

But does Tommy actually have to hit the target to have an effect? It might be enough to get a near miss, which would frighten the enemy into lying on the ground thus being out of combat. This is known as suppression and can be achieved in two ways. The first is to get an explosion close to the enemy, which will concuss him. This is a physical effect, and is primarily caused by blast over-pressure, of which more later. The other way is to get lots of bullets close enough to the enemy to terrify him. This is a psychological effect. Most people experiencing lots of bullets passing close enough to their person will concentrate on survival – which usually means throwing themselves to the ground and hiding rather than trying to kill Tommy.

The key questions are how many bullets and how close? Ask yourself. How many bullets would have to land round your feet or go past your ear (you'll hear the crack of their supersonic passage) before you hit the deck and start praying? One a second? Two a second? One a minute? It's your life, so it is your call. Tommy underwent "battle inoculation" as part of his training which involves having bullets fired relatively close to him, so he's a bit less distressed than you would be[38].

The more interesting question is "how close?" Well, they have to be close enough for you to be aware of them, which means you either need to see them hitting the ground near your feet or hear the crack of them passing your head.[39] Battlefields are busy places, so you may not actually be able to see fall of shot more than a couple of metres from you. If they're in the air and you hear the crack, does it tell you how close it was? No - but you might infer that it was too close for comfort! For as good a visualisation as any of what it is like to be under fire watch the opening sequence of *"Saving Private Ryan."*

This throws up a couple of interesting corollaries. There is a school of thought that the best sound you can hear on a battlefield is the crack of bullets passing you, as it means the enemy can't shoot straight.[40] There is an excellent description of this in *"Once a Warrior King"* by David Donovan where he describes an incident during the Vietnam War in which he was ambushed. His soldiers threw themselves to the ground and refused to return fire. It is an Officer's lot to encourage the men under his command to advance into enemy fire by example, so Donovan found himself standing with bullets whistling past him as he walked up and down the line of his troops, shaming them into joining the battle – which they eventually did.

---

[38] In theory – when he underwent battle inoculation Tommy knew that the rounds were supposed to be close, but safe. It's a bit different when they are actually being aimed at him. Tommy is still less distressed than you would be as he has trained for (and often experienced) this scenario and knows what to do.

[39] Most bullets travel at greater than the speed of sound, which is around 330metres per second. This means that they generate a supersonic shockwave. This manifests itself as a crack.

[40] In his memoirs, Winston Churchill describes the elation of being shot at with no ill effect. Balance this with the famous last words of US General John Sedgewick, who found himself in similar circumstances to Donovan at the Battle of Spotsylvania Courthouse. *"Don't worry men; they couldn't hit an elephant at this range."* He was killed by a bullet to his head a few moments later.

The second corollary is how do you suppress a deaf man? If he can't hear the bullets passing he won't know that you're shooting at him. What is a deaf man doing on the battlefield? One of the effects of blast, from say an artillery barrage, is bursting eardrums, thereby rendering someone deaf, and unable to hear the bullets that are supposed to be suppressing him. Tommy's world is sometimes rich in irony.

There has been much theoretical work done on suppression, which we can summarise with the assumption that if Tommy gets a bullet within 1 metre of an enemy's head, they'll notice it and it will have a suppressive effect. If Tommy can get enough of them there, and keep them coming, he will achieve suppression and the enemy will seek cover and not shoot back, at least until the Tommy has to change magazines.

Hitting the Target

Getting the bullet out of Tommy's weapon was, of course, the easy bit. Arranging for it to hit the enemy is hard. How hard? Let's say the enemy is a man on his belly – say 0.5m wide and 0.4m high- at a range of 300 metres. Assuming that we aim at the middle of the enemy, Figure 10 shows the angular accuracy we have to achieve. Before you look at it, I need to introduce you to another way of measuring angles – the "mil". One "mil" is the angle between two points 1000 metres away and 1metre apart.[41]

Figure 3.2 Tommy Shooting the Enemy at 300m

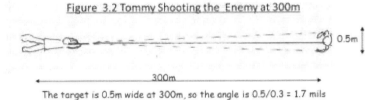

The target is 0.5m wide at 300m, so the angle is 0.5/0.3 = 1.7 mils

As we can see that the angular accuracy required to hit the target is +- 1 mil. If this sounds tough, it is. To make a comparison, consider

---

[41] This is effectively the definition of a milleradian (mil). Consider a circle of 1km radius. We know that the circumference of the circle is $2\pi r = 6,283m$. For simplicity there are considered to be 6,400 Military Mils in a full circle. One mil is therefore 360/6,400 or 0.056 of a degree,

golf, where the object of the exercise is to hit a ball into a hole 108mm wide. The level of accuracy required of Tommy is equivalent to sinking a 210 foot putt! Tiger Woods' longest putt is around 120 feet.

We can therefore see that at 300 metres we are setting Tommy a tough task. Although on a range he will hit a target this size well over 50% of the time when shooting from the prone position, it's more difficult from other positions – or in combat. Tommy learns to shoot in the same way as Mr Woods – practice, and lots of it. If Tiger misses he may lose the hole (and even the match) but he gets another chance – on the battlefield Tommy has no similar guarantee.

However if all Tommy needs is to suppress the enemy the target becomes the suppression bubble, which is five times wider. This is still equivalent to a 40 foot putt. Tommy can then hit the ground and take a more considered shot from the prone position. By having the option of single shot or automatic Tommy can seize the initiative with a quick burst at the suppression bubble and then complete the kill with a well-aimed, single shot.

One problem with automatic fire is that it uses up ammunition at prodigious rates –firing single shots Tommy might use 10 rounds per minute; on fully automatic he can manage that in a couple of seconds. Tommy cares about this as he carries his own ammunition, which is heavy. The more he thinks he will use, the more he has to carry. The last thing Tommy wants is to run out of ammunition as then he'd become the idiot who brought a knife to a gunfight- and there's no future in that.

DAMAGING THE TARGET

According to the US Army it takes about 80 Joules of energy to incapacitate a man target[42]. When the bullet left the muzzle it had a kinetic energy of about 3,400 Joules[43]. By the time it gets to the

---

[42] Hatcher's Notebook, by Major General Julian S Hatcher. He actually quotes 60 foot pounds, which is about 80 Joules.
[43] Taking the NATO 7.62mm 51 bullet. Kinetic energy = ½ x mass x velocity squared. =1/2 x 0.0095 Kg x 850 metres per second x 850 metres per second = 3,431 Joules.

target it will have slowed down a bit to about 700 metres per second, which still leaves it with 2,300 Joules - more than enough for the challenge is to dump this energy in the body of the target. If the bullet goes straight through the target's body it may not dump enough energy to kill. This can happen if the bullet passes through flesh without hitting bone. Of course it may eventually kill though blood loss and the target may well be incapacitated through pain. But in the ideal world Tommy wants instant incapacitation of the target.

When the bullet hits the body it starts to decelerate. The forces (i.e. friction from the target's body) doing this will tend to make the bullet start to topple and change direction. Although the bullet is hard compared to flesh it will start to deform, particularly if it has bounced off a bit of metal (say a rifle barrel) that the target is holding. It will therefore stop being the highly streamlined object that it was, thereby becoming more potent as a destroyer of flesh and bone. The bullet will continue through the body, cutting through tissue, bouncing off bones (probably breaking them) until either it runs out of energy or it comes out the other side of the body.

There are some designs of bullet that significantly reduce the possibility of bullets passing through the target's body. The most complex is an "explosive" bullet. While this does not have explosive in it, the nose of the bullet has been hollowed out and a drop of dense liquid such as mercury put in. When the bullet strikes the target the drop comes out and spreads out through the body – effectively making the bullet bigger. More direct damage is done to more parts of the body. For a graphic demonstration of the effect, watch the film "*The Day of The Jackal*". The problem with explosive bullets is that they are expensive to make. They are also more complicated in flight due to the effects of the liquid within the bullet. A simpler alternative is to carve a cross in the end of a lead bullet. This is the original Dum-Dum. When the bullet strikes, the cross increases the amount by which it spreads out. It may even turn into four smaller bullets on slightly different paths. Again the result is more damage to tissue over a wider area. The problem with Dum-Dums is that not many bullets now have lead on the outer skin, and those that do tend to be low velocity bullets for things like pistols. The solution is to make a hollow point bullet. This is like an explosive bullet, but without the mercury filling. It acts like a Dum-Dum, as when it hits the target it will deform and spread. These projectiles are controversial, as they have been banned under the Hague Conventions[44]. They are particularly useful in some special forces and law enforcement scenarios, such as shooting terrorists on an aeroplane, where the bullet must stay in the target's body to prevent it from penetrating the aircraft fuselage – or indeed hitting someone else.

It is not just the bullet that will be doing damage. Remember it arrives at about Mach 2, with a supersonic shock wave. This shockwave will also spread through the body, disrupting organs that are not in the bullet's path. The chance of anyone shrugging off the impact of a bullet penetrating their torso is not high.

If the enemy is lurking behind a wall, wearing body armour or in a vehicle then Tommy needs to inflict more damage to the target to get to the enemy's body and incapacitate him. The ability to damage is limited by the kinetic energy of the bullet, which is related to its mass and velocity, the faster and more massive a bullet is the more damage it will do. The downside is that it will require a bigger gun to launch it, will create more kick, will cost more and be heavier.

There are two approaches to getting more energy into the target. Either we can send more bullets by using a machine gun or we can put explosive in the bullet, turning it into a shell, and use the chemical energy from explosive. If you're wondering whether we can do both then you will be delighted to know that yes, we can and we'll get to that. But let's start with machine guns.

---

[44] The Hague conventions of 1899 and 1907 relate to what uniformed soldiers may do to other uniformed soldiers. Whether a terrorist is a uniformed soldier is, of course, debatable. The consequences of an explosive decompression of an airliner caused by a bullet passing through a terrorist and penetrating the fuselage are factual, hence the special case.

MACHINE GUNS

A machine gun reloads itself automatically.[45] Typically a machine gun fires about ten rounds per second. That's ten times as much energy being sent at the target – the question is whether it will get there, as Tommy will have to deal with the jump from the first round before the second round is fired one tenth of a second later. This is unlikely, so to control the aim we simply remove or reduce the weakest link, which is Tommy. Rather than fix the MG to his shoulder we'll put it in a tripod, securely embedded in the ground. Being a heavy bit of metal it will increase the inertia of the system, effectively ensuring that the recoil effects of firing one round are reduced and the barrel returned to pointing at the target by the time the second round is fired.

Now a tripod is heavy, and Tommy hates carrying unnecessary weight. For lighter machineguns, typically with a calibre of 7.62mm or less, there an intermediate solution, called a bipod. This is a device with two legs clipped to the machinegun close to the muzzle end. It is used as a support, its weight increases inertia and Tommy hangs onto the other end.

Firing so fast generates lots of heat, which might melt the barrel, or at least make it expand enough to reduce accuracy and (possibly) ignite ammunition in the breech before the firing pin hits the primer. There are common ways of preventing this. Firstly, make the barrel heavier, which allows is to soak up more heat and, if possible, put fins on it to increase the outer surface area to speed heat dissipation. Second carry a spare barrel or two and build a quick barrel change mechanism into the machinegun's design. The third solution is to maximise the airflow through the inside of the barrel. While a rifle has its breech closed between shots, in most machine guns the breech is only closed when the round is being fired and the bullet is still in the barrel. The rest of the time cooling air can get in. The potential problem is further reduced by Tommy firing in bursts, rather than continuously (which is also more accurate and saves precious ammunition).

---

[45] The detail of how it achieves this is in Appendix One

Older machine gun designs, such as the Vickers gun, had a water cooling jacket. These added hugely to the weight and bulk, but gave great reliability and availability – enabling the gun to fire almost continuously and indefinitely. Although most modern machine guns do not have such cooling, it is not unknown for urine to be used to cool them in extremis.

As we're using bigger guns we can expect the bullets to travel further. The good news is this implies that we can start killing the enemy further away; the bad news is that it will make observing the fall of shot harder. The solution is a tracer bullet, which is a normal bullet with a small piece of chemical attached to the back end. When the gun fires the chemical ignites and burns, typically producing a trail red or green light all the way to where it lands. We can therefore watch the bullet as it flies towards the enemy. The amount of tracer to "ball" (as normal bullets are known) varies from 1:1 to 1:4. Tracer rounds are just as lethal as ball rounds, so we are not sacrificing firepower.

Because we are now firing groups of bullets – typically a bust of 15 to 20 rounds – we need to consider how they may disperse. This dispersion is caused by vibrations in the firing platform arising from jump and recoil and the fact that the second and subsequent bullets leave the muzzle into an area of turbulence, caused by the preceding rounds. These fly through the air as a "cone of fire" emanating from the machine guns muzzle. For targets such as light vehicles, which are predominantly vertical, the cone of fire is used to engage. This is shown in Figure 3.3.

Figure 3.3 Cones of Fire and the Beaten Zone

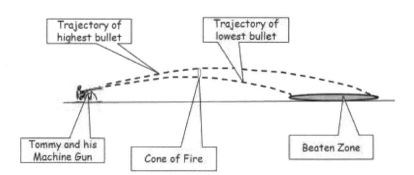

As the bullets continue they disperse further and start to tip to earth. When they strike the ground they will cover an area, known as the beaten zone. Typically for a machinegun at a range of 600 metres it will be some 1 metre wide and 60 metres long. Anyone on the ground's surface in that zone will be hit. Canny siting of machineguns to a flan enables a wall of bullets to be laid across an enemy's advance, as shown in Figure 3.4 below. Machineguns are at their most effective when firing from a flank, as the First World War repeatedly demonstrated.

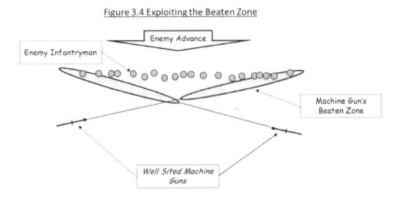

Figure 3.4 Exploiting the Beaten Zone

There are two further evolutions of the machine gun concept; Gatling guns and chain guns. These are described in Appendix One. Meanwhile we'll move onto firing larger projectiles, which may be necessary to deal with enemy who are dastardly enough to lurk in buildings or armoured vehicles – thereby being immune to bullets.

RECOILLESS RIFLES

One of the physical limits on the size of projectile that Tommy can fire is caused by recoil – too much recoil and Tommy will break his shoulder; the heavier the projectile the greater the recoil. In practice a projectile of over 100 grammes is going to cause problems with its recoil. One solution, adopted by the Barrett .50" sniper rifle, is to build a recoil system into the rifle. This is heavy, complicated and expensive, but does enable a bullet mass of around 750 grammes. The alternative is to remove the recoil. This is common in hand held anti-tank weapons such as the British LAW80, American

M72 and the ubiquitous Russian RPG-7. Take a look at the diagram below:

Figure 3.5 A Recoilless Rifles

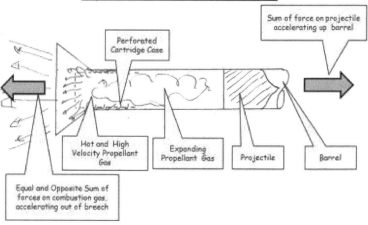

You'll remember that the recoil on firing (which is what causes "jump" and makes hitting the target hard) arises from Newton's 3rd Law which compels the entire rifle has to accelerate in the opposite direction to the bullet. By having no breech block and using a perforated cartridge case, it is the propellant gas itself rather than the weapon that accelerates in obedience of Newton's Law, while the projectile accelerates down the barrel. There is no need for the entire weapon to move, so it doesn't – hence being known as recoilless.

There are a couple of problems. For a start, all that hot and fast gas creates a huge back blast. Dimensions vary, but typically plan on 45 degrees either side of the tube for 25 metres behind the launcher. Anyone in that area will suffer from blast effects – which can be lethal. This back blast makes firing from buildings perilous to the point of impossibility[46]. Secondly, although there is no (or little) recoil per se, Tommy certainly knows when he's fired. The rapid movement of air creates all sorts of pressure effects, and the bang is very loud. In addition, the amount of smoke and dust generated is significant which makes it easy for the enemy to identify Tommy's location an exact vengeance. For some weapons, the smoke itself it

---

[46] There are ways round this – see Appendix one.

is toxic, meaning Tommy has to wear his gas mask when he fires. Still, on the upside he has just launched a projectile containing several kilogrammes of high explosive at the enemy. Accuracy isn't great as the projectile is relatively slow (sub 300 metres Maximum effective ranges are around 300 to 500 metres, and the effect at the target end will be gratifyingly dramatic. The enemy might survive a hit on the front of his tank (if he's in one) but otherwise it's going to make his eyes water.

But recoilless rifles are large and heavy. If Tommy is carrying one of them he is unable to carry a rifle, which means he's only useful when the enemy is in bunkers or armoured vehicles. The rest of the time he's a bystander. There is another approach.

GRENADES

If Tommy throws explosives at the enemy the energy from the detonation of the explosive will provide ample destructive power, so we don't need to worry about kinetic energy for any effect on the target. This means that we only have to give the projectile sufficient kinetic energy to reach the target. This can be achieved with a much lower velocity, proportionately reducing the recoil (don't forget that the explosive filled projectile is much larger and heavier than a bullet).

We had better be precise about what Tommy needs to achieve; he needs an explosive shell which is safe to carry about while he is doing all sorts of soldierly things like wading rivers, crawling under wire and jumping through windows but, at a moment of his choice, transforms into something murderously lethal. This is what a fuse does, with some arming mechanism that prevents it becoming lethal without Tommy instructing it to. Inevitably the fuse adds weight, bulk and complexity.

The simplest shell is a hand grenade — again something you're probably familiar with from war films. Like all shells, it comprises an explosive charge, a fuse, an arming mechanism and a casing. Let's look at one in more detail.

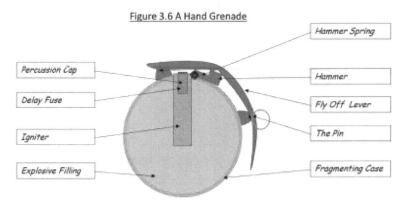

Figure 3.6 A Hand Grenade

Percussion Cap

Delay Fuse

Igniter

Explosive Filling

Hammer Spring

Hammer

Fly Off Lever

The Pin

Fragmenting Case

The arming mechanism is the pin, removal of which makes it possible for the fly-off lever to release the hammer which in turn strikes the percussion cap. Provided the fly-off lever is held in place and not released it is possible to disarm the grenade by re-inserting the pin. In practice, this is rarely done, removal of the pin being part of the delivery process.

When the grenade is thrown the fly off lever flies off, thereby releasing the hammer which hits the primer. This ignites the fuse, which is a simple time fuse. After around three seconds the fuse then detonates, setting off the igniter and then main charge. This in turn shatters the casing, producing high velocity grenade fragments, called shrapnel[47], and a blast wave. The blast wave propagates outwards at the speed of sound, some 330 metres per second. Note that the blast pressure reduces as a cube of the distance from where the grenade lands, as shown in Figure 3.11 below. The important point is that if we wish to double the effective radius of the blast we have to raise the pressure generated by the explosion by eight times. This can be achieved by either using a higher powered explosive or by using eight times as much of the standard one. As always, in practical terms this is limited by cost and weight – the latter having an effect on range as well as how many Tommy can carry.

---

[47] There is a subtle difference between "Shrapnel" and fragments. The former arises from material like ball bearings or pre-fragmented wire placed into the projectile. The latter means part of the projectile casing. As this difference is not apparent at the target end in common usage the words are interchangeable.

The shrapnel fragments are not aerodynamic so their speed reduces quickly due to air friction. But they don't have far to travel. They damage flesh in the same way as a bullet – although their blunt shape may well lead them to dump more energy into the target. Note that the concentration of fragments reduces as the square of the distance from the detonation point, and not all fragments are going in a useful direction. They have limited penetrating power – certainly a masonry wall will stop them.

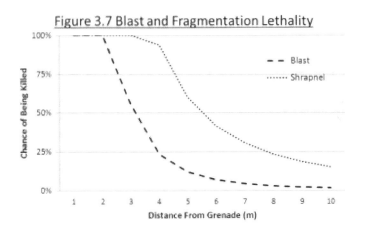

Figure 3.7 Blast and Fragmentation Lethality

The net result is a kill radius of 5 to 10 metres, and a wounding radius of perhaps 15m. In common with all blast and fragmentation weapons and unlike aimed gunfire, the grenade is very egalitarian. It will kill and maim those within its effective area irrespective of whether they are friend, foe, non-combatant, male, female or a child. One of the fundamental skills of throwing a grenade is to ensure that one is not in the lethal area at the moment of detonation!

Note that at the time of detonation Tommy does not have to have a line of sight to the enemy – indeed if he can deduce that the enemy is the other side of a wall, maybe by hearing them talk, to within a couple of metres accuracy and toss the grenade over then Tommy can kill the enemy without exposing himself to the enemy target at all. This is generally an attractive option.

The range is determined by how hard Tommy can throw the grenade, itself a function of the grenade weight, Tommy's strength and whether he is standing or prone. It is possible to design a grenade that can be thrown further – the easiest way is to put a handle on it as per the WW2 German "Potato Masher", but the ultimate limits remain Tommy's strength and posture. [48]Generally Tommy can throw a grenade about 30 metres from standing, and a lot less if he's lying down. Given its effective radius, you can see that the potential for damaging yourself with your own grenade is significant unless there are features such as walls, trenches and ditches that to constrain the blast to the immediate area of the enemy. The classic times to employ a grenade are assaulting enemy in trenches and fighting in buildings, when the enemy is in the next door room. As the consequences of a miss are significant it may be that Tommy prefers to get close, and "post" the grenade into a trench rather than seek to lob it in from further away – risking a miss and being wounded by his own grenade. Of course, he has to balance this with the inherent risks of getting closer to the trench.

There are two variants of a hand grenade that are worth mentioning. The first, which removes the problem of shrapnel hitting the thrower, is the blast grenade. This has a cardboard or plastic casing which disintegrates when the grenade detonates. There is therefore no fragmentation and only a blast effect. These are the stun grenades made famous by hostage rescue teams – the flash and bang of the explosion being enough to incapacitate people close to it. Some armies use stun grenades in place of fragmentation grenade when attacking.

The other version is the smoke grenade, of which there are two types. The simple ones produce coloured smoke through a chemical reaction. Typically they burn for 30 to 90 seconds. The smoke can be used to screen movement (although it takes a while to build up) or to indicate positions and wind strength and direction to helicopters and aircraft. The smoke may or may not be an irritant – the best example of an irritant is the CS (or tear gas) grenade – which produces an unpleasant smoke, useful for dispersing crowds. We'll consider this sort of thing in another chapter.

---

[48] As a grenade is about the same size a tennis ball, although it weighs about 500grammes, you can try for yourself. Just get an old tennis ball, slice it open and fill it with stones or coins to get the weight right

The more complicated smoke grenade uses white phosphorous. Phosphorous reacts spontaneously with air, burning and producing lots of hot, white smoke. The grenade works by having a small bursting charge which spreads the phosphorus into the air which ignites it. If there happens to be an enemy infantryman about and a piece of phosphorous sticks to him it will burn him too. Phosphorous burns are horrific, as the fragment will keep burning and penetrating flesh. The smoke is pretty unpleasant as well, and chokes. Now, the Geneva Convention does not approve of the use of white phosphorous as an anti-infantry weapon, but it is allowed as smoke. While it is a moot point as to whether tossing a white phosphorous grenade into a bunker to "smoke out" the occupants is lawful it is certainly effective.

GRENADE LAUNCHERS

So, we have given Tommy a highly effective weapon, with the caveat that to use it to full efficiency he needs to add the skills of Freddie Flintoff to those of Tiger Woods. Even then its range is limited. To send the grenade further he needs some form of launcher. The simplest method is to give him a gun capable of firing an explosive shell. The most common in western use is the American M79, which will propel a 40mm diameter grenade containing around 250 grammes of explosive up to about 300 metres. These were introduced in the 1960s and are still in service today. Essentially it is a short barrelled (in relation to its calibre) single shot gun.

Now that we know all about guns we can see that there is going to be a bit of a compromise to be struck here. If the effects of firing a 50 gramme rifle bullet at 750 metres per second are a limit, we are going to have to fire the heavier 250 gramme 40mm grenade much slower to avoid breaking Tommy's shoulder. The M79 muzzle velocity is about 75m/s. This lower velocity means that we're going to have to fire it on a higher trajectory to overcome gravity and its long time of flight, say 5 seconds to 300 metres, means that wind effects are going to be significant and we may well miss the target.

The projectile needs an arming system, to make the round safe to carry, and some form of fuse. The hand grenade is armed by pulling a pin. On the M79 the projectile arms itself using the centrifugal forces caused by the spin from the rifling. This takes time and there is a short moment when the projectile is flying through the air before it is armed. This creates a minimum range[49] - on the M79 about 30 metres.

Having got the round heading for the target and armed, we now need to get it to detonate when it gets there. We can either use a simple impact fuse or a more sophisticated centrifugal fuse, which detonates the grenade when its rate of spin reduces. The latter has the advantage of working if the nose of the round does not hit a hard enough target – it is sometimes called a glancing fuse.

The only other problem is that whoever is carrying the M79 either has to carry two weapons or not carry a rifle. Generally the two weapon solution is preferred, but of course the M79 and its ammunition add more weight to Tommy's burden. There are also time delays, as even Tommy cannot aim and fire two weapons at once. Mounting a grenade launcher on Tommy's rife is a common compromise. While it increases the rifle weight it does make both weapons available all the time. In most armies the M79 has now been largely replaced by the M203 grenade launcher, which is fitted under the rifle barrel. This delivers the same grenade, although the maximum accurate range is about 150 metres.

An alternative, which has intermittent popularity, is to use a rifle launched grenade, using the rifle barrel and ammunition to provide the launcher for the grenade.

---

[49] Of course, being hit in the chest or head by a ½ pound lump of metal travelling at 270mph may well be fatal anyway.

Figure 3.8 Rifle Grenades

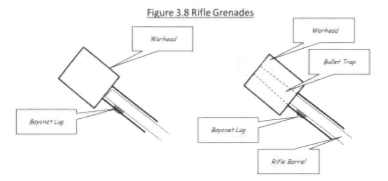

The basic rifle grenade slots on the end of the barrel in the same way as a bayonet.

To fire it, Tommy has to load a special (bullet less) cartridge – otherwise he risks blowing his rifle's barrel apart.

The "bullet trap" rifle grenade slots on the end of the barrel in the same way as a bayonet.

The advantage is that Tommy can fire a normal bullet, which will pass through the tapered bullet trap, thereby imparting momentum to the grenade without blowing up the barrel or requiring Tommy to waste time loading a special propellant round.

This reduces the weight carried by the rifleman. It also means that the only cost is the grenade, so all Tommy's colleagues can fire grenades, as opposed to only those equipped with M203/M79. If the M203 man is hit the section loses its entire capability whereas with a rifle grenade the survivors can carry on. The British Army used the (Belgian) Energa grenade in the 60s and 70s. They then went out of fashion as the M79 / M203 became dominant. The logistics argument is compelling and rifle grenades might yet make a comeback[50].

Of course, if you wish to get more than a grenade's worth of explosive onto a target it is possible using mortars, artillery and the like. It is also possible to mount bigger guns in vehicles, and use them for direct fire. We'll get to all this, but now that we know about ground and Tommy's direct fire weapons its time accompany Tommy into a small battle to see them in action.

---

[50] The Israeli and French armies use them.

Chapter 4 Tommy's (Basic) Tactics

Now that we understand about ground and some of Tommy's weapons it's time to see them in action. Let's go into battle! Its early stages, so we'll keep it simple. However as land combat is a team game we need to get Tommy some company. Let's promote Tommy to Lance Corporal[51], which makes him a fire team commander. His fire team comprises Tommy himself, a rifleman, a grenadier [with an M203] and a light machine gunner, who carries a Minimi rather than an SA80.

The fire team is the smallest fighting unit in the British Army, or indeed any other. Although a fire team will occasionally perform a task by itself it will usually work with at least one other team. In the British army two fire teams make a section. The other fire team will be commanded by a full corporal, who will both command his fire team and direct Tommy's team

This is a good time to consider what Tommy actually carries with him as a personal load. The table below makes it clear:

Item	Quantity	Total Weight (Kg)	Comment
SA80	1	5	Includes sight and one magazine.
Loaded Magazines	4	2	Each of 30 rounds.
200 round bandoleer	1	3	Additional loose ammunition for Tommy to refill his magazines whenever he gets the chance.
100 rounds link		1.5	For the fire team Minimi light machine gun (LMG).
Grenades	2	1	

---

[51] There is more on organisations, ranks and structures in chapter 10. We'll get there in due course.

Helmet	1	1	
Body Armour	1	10	Weight varies depending upon type of armour.
Radio & Batteries	1	1	Personal Radio. Platoon and company radios are much heavier.
Other Stuff	1	5	Water bottle, food, field dressings, Respirator etc. and a brew[52] kit.
TOTAL		29.5	

Tommy is going into combat carrying at least 30 kg of kit, over 30% of his body weight. Note that this is his basic combat load. It could easily be increased with anti-tank weapons, more radios and other specialist equipment which could make a total load of over 50kg, or 8 stone[53]. And of course on some operations he'll be needing sleeping bags, more food and water, more batteries etc. Tommy needs to move everywhere with it on, quickly and with agility; he must be able to pull himself up to windows, vault walls and jump ditches. Tommy is very fit, probably 6 foot tall and weighs in at around 90kg. Most hiking and rambling organisations quote the maximum backpack weight for a fit person as 33% of their body weight. Tommy is over that limit before he picks up any specialist equipment, or indeed his backpack containing spare clothing, more food and a sleeping bag. The load and strain on his back and lower limbs is significant and injuries are common, particularly in

---

[52] A brew kit is the equipment required to make a hot drink. At the minimum it is a cooker, a metal mug and a teabag. British Infantry is (rightly) famous for its ability to produce a mug of tea at time and in any conditions.

[53] In Afghanistan the "average load" is quoted as 110lbs, or 50kg. Small wonder that it is so hard for soldiers there to perform their traditional task of closing with the enemy. Much of the weight comes from body armour and other forms of protective equipment. There is a trade-off between levels of protection and effectiveness on the ground.

training[54]. Tommy is, in fact, a professional athlete – albeit without the sponsorship deals or celebrity lifestyle.

The sheer physical strength required to be an infantryman is one of the major reasons why few armies have infantry-women[55]. The simple fact is that the majority of women lack the basic physique to be able to perform the same job as Tommy. While some women may be able to develop the fitness and strength required, the overwhelming majority will not and thus it is not economically sensible to make the investment required. Remember also that the only way in which it can be definitively established that Thomasina can or can't make the grade is to load her up and test her. The risks of injury to her are absurdly high.

Of course, it would be possible for a woman (or anyone else weaker than Tommy) to be an infantryman (or infantryperson) if she was required to carry less equipment. But that leaves the stark question of who is going to carry it for her? Going into battle with insufficient ammunition is a step on the path to the mortuary and no one benefits if Tommy has to carry yet more ammunition to cover the shortfall arising from Thomasina's lighter load.

The harsh physical requirements of infantry soldiering do not prevent women from filling most other roles within the Army – which they do, with distinction as we shall see later. Those who seek perfect equality between the sexes and demand female infantrypeople are seldom those who would actually join and endure the tribulations of soldiering. The bottom line is that warfare is a violent statement of political intent, not a demonstration of political correctness. If you can't carry 50 kilogrammes or more you can't work with Tommy.

Back to the battle: we have the good guys, what we need now is an enemy. Imagine that Tommy's bit of the Army that he is in is

---

[54] Getting Generation X fit was hard. The play-station generation have caused military training establishments to accept physically weaker candidates and invest heavily in getting them physically strong enough. This is only a problem for developed world armies.

[55] Of course, some armies manage with less kit, particular "irregular" ones (aka "freedom fighters"). The reduction in personal load makes it possible for a higher proportion of them to be female.

advancing. His corporal has just been ordered to secure the top of a small hill about 500 metres east of the advancing main body. He has also been told that there might be a party of two or three enemy soldiers at the top. Have a look at the map below.

Figure 4.1 – Tommy's First Battle

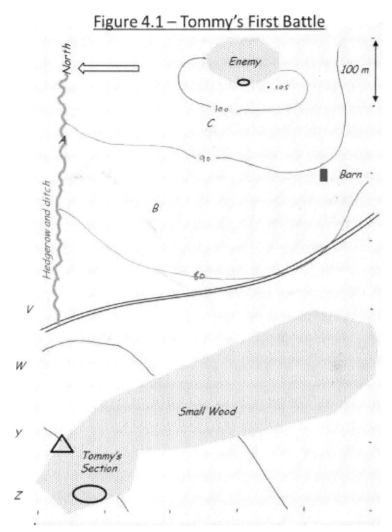

Tommy and his section are in the north-western corner of Small Wood preparing for battle. While the men will be checking weapons, filling magazines and applying camouflage. Tommy and the Section Commander will find an observation position (or "OP" in the jargon), have a look at the ground through their binoculars, and work out a plan. Let's join Tommy and his corporal, who are looking over the ground from their OP shown by the triangle. They're looking for the best way to get from Small Wood to the top of Hill 105[56], 400 metres to the east. (In this context "best" means the one least likely to get them killed, while still achieving the task that they have been given. Staying in Small Wood is not an available option).

If the enemy are on Hill 105 they will be able to see the Eastern side of Small Wood, everything south of the hedgerow and ditch, round to the barn. They can't see north of the hedge and ditch, south of the barn. Nor can they see the road. There is also some dead ground to them between the 80 metres and 90 metres contours. At the same time, from where Tommy is he can't see the top of Hill 105, although he can see most of the trees.

The spot marked A is interesting, as there is an approach to it in dead ground, and from A Tommy and the corporal can continue east in the ditch behind the hedge right up to the top of the hill. Alternatively they can move in the dead ground to the West of Small Wood, move over the spur and then head up the hill past the barn. Finally they could walk straight from Small Wood to the dead ground at B. They would then continue to C, where they would be emerging from the dead ground, and have to start fighting from there.

Each route has its attractions and disadvantages. After some reflection, the section commander decides to go for the first option, and sneak up to A. Like Fagin, he will continue reviewing the situation as it develops. Having made his decision, he returns to the section on the west of Small Wood. He tells Tommy to make a model of the ground, carving it out of the earth with his entrenching tool, a 5 minute job and a key skill that Tommy learnt en route to his promotion.

---

[56] The "105" refers to the height of the hill marked by the spot height. It's an easy way of identifying otherwise un-named hills on maps. Some hills named on this basis have actually become battle honours, for example Hill 60 is a First World War Battle Honour for many infantry regiments. Hill 60 was part of the Ypres Salient, and the scene of vicious fighting in April and May 1915.

The corporal now gives the entire section its orders, describing the enemy, the ground, what they have to do and, crucially, why. He'll run through actions on likely events such as encountering mines or wire. He'll describe what he anticipates doing if the enemy engage them from either Hill 105 or other locations. He'll cover formations to be used, hand signals, radios, who is to carry what and the chain of command should he become a casualty. Tommy is second in command, so he is the first choice. Then it will be the riflemen in order of experience and aptitude. Once he has answered any questions he will question the soldiers on the plan to ensure that they know what to do. If there is time they'll conduct a quick rehearsal of the key actions. Once the corporal is satisfied and camouflage has been applied, he'll give the order to "make ready" (i.e. cock the weapons so that they are ready to fire) and set off. Let's tag along with them.

From Z to Y to W the section moves as two fire teams, one lying prone, covering the likely enemy positions and the other walking, with five to ten metres between soldiers[57]. Once the corporal's team [known as the Charlie team] is at W they will halt and "go firm", covering likely enemy locations while Tommy brings the Delta team down the same route, and then continues on to V, where he goes firm.

The corporal then brings up the Charlie team, and heads up the ditch towards A. Once he is there Tommy and the Delta team join him. So far so good; they have got to within 150 metres of the enemy without incident. They have covered some 500 metres, which will have taken about 15 minutes. If that seems slow, remember that they have been moving as two fire teams, with one of them static at any one time. The soldiers have been walking at a steady, but not brisk, pace. Partly this is because they are heavily laden, but more because they are continually looking for the enemy, mines and wire, averaging 1 metre per second, about 3.5 km/h.

---

[57] Spacing is one of the major compromises of infantry life. The further apart the soldiers are, the less likely they are to all become casualties from one burst of fire or explosion. However they are also less able to concentrate their fire and are far harder to control. They can also get lonely and frightened – the tendency to bunch together is endemic.

Unfortunately the ditch is blocked by fallen trees, and the hedge is too sparse to give much cover. The corporal therefore decides to head from A to C, just on the edge of the dead ground. After a quick set of orders, the section fixes bayonets and continues, moving first one fire team and then the other. They start on their feet, but as they get closer to C and D they drop to their hands and knees and thence to their bellies.

Suddenly the peace of the countryside is shattered as the enemy spots one of the Tommy's team and starts shooting. The first the section knows of it is the crack of bullets over their heads, the whine of ricochets from bullets hitting the earth and a shout of pain from one of the Delta riflemen, who has been hit in the arm. This is when Tommy and the corporal start to earn their pay. The diagram below shows the situation.

Figure 4.2 – The Fire Fight Starts

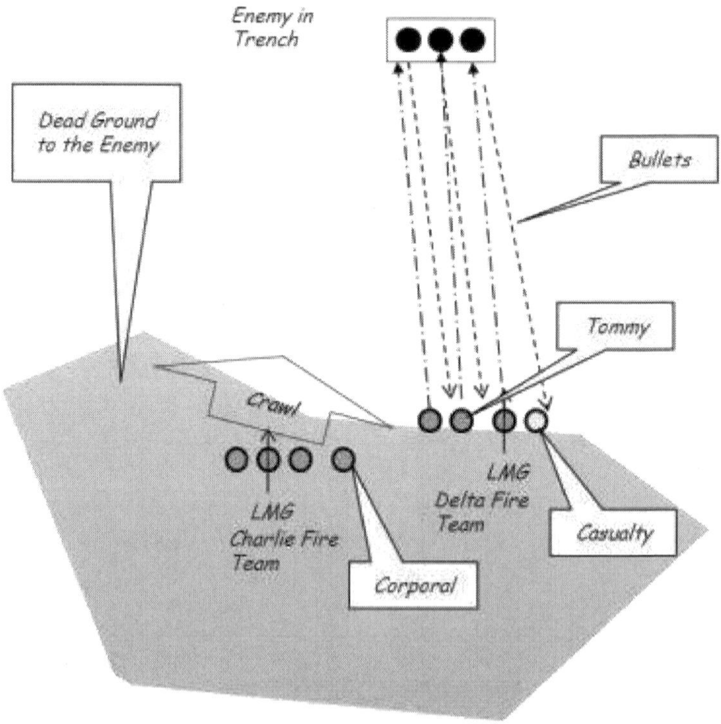

Enemy in Trench

Dead Ground to the Enemy

Bullets

Tommy

Crawl

LMG

Delta Fire Team

Casualty

LMG
Charlie Fire Team

Corporal

The good news is that the Delta LMG man next to the casualty has seen the enemy trench and the men in it. He starts to engage with the LMG, putting down bursts of 3 to 5 rounds. The tracer shows everyone where to look. The LMG gunner also shouts a target indication,

"100 metres, 12 o'clock, 3 enemy in trench, watch my tracer."

Tommy's job is now to relay the information he has to the corporal and get his fire team engaging the enemy. The section is now in a firefight, and the immediate task is to win it – quickly. Simple, but not easy.

The bad news is that Tommy's team is already down to 3 men, on their bellies in a line about 15 metres long. He is engaged by three enemy riflemen in a trench (thankfully, the enemy don't have a machine gun). To win the firefight Tommy's team, and the corporal's as it closes in, has to get sufficient weight of fire onto the trench to make its occupants duck. But the section does not have unlimited ammunition – very much the reverse. And of course, until they win the firefight the enemy, of near equal strength, is trying to kill Tommy's team.

Let's move on a few seconds. All of Tommy's team have identified the target and are engaging. Tommy will start controlling the fire, probably ordering grenades to be fired. He'll also be making sure that the LMG doesn't use its ammunition too quickly, while arranging for the fire team members to pass their belts of link ammunition to the LMG man to feed his Minimi.

The corporal will also be bringing his fire team into the engagement, and issuing similar orders. He also has a few other tasks. First of all, he needs to get on the radio and report the fact that he is in contact with the enemy to his commander.

"Hello India One Zero Alpha this is India One One Charlie, Contact! Wait Out".

The diagram shows the new, improving situation.

Figure 4.3 – Winning The Fire Fight

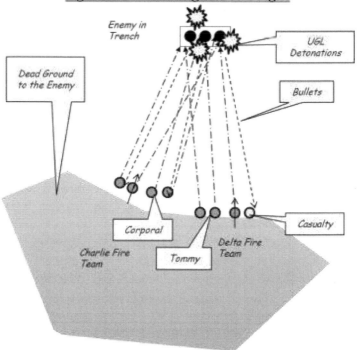

Notice that the effect of the Charlie fire team engaging is to double the amount of fire on the enemy and to halve the number of shots fired at each individual on the Tommy's side. The chance of killing the enemy has doubled AND the chance of becoming a casualty has halved. They have also fired a salvo of grenades from their M203 underslung grenade launchers ("UGL"). This is known as creating peace through superior firepower - winning the firefight is now possible.

The corporal now needs to work out what enemy he has met and how many there are. If there are fewer than two or three men then he can destroy them himself – any more than that then his section is not strong enough. The basic rule of thumb for a section commander is that if there is no machine gun the position is small enough for him to take on himself. Any sign of a machine gun and it's too big for a section. In this case the enemy has no machine gun, and so the section can take it on. Great, but how?

To be confident that the position is destroyed, the section needs to assault the trench currently occupied by the enemy. To do that the corporal needs to fire and manoeuvre a fire team forward (under covering fire from the other fire team). Once he is close he needs to take his team to a flank and with one other man crawl up as close to the trench as he dare. He will then "post" a grenade into the enemy trench. Once it has detonated he'll leap into the trench, dispatching any surviving enemy with his bayonet. Simple, but dangerous.

The contact has been raging for a couple of minutes, and it seems that the salvo of grenade launcher rounds has had an effect, as the volume of fire coming back at the section seems to have diminished. It's now time to hit the radios. Firstly the corporal must let the platoon commander know what is going on, so he gets on the radio.

"Hello India One Zero Alpha this is India One One Charlie, contact 11:00, grid 122479, three enemy in trench engaging me. I am assaulting. Out."

Then he shouts orders to Tommy[58] to make it happen.

"Tommy, fire and manoeuvre forwards, Charlie to move first,"

And wait for Tommy to shout an acknowledgement (*"OK"*). Then he shouts to his fire team *"Charlie Fire Team prepare to move...move"*

While the corporal and Charlie fire team crawl or sprint forward five metres, Tommy and Delta will provide covering fire at the trench. When Tommy hears the Charlie team open fire he'll order *"Delta Fire Team, prepare to move...move,"* and advance while the Charlie team provides covering fire. The section will continue like this until it gets to the position below. If they continue much further they will start blocking each other's fire. The corporal will order the delta fire team to stay where they are, while he takes his team left flanking, as shown below.

---

[58] Or use the personal radios, if they have them.

Figure 4.4 – Closing to Assault

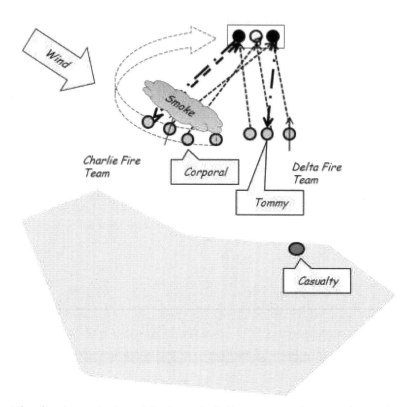

They've been lucky with the wind direction and strength so they cover[59] the move with smoke. On his route to the flank, he will drop off his LMG, and possibly one man as a point of fire. This time he can't as the rifleman has been hit. He and his accompanying rifleman then crawl to within a few metres of the enemy trench and throw grenades at or (ideally) into it.

---

[59] Cover from view, not fire. Many armies fire into smoke as a matter of policy and some thermal imagers can see through some sorts of smoke.

Figure 4.5 – The Assault

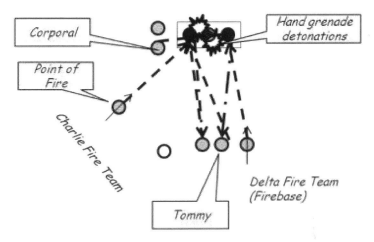

When the grenades detonate it tells the point of fire and Tommy's team that the corporal is assaulting. To avoid shooting him they prepare to switch their fire to another target, if there is one, or (in this case) cease. But they must keep the enemy supressed until the corporal is in the trench. Meanwhile the corporal dashes forward and into the trench, bayonetting or shooting the occupants. Quiet descends. The position is captured.

Of course, the corporal's work isn't over yet by a long chalk. If the enemy is competent there will be a counter-attack already heading his way. The corporal needs to reorganise his section to defend the position. He starts by shouting "Re-org" and the Delta team plus the point of fire will come in to him as fast as they can. The corporal will place them in position and point out their left and right of arc. At the same time they'll run through who is alive, who is wounded and how much ammunition they have. In order the members of the section will call out something like

"Smith, OK, two and a half magazines, 100 link, full bandolier, two grenades, one smoke"

Once they know what they have left, Tommy and the corporal reallocate ammunition, search the position, and find their own wounded. The riflemen get their entrenching tools out and start digging shell scrapes[60]. Meanwhile, the corporal tells his platoon commander what the situation is by radio:

"India One Zero Alpha this is India One One Alpha. Sitrep. Enemy position captured. Two enemy dead and one wounded POW. Own forces, two casualties, am holding position. Ammunition OK. Request medical support and escort for POW."

You will notice that the wounded have been left alone until the contact is over. The reasoning behind this is that the biggest danger to the wounded men is the enemy[61]. If the attack is not prosecuted quickly and effectively then the enemy has the opportunity to reinforce, counter-attack and call in artillery, none of which is healthy for the wounded. Moreover, if one man starts to tend his wounded colleague then neither man is winning the firefight, which reduces the odds of success. Losing the firefight is not a path to health and happiness for the wounded man either. There is also the question of how much help one man can give another with enemy bullets flying past and landing close. The immediate answer is that other than sticking on a field dressing and possibly administering morphine, there isn't much. Remember also that we are looking at the simplest, smallest battle. If we considered the next level of command, a platoon, we would find medics available there, and they will deal with the injured as the firefight is won[62].

The corporal also has a prisoner of war to deal with. The POW is a very lucky chap, as he managed to make his surrender clear before the corporal bayonetted him – not an easy task. The POW was wounded in the assault and is now a casualty who, once he has been disarmed, will be treated as an equal priority to the section's casualties. If he is badly wounded then he can be left with the friendly casualties. If he is not badly wounded then he is liable to

---

[60] A shell scrape is a shallow trench, maybe six inches deep that lowers a soldiers profile when he lies in it. It therefore makes him less vulnerable to direct fire and artillery.

[61] This is NOT the case in a counter insurgency operation, where a wounded man is vulnerable to having his throat slit (or unspeakably worse) by the local population. We'll get to that later.

[62] Or as soon as they can get forward to the casualty. Some battlefield medics are astonishingly brave, which is why they have a disproportionately high rate of award of gallantry decorations.

get in the way, and of course, is a potential threat should the enemy counter-attack. POWs need guarding, and they need controlling.

Let's just review the section's current situation as they reorganise. They started with eight men, two of whom are wounded and being tended by one other. That leaves five at the enemy trench. The corporal and Tommy are busy organising the defence of Hill 105, working the radios to get casualties in and having a look to the east in anticipation of the counter-attack. That leaves three. One of these will be on an LMG, covering the most likely enemy approach. That leaves two, who should be digging and supporting the LMG man. There is no-one spare to guard the POW.

The most likely outcome for the POW is that he will be blindfolded by having a sandbag placed over his head, have his hands tied and be forced to lie down and keep still and quiet. It is imperative that he is subdued, or otherwise he could easily require two of the three available men to restrain him. While the desperate circumstances of the section should not be an excuse for abuse, it is understandable that the prisoner is going to be robustly handled to prevent him from jeopardising the section's security. He will be sent rearwards as soon as possible, but if the corporal decides that the best place for him to be is in the trench the POW may find himself at the bottom of it, with a rifleman standing on him. There is a difference between the robust handling of a potential threat and torture that it entirely obvious to Tommy and the POW himself, but may be less obvious in a court or to an impartial civilian observer.

The dead enemy (or what's left of them - grenades are nasty things) will be removed from the trench and covered with a groundsheet. Again, when the platoon gets to the section a decision will be made about where to bury them and how to mark the grave. However the priority is dealing with the living.

This time the intelligence was correct, and no counter-attack or bombardment materialises. It is now some 30 minutes since the section left Small Wood, 10 minutes since the firefight erupted and just five minutes since the assault. It's been a busy time for Tommy and his mates, and the six survivors are now ready for their next task. The table below summarises their individual experiences:

Person	Time in combat	Rounds fired	Grenades Used	Comment
Corporal	8 minutes	77	One HE One smoke One M203	Shooting for four of the eight minutes at rapid rate of 20 rounds per minute.
Charlie Rifleman 1	8 minutes	93	One HE One smoke One M203	Accompanied corporal on assault. Fired more as didn't have to command.
Charlie Rifleman 2	6 minutes	84	None	Wounded as the flanking attack started.
Charlie LMG	8 minutes	329	None	Was the point of fire. Using LMG to fire a burst of five round every five seconds
Tommy	10 minutes	113	3 M203	First in contact and won the firefight. Provided covering fire when Charlie team went flanking.
Delta Rifleman 1	0 minutes	0	0	Hit in the opening exchange.
Delta Rifleman 2	10 minutes	143	4 M203	Fired a bit more than Tommy as didn't have a command role.
Delta LMG	10 minutes	417	None	Started the firefight and responsible for getting the first rounds down.

A quick bit of maths shows that we have used 1,256 rounds of 5.56mm, nine 40mm projectiles and two hand grenades to kill two of enemy and wound a third. Clearly most of the rounds did not hit the enemy, which rather begs the question of where they went. While many will no doubt have gone into the ground and tree trunks close to the trench, a 5.56mm bullet can travel over 1,000 metres[63].

Even this minor action requires a significant amount of coordination. The key to success at the sharp end is training, training and more training. The battle of Waterloo may or may not have been won on the playing-fields of Eton, but the current engagements of the British Army are definitely won on the training areas of Thetford, Sennybridge and Salisbury Plain[64].

If you have formed the impression that this battle was a hard, savage and brutal conflict between two groups of desperate men in mortal peril you would be correct. Hold onto that thought, as the action that we have just witnessed (and myriad others like it) is the inescapable result of any decision to go to war.

Most of the ammunition was expended winning the firefight, which Tommy had to do in order to be able to close with the enemy to capture the position. That process could only start once Tommy had found the enemy and was in line of sight of them, using direct fire weapons. Of course, this gave the enemy the opportunity to fight back, wounding 25% of the section. If it were possible to suppress the enemy without having to be in line of sight and direct fire range, then Tommy's assault would have got off to a better start. There is

---

[63] While this may not be a problem in all-out warfare, one can imagine that in a peace support operation a couple of hundred bullets heading across a town full of non-combatants could set a "hearts and minds" campaign back a bit. We'll pick up this point in a later chapter.

[64] It is an unfortunate aspect of defence accounting that training budgets are easily cut when equipment programmes go over budget (as they always do). It is unforgivable that senior officers connive at this direct threat to Tommy's life imposed by mandarins and accountants. We shall return to training in Chapter 15. Until we get there remember the maxim "Train hard, fight easy."

a way to do this, using indirect fire. So let's leave Tommy sneaking a cigarette and a "brew" and take a look at indirect fire in more detail.

Chapter 5 Tommy's Best Friend (and Worst Enemy); Indirect Fire

So far we have seen that supressing the enemy quickly[65] extends Tommy's life expectancy and is fundamental to him being able to achieve his mission. We know that the amount of firepower that Tommy can deliver himself is limited by how much weight he can carry and how strong a recoil force he can withstand. We also know that being in the enemy's line of sight is dangerous as it exposes Tommy to the enemy's direct fire weapons. There are therefore two broad ways of getting more firepower onto the enemy position. One method is to produce a vehicle that has protection and firepower that enable it to operate in line of sight of the enemy. This is armoured warfare, which we will look at in the next chapter. The other method is to arrange for someone outside of the enemy's line of sight to be able to shoot at Tommy. This is indirect fire, artillery and mortars, which we shall look at now[66].

If we are firing at the enemy from beyond his line of sight we are almost guaranteed to be firing at longer ranges than a direct fire weapon. This in turn means that the projectile will be more exposed to wind and therefore less accurate. Compensating for this inherent inaccuracy requires an explosive shell. As we saw with the hand grenade, the lethality of an explosion deceases at the square or cube of the distance from the explosion. If the 250 gramme charge in a hand grenade has a lethal radius of five metres, getting a lethal radius of 50 metres (necessary to overcome the inaccuracy) will require a charge about 100 times larger, or 25kg. The recoil forces associated with firing such a heavy projectile are substantial.

---

[65] Known in the trade as "winning the firefight."

[66] Historical note: it was only really in the First World War that indirect fire became common. Prior to that, including during the Boer War, it was usual for artillery to engage the enemy directly. As we shall see, indirect fire requires communications over long distances which only became practical with the invention of the telephone – although it took the radio to actually make indirect fire effective in the attack.

Mortars

The simplest solution to the recoil problem is to dump it into the ground by resting the breech end of the weapon on the earth, thereby transferring the recoil forces directly. This is known as a mortar, and the general arrangement is shown below.

Figure 5.1 General Layout of a Mortar

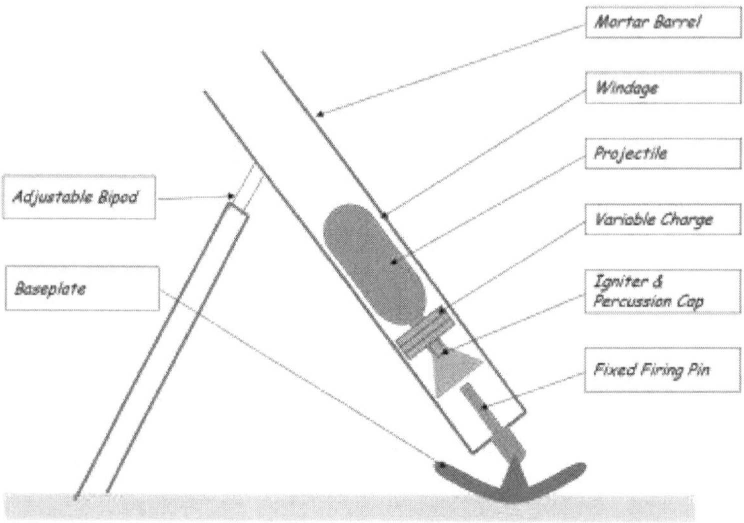

The projectile is dropped into the barrel, which it slides down. The air below the bomb escapes past the drive band, in a gap known as windage. When the projectile gets to the bottom it strikes a firing pin, which ignites the propellant, which sends the projectile back up the mortar barrel and on towards the enemy. While some of the propellant gas escapes through the windage[67], most doesn't and therefore accelerates the projectile up the barrel. The recoil forces are passed through the baseplate to the ground. The mortar is aimed by adjusting the angle and direction of the barrel. The system is simple and robust, and capable of high rates of fire.

Evading the need for a recoil system makes mortars relatively light and most can be broken down into man portable loads. This is very convenient in underdeveloped or inaccessible areas that are

---

[67] Some mortars, such as the British 81mm, have clever munitions that have a flexible drive band. This reduces the loss of propellant gas to near zero, thereby increasing both range and accuracy.

impassable to vehicles. But what is "man-portable"? The British 81mm mortar has a total weight of about 45kg and breaks down into three loads. The heaviest two, the barrel and base plate, are each over 15kg. This is, of course, to be carried in addition to rifle, ammunition, helmet, food, body armour etc. Mortarmen are almost weightlifters, and the more cynical of them understand "man-portable" to mean something heavy with a handle!

A mortar is useless without ammunition, and lots of it. If there is no vehicle to carry it then the infantry must. Typically each of the 600 or so men in a battalion will have to carry two mortar bombs each (another 5kg per head), which they will drop off as they pass the mortar firing position. Before he gets into combat Tommy is often a beast of burden.

 Using the earth for recoil does have a downside. As the firing angle, known as elevation, gets close to 45° we start to risk the recoil forces making the base slide along the ground. This would be exciting, but not conducive to safe, accurate fire. Mortars are therefore only fired at elevations of greater than 45°, known as the upper register. In practice the firing elevations are usually in the 60° to 80° range. This means that the mortar round is following a high trajectory, travelling a long way vertically in comparison to the horizontal distance travelled. This is not a problem in itself but it does significantly increase time of flight, and thus vulnerability to wind errors. These are complicated by the fact that wind speeds and directions change with height above the surface. The chances of a first round being on target are therefore reduced.

Restricting the allowable elevation means that there is a narrow band of effective ranges. However this is easily solved by varying the size of the propellant charge. A larger charge (charge 3 in the diagram) will send the round higher and further compared to a round fired with a smaller charge fired off the same elevation setting. The figure below shows a typical set of elevations and charges. Of course, the higher rounds will suffer more from wind than the lower trajectory ones. Note that to make the round travel further you DECREASE the elevation. This is the opposite to direct fire (or any fire with an elevation of less than 45 degrees – the lower register).

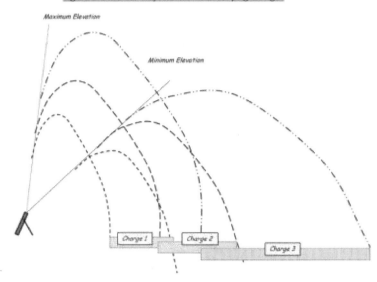

Figure 5.2 Mortar Trajectories With Varying Charges

Broadly there are three categories of mortar. Light mortars have calibres up to about 59mm. They are usually operated by one man and have a range of up to 1000 metres. Medium mortars have calibres of 60 mm to 120 mm. These are operated by a three or four man crew, and have ranges of up to about 8,000 metres. Heavy mortars have calibres. These may well be vehicle mounted or towed – they certainly are not man portable.

So far we have worked out how to get rid of the recoil and how to load the tube. Because mortars are muzzle loading we just need a quick thought about how they work. There is no cartridge case, so the propellant is carried into the breach on the projectile. In Figure 5.1 we have three charge rings attached, with space for three more. Just before the round is loaded the crew set the charge, in this case charge 3, by removing the three unneeded propellant rings[68].

When the projectile reaches the bottom of the mortar barrel, the cartridge strikes the firing pin. As with a rifle, this ignites the primer which ignites the propellant and accelerates the projectile back up

---

[68] The excess propellant rings are usually burnt in situ on the completion of the firing. In open air modern propellants burn quite benignly, it is the containment of the barrel, breech and projectile that make their combustion more violent.

the barrel. The net result is that our projectile, which for a medium mortar will weigh about 4.5Kg, will exit the muzzle at around 225 metres per second, depending of course on the charge used. Note that because of the windage the mortar is not spun by rifling grooves in the barrel, as it never touches them. Instead the tail fins generate spin, which ensures a stable flight and provides a mechanism for arming the projectile through the use of centrifugal force.

Once the projectile clears the mortar muzzle the crew just has to check the sights, and then load another. Mortars are capable of a high rate of fire, normally 10 to 15 rounds a minute and possibly as much as 30 for short periods if the tube is well bedded in (so the base plate doesn't move between shots) and the crew are fit and fresh. There are usually at least 6 medium mortars in a mortar platoon so if Tommy gets their support his enemy is likely to have 60 odd mortar rounds, each containing around 1 Kg of explosive, bursting on or above him in a 15 to 30 second period. That is the equivalent of about 240 hand grenades, which should dampen the enemy's will to fight.

However, sometimes Tommy is going to need a bigger bang than a mortar can provide, or want to hit the enemy further away than the mortars can reach. We now enter the world of artillery.

Guns and Howitzers

Mortars are generally carried, operated and controlled by Tommy and his infantry chums. Artillery is a whole bunch more complicated, and there is a separate part of the army which deals with it. Meet Gary the Gunner. It's his job to make sure that when Tommy asks for support the rounds arrive on target, on time. As we shall see, this isn't as easy as it sounds.

If we want to send a bigger round further then we have to revert to the rifle concept, and replace the windage with a driving band. This means what we can't muzzle load, so we need an opening breech. This in turn means that we can't use the ground to absorb recoil, because if we did the clever opening breech would be bashed into the ground. Instead we need to create a recoil system. The general arrangement is shown below:

Figure 5.3 A Standard Recoil System

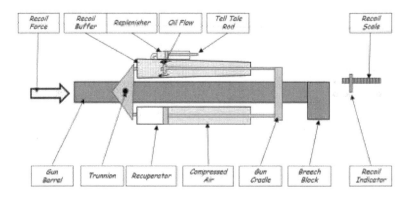

The gun barrel is held in a cradle which is in turn attached to the recoil damper and recuperator pistons. The recoil damper and recuperator are attached to the gun mount. When the gun fires, the recoil forces the barrel and cradle backwards, whereas the gun mount does not move (as it is attached to the earth). The pistons are dragged backwards. The recoil buffer is full of oil, which has to flow past the piston. Doing this absorbs energy from the recoil. The recuperator is full of compressed air, which is further compressed, absorbing more energy. When all the recoil energy has been absorbed the gun stops moving backwards – the breech presses against the recoil indicator, moving it along the scale. The recuperator is now full of very compressed air, and so starts forcing the piston (and the gun) forward again – with the recoil damper now acting as a shock absorber in the other direction. When the gun is fully forward (in the firing position) movement ceases.

Of course, if the gun is fired repeatedly the oil in the recoil buffer will get hot and expand. The replenisher allows for this. However as the oil gets hotter it also gets less viscous, so it absorbs less of the recoil.   The tell-tale rod on the replenisher and the recoil indicator are there to warn the crew if this is happening; they will have to cease firing to allow the oil to cool. If they don't at some point the gun would smash the cradle, which would be dramatic and life threatening.   And of course, that would mean less fire support available for Tommy, putting his life in jeopardy as well.

One further refinement to reduce recoil is a muzzle break, which is fitted to the end of the barrel. Once the projectile has left the barrel the propellant gas expands.

Figure 5.4 A Muzzle Brake

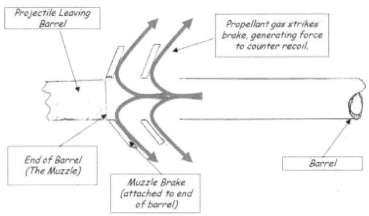

Some of this gas is deflected by the muzzle break, creating a force in the opposite direction to the recoil forces, thereby reducing it. Reductions in recoil of 20% to 30% can be achieved, with commensurate savings in the work required of the recoil buffer. There are a couple of downsides. Firstly a muzzle break adds mass, in particular at the end of the barrel. This means that the barrel has to be stronger, and therefore heavier and more expensive. The second is that the deflected gas has a significant pressure and velocity. It is also hot. While firing at high elevations (long ranges) this is not a problem, but at low elevations the muzzle is close to the ground and the high velocity gas kicks up dust – not a problem in itself but anything lying about may get damaged. The advantages outweigh the disadvantages and it is now rare to see artillery guns without muzzle brakes.

Artillery comes in a range of sizes. Nowadays the lightest gun is of about 100 mm calibre, the heaviest of about 200 mm. The most common calibre in the west is 155mm. Guns of this calibre are now capable of firing a 40kg shell containing 11kg of explosive some

30km – possibly 40km with rocket assistance[69]. Gary's first job on the gun line is likely to be feeding these 40kg shells to the gun as fast as he can. Upper body strength is a feature of artillerymen.

Range

There are three main benefits of having a longer range. Firstly, in a conventional war neither side's artillery engages in direct combat so artillery guns are sited to the rear. The longer the range, the further back artillery can sit and still be effective. From any one position a longer ranged gun can provide support further towards the enemy.

The second reason is that more guns can be brought to bear on any one target. This increases the intensity of the bombardment. Remember, it's the early rounds that do the most damage to the target end (as the survivors of the first salvo will have moved, or taken cover).

Finally, artillerymen enjoy shooting at each other - technically known as "counter battery fire". The longer the range, the more you can hit. Better still, if your gun has a longer range than the enemy's, you can lob shells at him and he can't shoot back. Unchivalrous perhaps – but safe and effective.

Figure 5.5 The Benefit of Longer Range

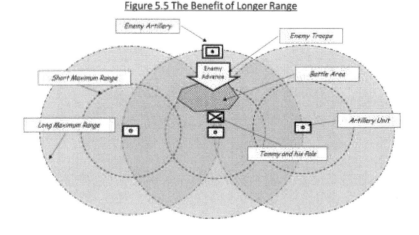

---

[69] A WW2 gun of the same calibre could throw a similar projectile about 15km. The increase is due to the onward march of technology.

As Figure 5.5 above shows, the longer ranged artillery means Gary can deliver three times as much firepower to Tommy. In addition, the enemy artillery is in range, and can therefore be engaged, preventing it from firing at Tommy.

Now, if long range is good, longer range must be better. There are limits on how much pressure a gun barrel can take, and therefore there is a limit on how much propellant can be burnt in a gun of any given calibre[70]. This puts the limit on the range that can be achieved from any one gun design.

Rocket Launchers

As we have seen, it's the early rounds on target that do the damage. Notwithstanding clever tricks with different charges and trajectories and having guns with longer ranges, there is a limit to how many rounds we can land on any one target at once, and that is the number of artillery pieces that we own. Artillery pieces are expensive and need lots of men to load and aim them.

In World War 2 the Russians came up with a brilliant solution, nicknamed "Stalin's Organ," which was to use rockets instead. The joy of a rocket is that there is no recoil to deal with[71]. All that is needed is a tube to keep the rocket steady until it has enough velocity for its fins to work. As there is little load on the tube, it is cheap and light. As it's cheap and light, with no recoil forces, lots of them (say 40) can be stuck together on the same launcher and fired almost simultaneously. Better yet, as they're all bolted together if we aim one we have aimed them all – so one crewman can fire all 40 rounds. Even better, because it is light the launcher can be mounted on a cheap truck. As they're cheap and don't need much of a crew we can have lots of them.

The Russians, and indeed the whole Warsaw Pact, went for this concept – big time. In 1963 they came out with the BM-21, which remains in production today. A battalion of 18 launchers is capable of delivering 720 rockets, each carrying 20kg warheads onto a

---

[70] The amount of propellant being brunt also affects the length of the gun barrel as it is (massively) inefficient for the projectile to leave the barrel before all the propellant has burnt. Or, in jargon, "shot exit" before "all burnt" is undesirable.

[71] Although there is a heck of a lot of back blast.

target in 20 seconds. That is three quarters of a ton of explosive per second which, as Tommy says, is enough to make your eyes water. This intensity of projectile delivery is also particularly useful for chemical weapons, which we'll come to later.

In the West rockets were less popular (except with the Germans, who presumably remembered the Wehrmacht's experience from the latter part of WW2, which they spent on the receiving end of Stalin's Organ). Rockets have some disadvantages. They are less accurate than an artillery shell and the range is shorter for a given payload. When fired they generate huge amounts of smoke, so they are easy to detect and thus vulnerable.   The rounds themselves are larger than artillery shells, and thus more expensive to make, move and store.   However the ability to get a large number of projectiles on or over a target simultaneously is compelling. Eventually the Americans developed the M270 MLRS[72]. This is tracked and armoured and carries 12 rockets with a range of over 30km. Each rocket carries a number of sub-munitions. In the First Gulf War[73] batteries of 9 MLRS repeatedly destroyed everything (literally, everything and everyone) in a grid square (1,000 metres by 1,000 metres or 100 Hectares) with one salvo, fired in less than a minute. God alone knows how many were killed.

Target Effects

On which sobering note it is time to have a look at indirect fire from the receiving end. From earlier chapters we know that we can kill a human with blast or shrapnel, and we have looked at this with hand grenades. The same effects are broadly true of artillery rounds and mortar bombs[74], but there are a couple of key differences.

---

[72] MLRS="Multi Launch Rocket System"

[73] The First Gulf War was fought in 1990-91. Iraq (a 3rd rate military power) invaded Kuwait, ended up in an armoured battle with the US, UK and French armour, which had been practising for such a battle (albeit in Europe) for over 40 years. In just 100 hours most of Iraq's combat power (including hundreds of thousands of Iraqi soldiers) was annihilated.

[74] Military pedants will argue for hours, or longer, about whether mortars fire rounds or bombs.

Firstly the projectiles[75] are bigger and have room for some clever fuses. This makes it possible to vary the burst height and detonate the projectile in the air. This saves much of the blast energy going directly into the earth without having the opportunity to pass through and damage one of Tommy's enemies. There are all sorts of ways of doing this. The oldest, devised by Lieutenant Shrapnel, Royal Artillery, at the end of the 18th century was by cutting a gunpowder fuse to the correct length to burst just before the projectile hit the ground. Nowadays, if timing is used it is likely to be electronic. There are also barometric pressure, laser and radar fuses, as well as the increasingly omnipresent GPS. Never forget that increasing complexity reduces reliability, and that an artillery shell accelerates up the barrel at over 50,000g so the circuit boards need to be tough.

So let's look at a bursting round as it hurtles towards Tommy's foe. At the designated moment the bursting charge detonates, rupturing the shell case. Note that all the fragments are already heading for the enemy at say 500 metres per second, the velocity of the shell. The bursting explosion just gives them an additional velocity away from the bursting charge, creating a cone of devastation. The fragments from the front of the shell hit the target before the fragments from the side hit the ground. This means that there is a variation in intensity, with the maximum concentration on Tommy's foe.

---

[75] Indubitably correct term — which will avoid long debates with aforementioned pedants. Beware though; they may mistake you for a ballistics boffin!

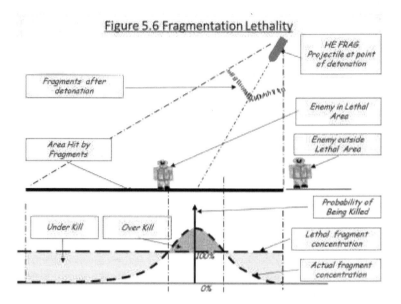

Figure 5.6 Fragmentation Lethality

As the chart shows, while this is lethal, it is not as efficient as it could be. Tommy's foe has been struck by enough shrapnel to kill him several times over, while his nearby companion has survived.

The solution to this is to create sub-munitions, each of which is smaller and separately fused. For the same effort in getting a projectile to the target area, we now have delivered more damage, effectively by taking the overkill and using it to cover the underkill. The same logic applies to bombs, which is why cluster bombs are now so widespread.

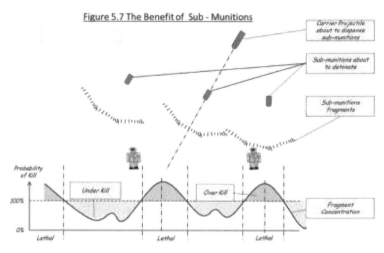

Figure 5.7 The Benefit of Sub - Munitions

The shrapnel pattern is not symmetric because of the descent angle and simple geometry. Blast effects add together in same way. As the diagram shows, the same projectile delivers over twice as much useful devastation.

Descent angle it is important if Tommy's foe is in a trench. A steeply descending projectile will still kill him, but a more gently descending one can't. Gary needs to know what he's shooting at so that they can pick the optimum trajectory and fusing option. This used to take lots of work with a slide rule and firing tables; of course today there are computers for it. Alternatively Gary could mix in some ground-bursting rounds to disrupt the trench – although as the First World War showed achieving significant disruption uses lots of ammunition. Gary's final option would be to use chemical weapons although the British Army eschews their use[76].

Figure 5.8 The Protection Given by Trenches

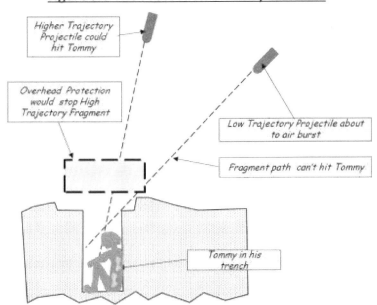

The other point about descent angles is that there are some targets that can't be hit - typically in mountain and urban combat. Of course, in the example in figure 5.10 below, it is entirely possible

---

[76] Chemical weapons are explored in Appendix Three.

that the lower trajectory round might destroy the block of flats, making it fall on Tommy. This is one of the reasons for the existence of large calibre mortars - they work well in modern urban terrain.

Figure 5.9 Terrain Masking Lower Trajectories

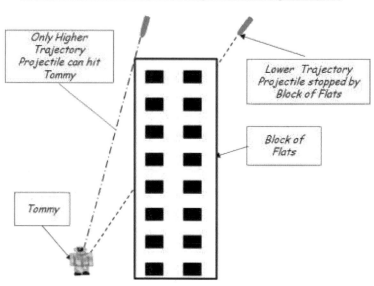

To sum up this chapter so far, we have now found a way of getting large amounts of explosive into the air. We have also seen how to maximise their effect once they get to the target. The slightly tricky bit is how we get it from the muzzle to the target, and that is what we'll look at now. It's a bit more complicated than shooting a rifle, as of course Gary can't see the target.

It is important to understand that artillery is generally an area weapon, not one that hits with pinpoint accuracy. The Royal Artillery, purveyors of indirect fire to the British Army, has the motto "Ubique." Gary maintains that this means "everywhere", as they're involved in all battles. Tommy, who is generally rather closer to the target area, believes that it means "all over the place" and tends to refer to Gary as a "drop-short". As Tommy says, being hit by artillery is never pleasant, but it's particularly galling if it comes from your own side. Inter-regimental banter aside, correctly handled mortars and artillery can generate a wall of death close to Tommy and thereby keep him alive and preventing him from being overrun, as the Taliban found out the hard way in Afghanistan – but we're getting ahead of ourselves.

Hitting the Target

First of all we had better define what and where the target is. We know it is an area so we can identify it on a map. If Tommy refers to grid 123 456 that defines a square 100 metres by 100 metres (i.e. a hectare) whose south-western corner is at 123 456. The next hectare north is at 123 457, the next one east at 124 456. So, if Tommy can see an enemy and work out on the map where that enemy is, he can pass that information to the gunners. Assuming that the gunners know where they are and have the same map, then they can calculate which way to point their guns and what the range is.

As ever, the practice is more complicated than the theory. For a start, Gary needs to know his own location more accurately than the nearest hectare. To do that he conducts a survey. Before GPS this would be to an accuracy of a 10 metres box, giving a grid of say 7890 1234. He would get this location using a theodolite[77] and a higher accuracy map. Of course, nowadays military GPS will give him an electronic location to plus or minus a metre of so, and more quickly. Whatever the case, Gary can't shoot until he knows where he is. But he also needs to have a reference point for directions, and so he has also to survey in a reference marker for his gun's sight – again modern artillery systems have navigation systems to provide this electronically. Without GPS it can take a well-trained crew 10 minutes to bring a gun into action.

Having surveyed the gun in, let's consider an engagement, or "fire mission," at a range 25km from the guns. Gary has to hit a target 100 metres wide. The angular accuracy required is therefore 100 metres/25km = 4 mils. Let's put that into perspective: a cricket pitch is around 20 metres long, so a similar angle would give a target of 8 cm wide. If you remove one stump from the wicket (not

---

[77] A theodolite is a surveying tool – in the non-military world you see them most commonly at roadsides, when surveyors are plotting the next bout of road works. The theodolite is the thing that looks a bit like a camera on a tripod.

the middle one) the angle is equivalent. How frequently would the average bowler hit such a wicket?

If line is a challenge, range is possibly worse, as Gary must also need to consider target elevation. Gary needs to consider whether the target is higher or lower than the gun, and adjust his settings accordingly.

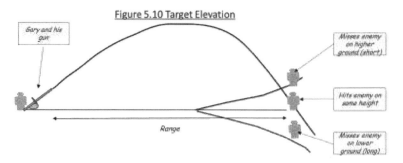

Figure 5.10 Target Elevation

Fortunately the map tells Gary the target's altitude, so another quick bit of maths gives him the angular correction[78]. His crew can now set the fuse on the projectile, load the projectile into the breach and ram it home, put in the correct amount of propellant and close the breech. All of this shakes the gun, so it can't be finally laid on the calculated bearing and elevation until it's loaded. It is then fired on Gary's order. As it is the early rounds that do the most killing (before the enemy has gone to ground), he will almost certainly ensure that all the guns fire together. This can get quite complicated when the guns are widely dispersed and therefore are firing at different ranges with different times of flight. Gary needs to get the rounds to hit the target at the same time which will involve firing at different, but tightly controlled, intervals. The technical term for this is "time on target." When Gary gets it right it can be devastating.

Once it leaves the muzzle, the projectile is subject to the same effects as a rifle bullet, but they last 100 times longer, as the projectile has about 100 times as far to go. The time of flight to 25km is likely to be over 45 seconds, during which time the forces and laws of nature are going to deflect the projectile from its target.

---

[78] Again, in really modern guns (artillery pieces ARE called guns), there are terrain databases that do all this automatically.

The biggest effect will be from wind. Even a light breeze of 10 km/h (at the surface) is going to move the projectile tens of metres at impact. Worse than that, because our projectile is going to reach a height above the ground of several thousand metres wind direction and velocity change significantly with altitude. Of course, having gone up the projectile will come down again, through a different set of winds (and weather). How often is the wind and weather the same in London and Guildford? Gary has the same problem.

And, as we know, it is not just wind. Atmospheric density and air temperature (both of which vary with altitude) affect the air resistance of the shell. So does the presence of water vapour, which is relevant if there is a cloud in the way. Gary (or his computer) also has to consider barrel wear, the breech and charge temperatures, what sort of round it is and who made it (shells are mass produced and different factories may have different tolerances). All in all, the hectare is starting to look like a very small target.

There are two things that Gary can do to reduce this challenge. The first, unsurprisingly, is to measure the wind. This is done by regularly sending up meteorological balloons, the data from which is then broadcast to all gunners. This provides a meteorological correction.

The other solution is to fire a smoke round at the target hectare and ask someone near the target where it went, make a correction and try again. This process is called registering a target, and adjusting artillery fire is something that every commander at every level should be able to do. Have a look at the diagram below.

Figure 5.11 Adjusting Artillery Fire

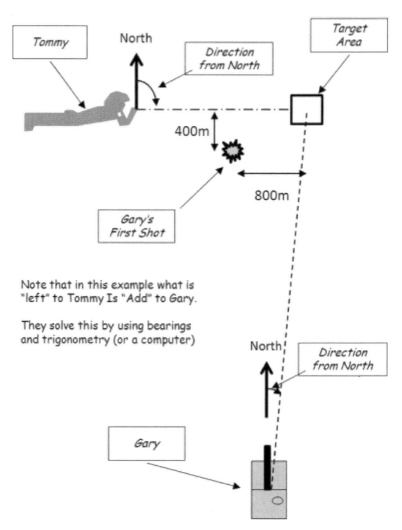

Note that in this example what is "left" to Tommy Is "Add" to Gary.

They solve this by using bearings and trigonometry (or a computer)

So let's see if Tommy is any good. His test is to adjust Gary's fire onto the target. They do this via radio. The sequence will be something like this:

What Is Said	What it means
"Hello GOLF 20 this is INDIA 31 Fire mission, Grid 123 456,	GOLF 20=Gary, INDIA 31 =Tommy

enemy infantry company in open. Neutralise at 15:30 for 2 minutes, over."

Note that numbers are said as their digits, i.e. "Golf two zero" not "Golf twenty."

This gives Gary all the information he needs to select ammunition and set fuses.

"GOLF 20 Fire mission, Grid 123 456, enemy infantry company in open. Neutralise at 15:30 for two minutes, wait out."

Gary repeats everything back as it would be embarrassing if a typo dumped this fire mission in the wrong place. There will then be a pause while Gary (or his computer) does the sums, loads etc. Then:

"Hello INDIA 31 this is GOLF 20. One gun adjusting, shot 45, over."

Telling Tommy that there is one round in the air, which will land in 45 seconds

"INDIA 31. One gun adjusting shot 45. Send splash, over."

Repeating. "Send splash" means "tell me when its 5 seconds from impact." (Remember Tommy could well be in a fire-fight, and can't spare 40 seconds).

GOLF 20. Send Splash out.

Repeating. Then, about 35 seconds later:

Hello INDIA 31 this is GOLF 20. Splash Out.

Tommy looks at the target and surrounding area to see where the round lies. If he can, Gary will have sent a smoke round to make it more obvious. When Tommy sees the impact he works out how much it has missed by (in metres), and sends a correction.

GOLF 20 this is INDIA 31. Direction 1550 magnetic, left

The direction is the bearing from Tommy to the target.

400, add 800 over.	Magnetic tells Gary that he will have to subtract magnetic deviation[79].
GOLF 20, Direction 1550 Mag, Left 400 Add 800 Out	Gary repeats what is said and then converts Tommy's left 400 (metres), add 800 (metres) to the correct alteration for the gun. Then relay and
"Hello INDIA 31 this is GOLF 20. One gun adjusting, shot 45, over."	Another round is on the way.
"INDIA 31. One gun adjusting shot 45. Send splash, over."	
GOLF 20. Send splash out.	
Hello INDIA 31 this is GOLF 20. SPLASH, Out.	Tommy looks up, and this time sees the round on target.
INDIA 31, on target. Fire for effect over.	i.e. get everyone firing.
GOLF 20 Fire for effect. Shot 45, over.	All the guns will have been following the corrections from the adjusting gun, and so can fire immediately, and keep loading. HE rains onto the target area until the rounds allocated for the task are finished. Then
INDIA 31 this is GOLF 20. Rounds complete. Over.	All the rounds have been fired although there may well be two or three still in the air. If Tommy is attacking, this is his cue to prepare to move

---

[79] Unfortunately the magnetic north pole moves, so north on the compass is not the same as north on a map. The difference is "magnetic deviation," which itself varies with time and from place to place. It's just one more thing for Tommy and Gary to remember.

INDIA 31 rounds complete, record as target, end of mission, over.	Repeating, then asking for a quick reference number for the target, and then confirming that the rounds have had the desired effect.
GOLF 20, record as target, end of mission out.	Repeating. Then:
INDIA 31 this is GOLF 20, target number ZW235 out.	That target is now ZW235 and the settings required to hit it are recorded.

By giving the target a reference, all the gun settings are recorded. If Tommy calls for that target again, Gary knows that he can hit it first time, and therefore can go straight to fire for effect, saving 2 minutes or so and thereby killing more of the enemy sooner. The other benefit is that Gary now knows the difference between his predicted shot and the corrected shot. The next time he fires in the area of ZW235 he can add the correction, saving a round and, more importantly, reducing the time between Tommy needing fire support and it arriving on target.

Of course, the best solution is to register the target before we need it. Provided he has meteorological data and the opportunity to check the odd target, once Gary has registered one target in an area he would expect to hit them first round – meaning he can go immediately to Fire For Effect, and rain death and destruction on the enemy sooner.

In the pre-computer age, this meant lots of writing and record-keeping for Gary. It's a bit simpler now, but of course no-one trusts a computer not to throw a wobbler at the crucial moment (or indeed, fail as a result of counter-battery fire) so the records are still kept and the manual skills practised.

FOOs, FDCs and MFCs

There is one refinement of the system. It's a long way from Tommy to the guns, and actually Tommy has plenty of other stuff to do, (like sticking his bayonet into the enemy's guts). Although he can adjust fire, there is usually another link in the chain, called a FOO

(Forward Observation Officer) if you have artillery support and MFC (Mortar Fire Controller) if you have mortars. Tommy points out the target to the FOO or MFC, and then the FOO takes over adjusting the fire.

Generally there is not an unlimited supply of artillery support; at any one moment there are more of Tommy's colleagues wanting artillery than there are guns. Their competing demands are sorted out and prioritised in a fire direction centre (FDC), which allocates guns to targets on the basis of urgency and opportunity to kill. The fire direction centre also has to deal with guns that are moving from one position to another, allocating guns for counter-battery fire and a myriad of other technical stuff that Gary understands but need not trouble us or Tommy.

We have now got to the state of warfare circa 1914[80]. We have a battlefield that is full of bullets, artillery fragments and explosions that can make life short, unpleasant and brutal. Being caught in the open is both probable and fatal. This makes it hard to attack and harder yet for an attack to succeed. However wars are not won by defence alone. We therefore need to find some protection, preferably mobile and from which we can kill the enemy while being safe from at least his indirect fire. We need tanks and other armoured vehicles.

So let's step up from the infantryman's pedestrian mud and move to the classier world of armour, tanks and the cavalry.

---

[80] Although in 1914 they did not have radios, which meant they had to use land lines to communicate with the guns. This is fine in defence as one can bury the lines in a trench to protect them. It's not so good in the attack as surface laid lines will get cut by artillery fire (your own or the enemy's), and with it the crucial link between the infantry (almost certainly facing a counter-attack) and the guns (which had the potential to destroy the counter-attack, enabling the infantry to advance further). This simple technical point explains much of the frustration of the First World War and the repeated failure of attacks to hold the ground captured or achieve a breakthrough. The significance has been missed by many most commentators.

Chapter 6 Tommy Goes Heavy Metal; Armoured Warfare

Chapter Four demonstrated the risks that Tommy has to take in order to close with the enemy and impose his government's will. Chapter Five explained indirect fire and how it is possible to rain destruction on the enemy (or close to him) without the person firing the gun having to be exposed to direct fire. Tommy can be killed by people who can't see him, as well as by those who can. This is approximately the state of warfare in 1916 – getting out of one's trench is dangerous.

The solution was to build a machine that could transport firepower to the enemy, while keeping the crewmen inside safe[81]. This concept became the tank, and eventually spawned a whole range of armoured fighting vehicles doing everything from killing the enemy to bringing up supplies and evacuating the wounded. They share a high level of mobility and a level of protection that is substantially higher than that of a man in the open. Armoured vehicles are complicated, and there is more technical detail in Appendix Two.

TANKS

The first thing to realise is that in the same way that all that glitters is not gold, not everything with tracks and a gun is a tank. Remember that and you know more about soldiering than most people. The history of the tank and its evolution has been better described by others and is beyond the scope of this book. For our purposes a tank is a main battle tank, like a Challenger 2, Abrams, T-72 or Leopard.

---

[81] The German for a tank is *panzer* (or, in full, *Panzerkampfwagen*). The word panzer also means a safe, so to a German a tank is a safe battle vehicle. "Safe" in this sense, is of course a relative rather than absolute term.

Figure 6.1 General Layout of a Four Man Crewed Tank

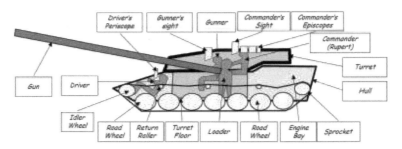

Look at figure 6.1, which shows a slice through a modern tank. The entire vehicle is designed around the gun, which is mounted in the turret. The turret sits on the hull and is capable of rotating through 360 degrees. The hull contains the driver at the front, the fighting compartment (the bottom of the turret) in the middle and the engine and transmission at the back. The power from the engine is taken through the gearbox to the sprocket, which drives the track. As the track moves forward from the sprocket it is supported by the return rollers until it gets to the idler wheel. It is then laid down on the ground, and the road wheels (which carry the weight of the tank) drive along it. To steer the driver applies a brake[82] to one track, which slows and the tank therefore turns.

THE CREW, AND LIFE ON BOARD

A tank has a crew of three or four comprising the Commander (who can usually also fire the gun), the gunner (who fires the gun), the loader[83], who loads the gun, helps the commander with the radios (and in a Challenger makes the tea) and the driver. The driver generally sits by himself in the hull, while the other three are in the turret.

---

[82] In British tanks he achieves this through pulling a lever (known as a stick). On some tanks he has a steering wheel.

[83] On three-man crewed tanks the loader is either replaced by an automatic loader, as on the Russian T-72, or the commander gets to load as well. While removing the crewman has the advantage of making the tank smaller and lighter, it does increase the workload on the rest of the crew – particularly during maintenance and on protracted operations

Inside the tank is very different to Tommy's world, and it attracts different people. Meet Rupert, a tank commander. Rupert is an officer, and so as well as commanding his own tank controls the actions of other tanks. Command is covered later in the book; at the moment just consider Rupert as a tank commander – not all tank commanders are officers.

As a fire team commander, Tommy can always see the three riflemen that he commands, and they can see him. If necessary, Tommy can grab them and boost their morale by some intense personal counselling. In contrast Rupert is almost touching his gunner, can see the loader (but is separated from him by the gun) and can't see his driver at all. Neither the gunner nor the loader have the ability to opt out of combat in the way that one of Tommy's infantrymen can by lying down and refusing to advance. But the driver, who is the only crewman who can drive the tank, can opt out by refusing to advance. While Tommy has relatively straightforward access to recalcitrant riflemen, Rupert (and the rest of the crew most of the time) can't even see his driver. The leadership challenges are significant.

While a tank looks big from the outside, inside it is small and cramped. (Figure 6.1 has left out most of the contents of the vehicle for simplicity and clarity). The driver usually has the most room and the most comfortable seat. Although he has intercom and can hear the radios, he lives in isolation from the rest of the crew. He can only get access to the turret when the gun is in a specific position, and that requires the litheness of a limbo dancer. The driver has his own hatch, and can raise his seat to drive head out. However if the turret is likely to rotate he will drive with his seat lowered and his hatch shut, using his periscope. If he stayed head up he would run the risk of being decapitated by the turret when it traversed.

The turret is dominated by the gun, which effectively divides it in two. The loader stands on one side, the commander and gunner sit on the other, with the gunner's head pretty much touching the commander's knees. The commander, Rupert, sits at the top, usually equipped with an array of episcopes[84] to give him 360°

---

[84] An episcope is like a periscope, but has a wide field of view and no magnification.

vision. He might have a tactical data display, and he'll probably have a GPS read-out. He has a map on his lap and dangling round his neck are radio controls. He has a set of gun control equipment, and his sight Is aligned with the gunner's sight. If at all possible Rupert will travel head up, as he has a much better view (albeit without the benefit of thermal sights) and the open hatch provides much needed fresh air[85].

The person closest to Rupert is the gunner, who sits literally at his feet. The gunner has a limited view out of the tank through the gun sights, and complex fire control systems to manipulate – his primary responsibility is acquiring and engaging targets. He is all too aware of Rupert's presence – particularly if baked beans have been on the menu. The gunner does not have his own hatch; he can only get in and out of the tank if Rupert gets out first.

Across the turret is the loader, who usually stands on the turret floor. As well as loading the gun, he also helps with the radios, encoding and decoding if necessary as well as switching frequencies. He is the crewman most likely to be injured; if he slips and catches his foot between the turret floor and the hull he will break his leg at the least. If he gets into the gun's movement and recoil area he will be pulped. The loader does have a hatch, which again will be open if it is prudent. On a British tank the loader also operates the "BV[86]". This is an electric water heater which produces hot water and enables canned and bagged meals to be cooked. The loader is also the only crewman who can get to the driver from the turret, and even then only with the turret in a specific position and the gun depressed, so the loader gets to be both chef and waiter.

---

[85] If the turret hatches are open many tanks take their engine air in through them, as there is less dust. This ensures a constant flow of air through the turret (or at least past the commander). It is very important to remember to switch the engine to its hull based air intakes before shutting all the hatches.

[86] The Boiling Vessel transforms the quality of life of an armoured soldier. Breaking the BV, which is something that fresh young officers are prone to doing, can lead to very full and frank exchanges of view – plus a miserable lack of hot tea. It has been argued that as the BV is at the centre of a tank, which must be the safest place, it is therefore the most important thing in the tank. Few tank men would demur.

When Rupert wants the tank to move he tells the driver where he wants to go. Wise commanders give the driver the maximum freedom to pick their routes, although it takes a while to get the hang of describing where to go to a person with a lower viewpoint. Once the tank is moving Rupert will be looking through his episcopes at what else is going on and the gunner will be scanning for targets through the main gun sight, continually moving the whole turret from left to right and back. Depending upon the terrain and speed, the loader will be either clinging on for dear life or looking out of his episcope – he is more likely to be standing on the turret floor than perched on his small seat. While there may be some chatter over the intercom the crewmen will also be able to hear the primary radio net[87] and generally will try to avoid speaking if there is something important happening on the net. Singing drivers are not appreciated.

Living in such enforced intimacy generates a less formal relationship within a tank crew than in an infantry section. Thus Rupert, who is in fact an officer and in the infantry would be called "Sir", is known as "boss" in his tank. Similarly, he'll use crewmen's nicknames (but never Christian names) rather than surnames when giving instructions. With the hatches shut the interior is dark, lit only by a couple of small lamps and the glow from some of the warning lights. There is an air supply, which blows in air that has been filtered to remove chemicals, bacteria and dust. Some tanks have heaters, some air conditioning, but the atmosphere inside any armoured vehicle is pretty fetid, with a strong odour of sweat, diesel and cigarette smoke. The crew can live inside for protracted periods (most tanks have some form of primitive toilet, typically a plastic bag and a seat, which does not improve the odour) but the noise and vibration make the environment very tiring. It's not a lifestyle for everyone.

The primary characteristics of a tank are firepower, protection, mobility and communications. Let's look at these features in more detail.

---

[87] And can speak on it from their positions

FIREPOWER

We'll start with fire power because we understand guns and delivering firepower is the prime purpose of a tank. Tanks are direct fire weapons whose primary job is knocking out other tanks[88]. Once they have destroyed the enemy tanks they are then virtually invulnerable and can provide Tommy with devastating direct fire support. We know that tanks are well protected so we know that knocking them out is going to require a lot of energy. This energy can be generated either kinetically (by firing a high velocity projectile) or chemically by filling the projectile with explosive.

Sabot Rounds

Kinetic energy is a function of the projectile mass and the square of the velocity. We need the energy to be high at the target end, so the projectile needs to be streamlined to minimise air resistance and thus preserve velocity. This is best achieved by using a sabot round – see Figure 6.2 below. The projectile, made of a dense strong metal such as tungsten carbide, is narrower than the barrel calibre. The gap is filled by a light carrier called a sabot.

---

[88] If this sounds self-fulfilling, remember that in the First World War, when only the British Army had tanks, and could therefore concentrate tank firepower on Hans (the German Infantryman), they won a series of spectacular successes such as at Cambrai in 1917 – finally achieving the ability to capture, hold and exploit from the German positions that had been more or less unchanged for the three preceding years.

Figure 6.2 A Sabot Round

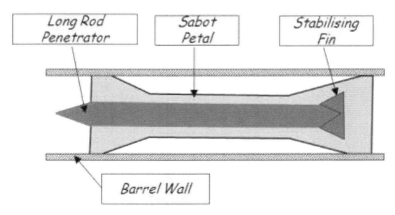

Once the projectile exits the barrel the light sabot falls away, leaving the bulk of the energy in the (heavy) long rod penetrator. It is the movement of these sabot "petals" that prevents tank guns from having muzzle brakes[89].

A modern sabot round weighs around 8.3kg and has a muzzle velocity of 1,750 m/s, over 5 times the speed of sound. This has a kinetic energy of 25MJ. That is the same energy that a hatchback car would have travelling at over 350 mph. The penetrator diameter is about 30 mm; when it hits the enemy tank all this energy is pressed onto a piece of metal about half the area of a baked bean can. The resulting heat and pressure makes the metals flow like water[90], and the penetrator slips though. As it emerges on the inside of the target tank it fills the target with high velocity, hot metal fragments, which will be on fire if the penetrator is made out of a pyrophoric[91] metal. These burning fragments will bounce around inside the target until they hit something inflammable, explosive or the crew. It may also trigger secondary explosions

---

[89] There is such a thing as a pepper pot muzzle brake that gets round this. See Appendix Two.
[90] Literally. The effect is called "Hydrodynamic flow" for the jargon junkies.
[91] Pyrophoric means it has a tendency to catch fire. Such metals include Zirconium and Uranium 238, which is also dense. This is why many anti-armour rounds are made of depleted Uranium.

within the tank, perhaps from ammunition being detonated, which will do neither the crew nor the tank any good whatsoever.

As well as giving the round huge amounts of energy, the high velocity makes it very accurate, particularly against moving targets. With a time of flight to a range of one mile of less than one second the target won't have moved far and there is less time for the wind to have an effect. Of course, getting the projectile up to Mach 5 requires an enormous charge, typically 15kg of propellant, and a long, strong barrel. There are also substantial recoil forces which have to be dissipated by the recoil system, which is pretty much the same as for an artillery piece – although bigger as the energy loads are higher.

Chemical Energy Rounds

Sabot rounds are best at destroying tank targets and are generally saved for them. However not all targets are tanks. There are abundant trenches, Infantry Fighting Vehicles, buildings, lorries and the like on the battlefield; tank guns have other types of ammunition to deal with them. These use explosive: the simplest is the high explosive fragmentation round. This is not an anti-armour round, but is used to kill infantry in a similar way to artillery (albeit, as a direct fire round it is much more accurate and can hit individual trenches). We learnt about HE-FRAG in the last chapter, so we won't cover it again.

The next type is the HESH (High Explosive Squash Head) round, which is fired by rifled tank guns[92]. When the projectile hits the target it forms an explosive "cowpat" on the outside, which then detonates. This sends shock waves through the target's armour, and bits break off the inside. These fragments then bounce around the inside until they hit something soft (the crew), important (all the electronics and the engine) or explosive (ammunition and fuel). Not fun for the occupants. However most tank guns are now smooth-bore (as this allows a higher muzzle velocity) and are therefore able to fire HEAT (High Explosive Anti-Tank) rounds.

---

[92] British tanks have rifled barrels. Most others have smoothbore guns, which enables the use of HEAT and the achievement of higher muzzle velocities. There has been no advantage to rifled tank guns for three decades, but you have to admire British persistence.

HEAT Rounds

HEAT warheads use a shaped charge to focus the explosion on a small area. These are the most common anti-armour warhead on the battlefield, and are worth considering in detail. As the armour penetration comes from the explosive in the warhead, the speed at which the round gets from launcher to the target is not a factor. Shoulder launched anti-armour rounds, such as the ubiquitous RPG-7, use HEAT warheads to achieve their effect as do larger missiles such as the Hellfire.

The key part of the HEAT warhead is the copper liner, which is shaped in a parabola[93]. Have a look at the figure 6.2 below:

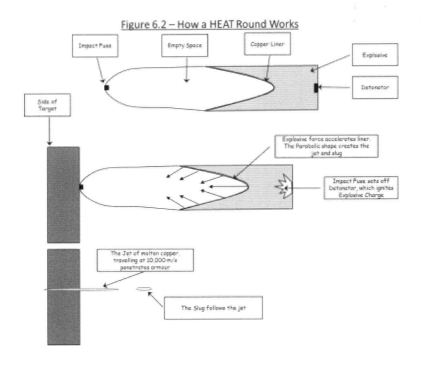

Figure 6.2 – How a HEAT Round Works

---

[93] A parabolic curve is the shape of the mirror at the back of a torch or spotlight; it reflects light from any angle into a beam. The precise detail of the shaping depends on the target, the type of explosive being used and myriad other technical factors. A simple cone works well.

When the impact fuse hits the target, it triggers the detonator which ignites the explosive from the back. This transforms the liner, usually copper, into a jet of molten metal travelling towards the target at about 10,000 metres per second and a "slug" which is less tightly focussed and travels slightly more slowly. The jet then uses its kinetic energy to cut through the armour, filling the inside with high velocity, molten metal.

The distance between the fuse and the liner is known as the stand-off distance. It is crucial to the penetration – if the warhead is detonated at any other distance from the target the jet will be "out of focus" and its penetration will be much reduced. The "cage armour" often seen on vehicles in Iraq and Afghanistan is there entirely to make HEAT warheads detonate early – thereby losing penetration. There is much more on the various sorts of armour in Appendix Two.

Rifled guns can't fire HEAT rounds because the spin of the projectile prevents the jet forming due to centrifugal force.

MACHINE GUNS

Some targets, like men in the open and light vehicles, are more economically engaged with a machine gun or chain gun. Normally a tank will have one mounted coaxially[94] with the main armament and another on the turret roof, operated by either the commander or loader. It is generally dismountable and used for local defence when the tank is parked in a hide (of which more later).

Most countries fit 7.62mm machine guns for the commander or loader. The exceptions are the Russians and Americans, both of whom of whom opt for something bigger. The Americans continue their long love affair with the Browning .50 and the Russians with their equivalent 12.7mm, although both have the lighter 7.62mm weapon as a co-ax.

---

[94] Jargon for "pointing the same way as." The co-ax is essentially mounted to the main gun, and therefore points the same way.

Smoke Dischargers

Every now and then even the best tank commander gets into the wrong place at the wrong time, and blunders into the sight of the enemy. Tommy solves this by throwing himself to the ground but Rupert in his tank does not have that option. Instead he uses smoke, generated in one of two ways. Some tanks have both.

One method is to fire a pattern of smoke grenades. Launchers are mounted on the front and/or sides of the turret. Rupert presses a button and they all fire, typically producing a cloud of smoke about 30 metres from the tank covering at least the frontal 180 degrees. These are usually white phosphorous and generate an instant screen –albeit with the risk of setting anything on the outside of the tank on fire. The advent of thermal imagers (which can see through some smoke) has led to more complicated grenades which are designed to produce a hotter smoke, impermeable to thermal imagers.

The other way is to inject diesel into the exhaust. This too generates smoke, although it is usually emitted from the exhaust ports in the rear of the hull – not a problem as the tank will be reversing out of trouble anyway. It takes some time for the screen to build up.

Fire Control Systems

As Tommy will tell you, being able to hit the target is one thing – actually hitting it is another. (We have already seen that it's tough for Tiger Woods and harder still for Tommy.) For Rupert, who may be shooting at something three metres wide at a range of 4,000 metres, it's harder still. Fortunately his tank comes equipped with sophisticated sights, thermal imagers, laser rangefinders and a clever computer. Assuming that he has performed all the necessary procedures and maintenance correctly (not as straightforward as it sounds – see appendix two) and that the wind behaves Rupert is pretty much guaranteed a first-round hit if the target is static and Rupert's tank isn't moving either.

Of course the problem is that most of the time one or the other of them will be moving, and sometimes both. Modern tanks have "stabilised" guns and turrets – which means that they point the same way regardless of the movement of the tank itself. Top flight tanks can therefore hit moving targets while they themselves are moving – provided all the systems are working. As you can imagine, there is quite a lot of complicated machinery and electronics involved in keeping a 15 ton tank turret pointing in one direction constantly while the tank hull hurtles across country, bouncing over bushes and ditches. Tanks are therefore not cheap, and consume many man hours of maintenance. But when 10 of them advance towards you at 30 mph, firing accurately three or four times a minute with lethal consequences, you'll agree that it was money well spent.

PROTECTION

In theory, protecting the tank is simple – just wrap it in lots of armour plate. In practice this is difficult. Modern anti-tank weapons can typically penetrate over 600 mm of rolled homogeneous armour ("RHA"[95]). Making all the armour on a tank this thick would produce something far too heavy to move. While there are now more sophisticated armours available, it is not possible to protect a tank completely from all angles as the weight and size of the ensuing vehicle would be impossibly large.

The best protection is not to get hit in the first place. We can achieve this through using the shape of the ground to hide most of the tank. As Figure 6.3 below shows, Rupert can hide most of his tank, even when he is engaging the enemy.

---

[95] RHA is the standard method of measuring the protection of armoured vehicles. In fact there are now more sophisticated armours, including ceramic, Chobham and reactive armour. These are discussed in more detail in Appendix Two.

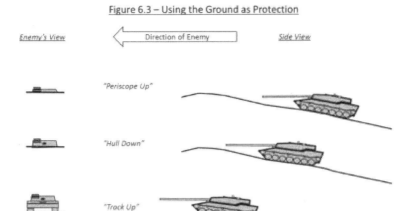

Figure 6.3 – Using the Ground as Protection

If Rupert parks his tank behind a crest, he can use the dead ground behind it for protection while still being able to see the enemy by being "periscope up."

If and when Rupert sees a target he can then move to "Hull Down" to engage. He does this by telling his driver to advance, slowly. If he goes too far then he will expose more of the tank than necessary – if he advances too little he may have a different problem. The gunner's sight is higher than the gun muzzle; it is therefore possible for the gunner to fire at a target that he can see fully but the round to hit the crest in front. There are various methods of checking "crest clearance" that involve levelling the gun and either the loader looking down the barrel (if it is not loaded) or the gunner using an emergency sight, which is mounted coaxially with the gun.

If there are more enemy targets Rupert can reverse to periscope up, if not he can then advance – exposing the whole of his tank ("track up") only when he knows that it is safe to do so and that his gun is loaded and ready to fire. Remember, tanks prefer to engage at ranges over one mile, which means that there is usually a convenient crest for Rupert to use. The process of using a crest like this to protect his tank while engaging the enemy is known as "jockeying" – it requires practice and clear communication with the driver (who can only see over the crest if he's gone too far forward).

You can also see that although the ridge protects Rupert's tank very well from the front, if an enemy did get onto the same ridge and look along it Rupert's tank would be very, very vulnerable. Using the ground to provide protection is fundamental to tank warfare, and is a skill learnt by practice. There are some terrains, such as the desert, where there are insufficient undulations to provide Rupert with something to hide behind. This was the case in the First Gulf War, and additional armour was added to tanks to offset this problem.

Of course, it is still possible that the enemy will see Rupert and shoot at him. However if Rupert is doing a good job then only part of Rupert's tank that the enemy will be able to see is the front of the hull and the front of the turret. So that is where tank designers put the armour plate. This is not to say that the remainder of the tank is unprotected – certainly it is impenetrable by small arms calibre rounds and artillery fragments. But it won't stop a HEAT round.

Size

As Tommy's girlfriend tells him, size matters. It's true for tanks as well. The smaller the tank the less it weighs for a given level of protection. A lighter tank requires a smaller engine for a given performance. A smaller engine consumes less fuel and so requires less space, so the tank can be smaller still. While this virtuous circle is lovely, it ignores one thing. Our tank exists to kill other tanks (and any lesser target) which requires a big gun firing heavy projectiles at high velocities, generating recoil forces. These, combined with the projectile's dimensions, fundamentally influence the minimum width of a tank.

Figure 6.5 The Turret Ring

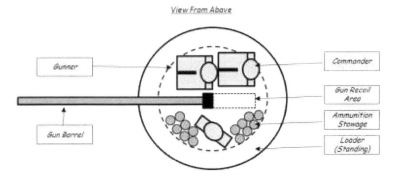

View From Above

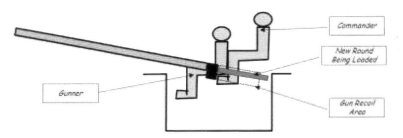

Side View, Without Loader and Ammunition

MOBILITY

Depending upon the crew size and level of protection, a typical tank weighs between 45 and 70 tons. Moving this about the battlefield is challenging. Firstly it needs something to stop it sinking into the ground.

Tommy weighs about 90kg and has feet with a ground contact area of about $0.015m^2$ has a ground pressure of about 55kPa, or 8psi. If he starts walking then the pressure doubles to 110kPa. Rupert's tank must have a similar ground pressure to Tommy's foot if they are going to cross the same ground, about 100Kpa. So a tank weighing 45 tons needs a ground contact area of $4.5m^2$. This would require an awful lot of wheels or a pair of tracks, each having a width of 0.5m and a length in contact with the ground of 4.5m. Heavier tanks need wider, longer tracks.

Fitting wheels large enough to deliver the required contact area would make the vehicle enormous and high. This of course is an impossible solution, as it would need more armour plate, which is heavier and so demand bigger wheels - a vicious circle. The wheel only becomes a viable option for cross country fighting vehicles weighing 15 tons or less.

Having decided upon tracks, the next challenge is power. Most modern tanks have a power to weight ratio over 20 horsepower per ton. While that is only quarter of power to weight ratio of a small family car, for a 60 ton tank that means that it needs 1,200bhp. Tanks need high power density; in other words the maximum power from the minimum volume (including all the power train and the fuel). Most common tank engines are up-rated[96] commercial 4 stroke diesel engines. Gas turbines are now more common, and are fitted in the Russian T-80 and the American M1. Their advantage is that they produce a very large amount of power from a tiny volume. The challenge is that they have a very narrow power band, which makes for a complicated gearbox and poor fuel consumption. They also need lots of clean air requiring lots of bulky air cleaners, and generate large volumes of high velocity, hot exhaust, which makes them easy to spot on thermal imagers. Certainly the M1 is no smaller than any other modern Western tank and the (three man) T-80 is not noticeably smaller than a (three man) T-72

Tanks almost always have their engines at the back, where they are out of the way and behind all the armour plate[97]. The engine is surrounded by metal with a minimum amount of airflow, so it gets hot and requires elaborate cooling systems. Tracked vehicles also vibrate far more than road vehicles and so engine reliability and life is much lower than it would be in a commercial vehicle. The net result is that Rupert and his crew spend much of their time maintaining and mending their vehicle.

To steer a tank, one track must sometimes go faster than the other. This is achieved through the use of an epicyclic gearbox, which work in a similar way to a differential. Most tanks are able to perform a

---

[96] Up rating means that the engine management system is adjusted to burn more fuel – which generates more power. Of course, you don't get anything for nothing and the price is paid in fuel economy and reduced engine life and reliability.

[97] The exception is the Israeli Merkava.

neutral turn, where one track goes forwards and the other backwards making the tank turn on the spot. The risk with this manoeuvre is throwing a track, thereby immobilising the vehicle and creating some hard work for the crew, plus abuse for Rupert.

The tracks are made from a number of steel links, which may have rubber inserts to reduce noise and vibration. They are held together by pins. Let's just consider the life of a track link.

Figure 6.5 Running Gear

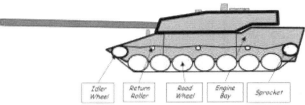

It starts on the ground, at rest with the tank's road wheels passing over it. Immediately after the last road wheel passes over it the link starts moving vertically to the sprocket. As it goes round the sprocket it loses its vertical velocity and is accelerated to twice the tank's velocity. At this speed it bounces across the return rollers and reaches the idler wheel, where it stops moving horizontally and is lowered to the ground. If the tank is doing 36Km/h or 10 metres per second, then the link is travelling at 20 metres per second on the top. It is accelerating to that in the time it takes it to travel the radius of the sprocket, which comes out at around 50g! One third of a second later it decelerates at the same rate at the idler, is lowered to the ground and then driven over by the tank. Unsurprisingly, tracks wear out quickly as the pins stretch – as do sprockets in particular and idlers. If a track breaks at high speed the results can be spectacular, often flipping the vehicle onto its back. This is not fun for the commander, whose head is often the highest point of the vehicle.

Moving the 40 to 60 ton tank across country at 30 miles per hour or so requires a hefty suspension system to smooth the ride. There are several main approaches to tank suspension. The first, and by far the most common, is to use a torsion bar, essentially a spring running across the hull bottom. Some tanks use gas and fluid in a tube, which has the advantage of combining shock absorption and damping in one unit. Motion sickness is a problem. In tanks the gunner, who generally has the worst view, is most susceptible. In Infantry Fighting Vehicles the entire dismount section is vulnerable.

One final peril is "hatch rash," which is a disease suffered by commanders when their open hatch breaks out of its retaining lock and slams shut. The usual symptoms are a sore head, concussion and crushed fingers. Crushed vertebrae are not unknown. Those who have had it once are very, very conscientious about checking the security of their hatch.

COMMUNICATION

Rupert's tank moves at about ten times the speed of Tommy on his feet, so   a tank commander has to consider ten times as much battle space, ten times as fast as a dismounted infantryman. It also means that an armoured battle space is large, with long distances between friendly forces opening up. Radio communications are fundamental to armoured warfare.

Tanks generally have two powerful VHF[98] radios, capable of transmitting over 25 Km or more. They might or might not have encryption, and they might have an ability to pass data as well as voice. The number of radios reflects the number of radio networks that can be monitored and spoken on simultaneously. Rupert will normally be commanding his tank crew over the intercom (both ears), listening to his boss and commanding his other two tanks on the squadron net (left ear) while monitoring his regimental command net in his right ear[99]. He's a busy bunny!

Tanks, and indeed all armoured vehicles, have plenty of electricity available and so are increasingly having other pieces of battlefield

---

[98] VHF=very high frequency, most commonly used for ground voice radio. UHF (ultra-high frequency) is used for ground and air to air. HF is available as a backup. The higher the frequency the more data can be passed, and the better the sound. Increasing frequency also makes the transmission more reliant on line of sight.

[99] There is more detail in this in Chapter 15.

command and control equipment added to them. In the same way that the infantryman regards anything new as another load to carry, tank crews tend to look at electronics boxes as another thing to bash their head on. Increasingly, armoured vehicles have a range of data displays, depicting ground and friendly forces locations. For now we'll focus on communication inside the tank.

FIGHTING THE TANK

Rupert sees an enemy tank. He immediately points the gun its general direction while starting to issue a fire control order. The intercom conversation sounds a bit like this:

Rupert	Loader	Gunner	Meaning
"Fin! *Tank...* *....On"*			Load a (fin-stabilised) sabot round.
			The tank that I want you to shoot is now by the aiming mark.
			(Rupert, who spotted the target first, laid the aiming mark close to the target when he took control of the turret – which he now relinquishes to the gunner).
		"On!"	I can see the target, and am starting the engagement sequence.
	"Loaded!"		A sabot round is loaded. I have made all the safety switches and the gun is ready to fire. I have another sabot round in my hands to reload.
"Fire!"			Nothing in the way, fire the

	gun.
"Lasing..."	I'm firing the laser range finder. The gun is about to move as it automatically elevates.
"Firing NOW!"	The aiming mark is on the target and I'm pressing the trigger. (British tank gunners are taught to fire on the "ow" of "Now.")
"Target!"	The round hit the target.
"Target. Stop."	Target is destroyed and I can see no others
"Loaded."	I've reloaded sabot. I have made all the safety switches. The gun is ready to fire again. I have another sabot round in my hands to reload.

The driver has said nothing, but that does not mean he is not part of the process, particularly if Rupert's tank is firing on the move. The moment he hears *"Fin tank on!"* he knows that he must drive as smoothly as possible, avoiding bumps and changing gear. He is also aware that an enemy tank is probably trying to engage him as the target – with potentially lethal consequences. Sitting by himself, he is likely to feel quite isolated in his fear[100]. There is absolutely nothing that he can do about this other than driving smoothly to help the turret crew.

Note also how few words convey lots of meaning, and disguise lots of activity. Of all the crew, it is Rupert who is most aware of the level of danger. If he wants to get the best out of his tank, it is important that the crew don't get frightened. Being able to use

---

[100] In the Second World War most tanks had two crewmen in the hull, the driver and the radio operator. Many veteran tank drivers tell of the comfort of having another human alongside them. Some held hands at moments of severe pressure.

familiar commands to generate familiar actions is fundamental to operating the weapon system. Training and practice is essential.

OTHER ARMOURED VEHICLES

Most armoured vehicles are not tanks, although almost all of them have been designed to exploit the speed and manoeuvrability that tanks have brought to the battlefield and many of them have turrets, guns and tracks.

RECONNAISSANCE VEHICLES

The role of a recce vehicle is to find the enemy. To do this they need to be mobile, and if possible small. Their weaponry is primarily for self-protection, although the ability to snipe and/or engage high value targets, such as headquarters, is desirable.

The vehicle has excellent sensors, and the ability to dismount a couple of men can be a benefit. Different armies have very different solutions to reconnaissance, and it is an area of great controversy and confusion[101]. The consequence is that recce vehicles vary in size from 10 tons or so to over 40 tons, range in armament from machine gun to anti-tank missiles and guns and crews range from two to six or seven.

INFANTRY FIGHTING VEHICLES AND ARMOURED PERSONNEL CARRIERS

The solution to enabling Tommy to keep up with Rupert is to give him a tracked vehicle too. Easily done, and we end up with an Armoured Personnel Carrier, or APC. It's an armoured box with a door at the back, typical examples being the British FV432 and the ubiquitous US M113 which carries a crew of two, plus a section of eight men in the back. Simple, relatively cheap and reliable, this

---

[101] In the UK controversy and confusion usually translates into delay. The author recalls being involved in trials for the replacement of CVR(T), the then obsolescent British reconnaissance vehicle, in 1987. He was involved again as an advisor in the late 1990s. The contract for its replacement was eventually announced in 2010, with an in-service date of 2015. CVR(T) will thus have managed 30 years' service as an obsolescent vehicle, on top of the 20 years when it was adequate. It makes one proud to be British.

now gives Tommy two possible homes. One is in a trench, holding ground; for this the APC is held in the rear. The other is advancing with the tanks, in which case Tommy is safe in his APC – which will protect him from artillery and small arms fire, if not from a direct hit. The risk of a direct hit rises as the advance becomes an attack and more so when that attack becomes an assault.

If Tommy is in his APC assaulting a position he will be in one of four APCs in his platoon, all of which will typically be supported by one tank. They can't all hide behind it, so there is an increasing risk from handheld anti-tank weapons. The tank is supposed to stop this, and indeed it does – usually by putting HE-FRAG of HESH rounds into any trench that it sees (and don't forget that Gary the gunner will be laying artillery on the front of the enemy position too – but this will have to lift as Tommy's APC gets close and Tommy is about to get out). But at all times the tank's priority is enemy armoured vehicles and not avoiding being engaged from the rear by enemy infantry with handheld anti-tank weapon. Tying the tanks tightly to the infantry compromises their ability to use ground to perform their (vital) primary task.

This dilemma took some time to solve. The Russians, who had a specific problem[102] and plenty of armoured experience, solved it first producing the BMP[103], which has set the baseline for Infantry Fighting Vehicles (IFVs) ever since. This had a gun turret, an anti-tank missile and outward facing seats with firing ports to enable the infantry to fire their weapons from inside – only dismounting if absolutely necessary. Twenty years later the British ended up with Warrior, which has a turret with an obsolescent 30 mm cannon, no anti-tank missile and no firing ports.

The theory of IFVs is that in the assault the additional firepower on the IFV adds to the suppression of the immediate infantry objectives – and being direct fire it is more accurate and therefore it can continue to fire at the enemy as Tommy dismounts and closes in.

---

[102] The problem was how to destroy NATO forces (primarily in West Germany) should The Cold War ever turn hot. They had to achieve this even if nuclear weapons were used.

[103] BMP stands for Boyevaya Mashina Pekhoty, which is the Russian for infantry fighting vehicle.

Ideally the IFV should be able to engage accurately as it approaches the dismounting point. That involves firing on the move which requires stabilisation[104] in order to be accurate. There are three broad options for when Tommy dismounts to fight, illustrated in Figure 6.6

Figure 6.6 – Dismounting Options

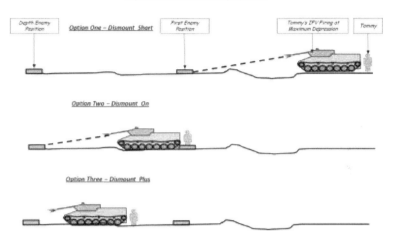

Dismounting short of the objective is easy for control, and provided the weapon on the IFV can depress enough, pretty straight forward. Tommy and the rest of his section then skirmish forward with fire support from the IFV, and capture the trench. The IFV can then move forward, pick them up if necessary and the process can be repeated.

Dismounting on the position has the advantage of getting direct from the artillery protection of the armoured box to the artillery protection of the trench. However it does run the risk of receiving a grenade inside the IFV, which would be catastrophic. There is also the complication of the driver stopping in the right place – he can't see the ground ahead of him if it's less than (typically) 5 metres away. However, if Tommy is in an APC (i.e. an unarmed vehicle) this is probably the best option.

Dismounting after the position gives the IFV the maximum opportunity to damage the trench and its occupants, and it can

---

[104] The US M2 Bradley has stabilised cannon. The British Warrior does not.

place itself between the target trench and any supporting trench. The disadvantages include the distance to travel, the vulnerability to enemy fire and the inability to provide Tommy with fire support as he assaults.

While none of these options is easy, the alternative of making the entire assault on foot is usually a whole lot worse[105].

Note that the size of a section has grown by 25% to provide the IFV crew and that while Tommy is still only working at 3mph when dismounted his vehicle and higher commanders still have to fit into the faster armoured battle. This can be quite a cultural shift. There are also questions about who is in command when the dismounts are out, and how best to lead. The answer is practice, and lots of it.

COMMAND VEHICLES

The armoured protection of combatants has spread to headquarters. Generally a command vehicle is based on an APC or IFV, often with added headroom. It will typically have at least three radios, an intercom system and a map board. Tactical displays and computers abound, and the crews are skilled at linking large numbers of command vehicles to form complete headquarters.

Some commanders need to get forward and into or close to the combat zone. These will have command tanks or IFVs, which are only distinguishable from the gun tanks by the presence of an additional radio antenna.

SELF-PROPELLED ARTILLERY

Of course, if Tommy and Rupert can now advance at 30 miles an hour, they need their artillery to be able to keep up. The solution is to give Gary as self-propelled gun. His artillery piece is mounted in a turret on a tracked chassis, almost always at the back. Compared to towed artillery, self-propelled artillery is better protected, more mobile and faster into action. In the digital age, it is also better connected.

---

[105] And, crucially, IFVs have BVs in them so Tommy is assured a hot cup of tea once he has completed the assault.

Gary will still need lots of ammunition, which has to be provided separately, usually by cross-country container lorries, although there are also armoured, tracked logistic vehicles. And now that he has a 40 tonne armoured vehicle he's going to need more fuel, mechanics and spare parts – Gary's logistic needs, always challenging, have become greater and more complicated.

We have covered a huge amount, and taken Tommy, Rupert and Gary from the technology of 1914 to the 21st century. They can now cross huge distances quickly, and kill the enemy from the relative safety of an armoured box. The cost of war has expanded, as has the lethality. In exchange for an armoured box to call home, Tommy has lost the ability to protect himself by throwing himself to the ground. Complexity has increased enormously, the armoured vehicles need far more support, training and maintenance. Tommy, Gary and Rupert need to learn more stuff and there are now proportionately more people involved in supporting their efforts – the proportion of manpower engaged in combat is reduced, although the combat effect[106] per head is massively increased. Costs have escalated spectacularly.

But the basic challenge facing Tommy, Rupert and Gary remains unchanged –find and identify the enemy without being found themselves. See without being seen and you can kill without being killed. It's time to consider target acquisition.

---

[106] Measuring combat effect is a fascinating and complex business way beyond the scope of this book. Think of it as the number of projectiles delivered on target per minute and you'll be on the right lines.

Chapter 7 Tommy Sees the Light; Surveillance and Target Acquisition

Now that we know how Tommy, Rupert and Gary can rain death and destruction on any enemies that they can see we need to understand how they see them – which is the tricky bit. That is what this chapter is about. By implication, it is also about how Tommy and his pals can avoid being seen by the enemy with concomitant benefits to their quality and length of life.

Like you, Tommy takes in the overwhelming majority of the information that he needs through his eyes. The human eye is an astonishingly capable sensor. In the jargon, it has a field of view of about 140 degrees[107] , full stabilisation and an integral coincident rangefinder. It is able to detect another person at about 1,000 metres. What does all that mean? Well, with the minimal amount of head turning Tommy can see to his front and flanks. His eyes work when he is moving, and his brain sorts out a coherent picture for him, even if he is jumping up and down the image stays constant. Because he has two eyes he can judge distance, and thus movement speeds accurately enough to catch a ball travelling at 100 kilometres per hour. With practice he can estimate distances accurately up to over 1,000 metres. Detection is more complicated.

DETECTION, RECOGNITION AND IDENTIFICATION

There are three key concepts in target acquisition.

> **Detection** means we know something is there, but we don't know what. It could be a tank, a person or a roe deer. You may scoff at confusing such different things, but it is possible if you are using a thermal imager (which identifies heat) or a Doppler radar (which identifies movement) or a trip flare, which goes off when anything disturbs a tripwire. Tommy was safe and content the moment before he detected something at the limit of his sensor's range. Now he is alert and worried; it might be the enemy.

---

[107] That is with two eyes. You have about another 20° on each side where you have only single eye vision, making a total of almost 180°.

Recognition happens when Tommy is able to distinguish between various target types. "It's a tank," or "It's an animal." Note that he still does not know enough to distinguish friend from foe, and so can't decide whether it's a threat or not. However Tommy now does have enough information to be able to aim an appropriate weapon

Identification is the ultimate stage – "It's a T-72," or "It's Corporal Smith," or "It's an enemy infantry section."

THE BATTLE PICTURE

Now, the sensor will give Tommy most of the information that he needs, and (if it is a weapon sight) will enable him to engage. However it is not the only source of information; other sensors and his knowledge of the state of the battle will also guide Tommy. Imagine Tommy is a sentry in a defensive position, anticipating an attack by an armoured enemy from the east. He has been told that there are no friendly forces to his front. He hears track and engine noises, and then makes out something through a thermal imager. Although this is only detection on the thermal sight, the track noises make it an armoured vehicle and the knowledge that there are no friendly forces to his front means that it's an enemy one. He has combined information from three sources to deduce what is happening and has achieved identification at detection range – a significant tactical advantage.

Conversely, imagine Tommy has been told that there are no friendly forces to his front, but that there may be refugees fleeing. He hears engine noises and through his thermal imager sees something. He has to wait until he can recognise the vehicle, "It's a car," before he can decide whether it is hostile or not.

Two points arise. Firstly, soldiers prefer sensors that can provide identification information as soon as possible – particularly if there are civilians about. Secondly, knowledge of the current battle picture is fundamentally important. The key word here is current, as battles change every second. It could be that the tank from the first scenario is one of ours, perhaps a straggler having broken down, but if no one has told Tommy he has no way of knowing that his battle picture is wrong. This dilemma is often referred to as "the fog of war", and is a primary cause of what the media term "friendly fire engagements[108]."   There are procedures to avoid this, and some technology sometimes helps.

Generally, a better trained army operates in a less dense fog – but tired people make mistakes. We'll cover the process and technology in the chapter on command, but understand now that as sensors become more capable detections, but not necessarily identifications come earlier.   Note also that being able to tell the difference between say a Challenger 2 and a T-72[109] through a thermal sight at extreme range is a key skill.   It can only be achieved through training[110].

ACTIVE AND PASSIVE SENSORS

One more concept that you need to understand is whether a sensor is active, which means it both emits and detects radiation, or whether it is passive and just detects the reflection. Active sensors have the advantage that they are not dependant on other sources of radiation (like the sun).   The big downside is that using them announces our presence to anyone with a passive detector – which is why competent burglars don't use torches. A human eye (passive light detector) can see a candle at over 1,000 metres.

OPTICAL SENSORS

Imagine two photons[111] of visible light that comes from the sun, make their way through the atmosphere, hit the surface of the earth (or something on it) and get reflected towards Tommy's eyes (one ending up in each of them).   In each eye, the lens in the pupil focuses the photons onto the retina, where the photon hits a rod or cone, depending upon how close to the centre of Tommy's view the

---

[108] One of Murphy's Laws of Combat is that "There is no such thing as friendly incoming fire".

[109] In the 2nd Gulf War someone confused the two and one Challenger engaged another. The good news that the Challenger ammunition worked was mitigated by its impact on the crew of the target Challenger.

[110] Much effort has been expended in the development of target identification algorithms. While they are improving, Tommy is better than a machine at target recognition. He is also cheaper.

[111] Or "beam" if you prefer.   This is not a book about particle physics (thankfully!).

object is. The rods, which are at the centre of the retina, need quite high levels of light and provide a colour picture. The cones, round the sides, require less light but provide less detail.[112] The rod or cone then generates an electric signal, which passes down the optic nerve and into Tommy's brain, which paints a picture for him based on the photon's frequency and energy (colour and brightness) and, as Tommy has two eyes both of which have seen a photon from the same place, the brain also works out the distance and produces a 3D image.

This is the basis of how Tommy sees the enemy. If there is insufficient light being reflected into Tommy's retina his brain can't construct an image, and Tommy sees nothing. Tommy gets more light by looking through magnifying lenses, such as binoculars, telescopes and gun sights. There is a trade-off between the amount of magnification and the field of view. Unaided, your binocular field of view at 1,000 metres is about 2,000 metres. Use a typical pair of binoculars and the magnification will be seven times, but field of view is a mere seven degrees, or one twentieth of the normal 140 degree field of view of a human. The SUSAT sight on Tommy's SA-80 has x4 magnification and a field of view of 10 degrees.

Of course, the enemy is not going to make it easy for us to see him even if there is enough light. He can disguise himself:

Figure 7.1 Background Contrast

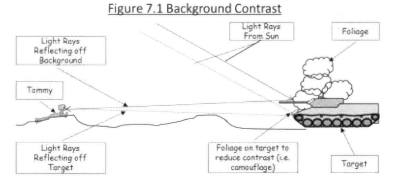

Have a look at Figure 7.1 If the enemy can make the light bouncing of his vehicle have the same (or similar) frequencies and amplitude

---

[112] Tommy has learnt that to see at night it is best to use peripheral vision and not to look directly at what he is observing – which is all fine and dandy until he needs to aim his weapon.

to the light bouncing off the trees beside it, then Tommy's brain will not distinguish them. The easiest way to do this is to cover the tank in branches from the same sort of tree. Welcome to the art of camouflage. A well-trained soldier who follows the rules of camouflage (shape, shine, surface, shadow and silhouette) can become indistinguishable from his background. Snipers rely almost entirely upon this for their protection, and have special ghillie[113] suits to help. Even normal combat clothing has pigments in it to try to mimic the reflectivity of foliage.[114]

Generally target acquisition is easiest for the defender, who can remain static (movement attracts the human eye) and has had time to select and conceal his position. Reconnaissance troops, who generally lead advances, often struggle to detect a competent static enemy without being seen themselves.

NIGHT

At night time there is less visible light so Tommy can see less. Weather has a great influence, as does the phase of the moon which, in the context of target acquisition, is a big mirror reflecting sunlight onto earth. However, even on the brightest night Tommy can't see as far as he can in daylight; as the reduced amount of light makes it impossible to distinguish the target from the background.

The obvious solution is to get more light to the target by shining a light at it. Until the invention of thermal imagers, all tanks had searchlights fitted to them and many second-rate armies still have nothing better. The problem is that a million candlepower searchlight is an active sensor and gives its position away[115]. Engaging with a searchlight is still more effective than firing and

---

[113] A Ghillie is a Scottish word for someone who helps stalk deer – and whose field craft is therefore outstanding.

[114] The British military habit of steam-ironing and starching their uniforms at every opportunity does not help these pigments at all, but it does make the chaps look smart.

[115] One way of getting found the problem of shining a beacon from your tank was to put on an infra-red filter – which meant that the searchlight beam was only visible to those with infra-red red detecting sights. As this included anyone in a tank and most of those with an anti-tank weapon the improvement was marginal.

missing, or not firing at all. If the tank crew is slick, the time between illuminating the target and killing it is short and they turn the light off quickly the method is still viable.

There is a more elegant searchlight based solution which is sometimes possible. It relies upon refraction[116], and using a hill or ridge to refract a searchlight beam, as shown in Figure 7.2. The neat bit is that the searchlight is reasonably well shielded from the enemy.

Figure 7.2 – Bending Searchlight Beams

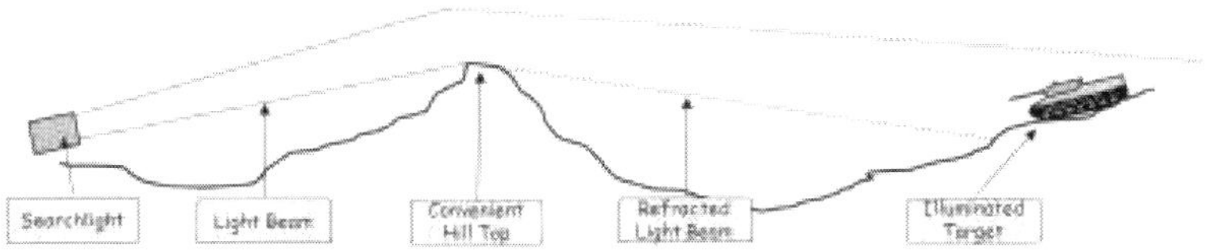

| Searchlight | Light Beam | Convenient Hill Top | Refracted Light Beam | Illuminated Target |

Of course, not everywhere is so conveniently located. So now we turn to indirect fire. One of the many types of ammunition available to artillery and mortars is an illuminating round – usually called ILLUM. It is simply a parachute flare that deploys above ground level. Typically the flare will last for 60 seconds, so keeping the target lit is straight forward and leaves plenty of tubes available to lob HE about the place. Meantime Tommy can stay concealed in the dark, shooting at the enemy – who may have lost their night vision. For minor engagements there are handheld rocket flares which achieve the same effect. Notwithstanding the availability of ILLUM, it is not ideal. We don't have sufficient ammunition to be able to fire enough ILLUM to transform night to day all night – and we wouldn't want to either because we'd wear our barrels and give gun positions away.

IMAGE INTENSIFIERS

Although there is not enough visible light falling on the earth for the human eye at night this does not mean that there isn't any light at all – just that there is not enough in the visible spectrum. The problem is that Tommy's eyes can't detect outside the visible spectrum, so he needs a converter. This is what an image intensifier

---

[116] If I tried to explain refraction I would end up writing a book on particle physics. Trust me, it works.

(II) does. Like any other optical device, it has a lens that focuses the incoming (invisible) light onto a sensor. This in turn releases a photon in the visible range, which is then focused by the human eye. Within the electronics there is an ability to amplify the light. The results are startling – the modern II sight available for SA-80 enables targets to be identified at around 300 metres.

Image Intensifying sights are now small enough to be helmet mounted, which makes them useful for patrolling and observation. However views tend to be foreshortened and it is still less than perfect so using them successfully requires practice. More importantly though, we now have got to the stage where we are doing as much as can possibly be achieved with ambient light. To see more or further requires another approach.

THERMAL IMAGERS

We have seen that any active source of electromagnetic radiation is potentially detectable. All things at a temperature above absolute zero are hot. This means that their molecules are vibrating, and in doing so they are emitting electromagnetic radiation, known as "black body radiation". Everything on a battlefield is therefore an active emitter of black body radiation, which is in the infra-red band. The tricky bit is finding a sensor that can focus and detect in this waveband. These now exist, and are called thermal imagers.

Focussing the radiation of this frequency requires a lens made from exotic materials such as indium, gallium and arsenic, which get very expensive very quickly. Detection is usually achieved on focal plane arrays that are cooled to -200°C or so by liquid air, or Stirling engines.[117] Again, expensive and complicated. However the results are worth it as Tommy and Rupert can now see anything that has a temperature greater than absolute zero, which is everything. The hotter a target is, the easier it is to see. Fortunately things of military interest (tanks, people) are hot. So are rabbits and other nocturnal creatures, but the quality of image means that we can distinguish them, and they're no more confusing that they would be in daylight.

---

[117] A Sterling engine is a very clever piece of thermodynamic equipment that is commonly used to cool things to minus 200C.

As the manufacturing techniques improve TI becomes cheaper and more common. Pretty much all modern western combat vehicles now have thermal sights, as do helicopters and attack aircraft, where it is often referred to as FLIR.[118] Within the constraints of fields of view, we now have turned night into day.

This has one interesting corollary. Before thermal imaging, moving at night was fairly safe. Provided Tommy did not get lost and kept about 300 metres (i.e. effective II sight range) from the enemy, he was pretty much invisible, and immune. He could therefore walk across open ground that he would avoid in daylight. When he was given TI he suddenly realised how vulnerable he was, and started to move at night in the same way that he had at day – which significantly slows his movement.

There are some things that TI can't do. It is not good at looking through dense fog (the water absorbs the radiation), glass (which is opaque to TI) or dense brush. Heat haze can also cause problems. However the bottom line is that with TI sights Tommy can use his weapons as effectively at night as day. This makes battle a 24 hour a day activity, which has implications for Tommy's fatigue levels. It also creates yet more costly, heavy and logistically demanding equipment for Tommy to carry. But the benefit is huge, particularly if Tommy is fighting an enemy who either doesn't have TI, or who has not trained extensively with it.

RADAR

Radar is an active source – it sends out a pulse of electro-magnetic radiation and then detects the reflection. By the time taken and the angle of reflection the radar can immediately produce an accurate location of the target. There are all sorts of radar bands, referred to by letters of the alphabet (e.g. S-band, X-band etc.). While this is of fascination to electronics buffs, it need not concern us. But we do have to revise one more bit of physics, which is the Doppler Effect.

Imagine a radar pulse heading out, as shown in Figure 7.3. The distance between outgoing pulses is W, the wavelength. When the first pulse hits the tank, it is reflected. During the time gap before the second pulse arrives the tank moves, and so the second pulse

---

[118] FLIR= Forward Looking Infra-Red

has less distance to travel. The wavelength is thus reduced to X, and the clever electronics in the radar use this to work out how fast the tank is moving towards the radar.

Figure 7.3– Doppler Radar

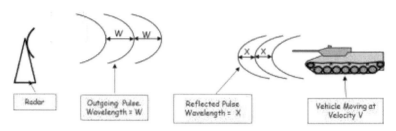

| Radar | Outgoing Pulse. Wavelength = W | Reflected Pulse Wavelength = X | Vehicle Moving at Velocity V |

The point is that the change in reflected frequency is a function of the speed and direction of movement of the target – which gives us even more valuable information, electronically in real time. Radars can reach to 30km or more, provided a line of sight exists. They tend to be sited on high ground, possibly on elevating masts.

On the battlefield, ground surveillance radars are used by reconnaissance troops and forward artillery observers[119] like Gary. (Artillery shells have metal cases and have high, changing velocity and therefore show up well on Doppler radars). Radars consume electricity and are heavy, so they are at their best when mounted on vehicles. They can be dismounted, with Tommy, and even Gary, becoming beasts of burden (again).

While detecting ground targets is challenging due to line of sight and ground clutter, detecting artillery and mortar rounds in flight is quite easy, as they travel high in the air. The joy is that once we have their height, speed and direction we know where they are on their trajectory, as the laws of physics are universal. We can therefore deduce where they are going to land and when, which gives us a chance to warn our troops, although we only have seconds to do this. Alternatively, we can work out where they were fired from, and can pass the grid reference to our own artillery to enable them to engage in counter-battery fire.

---

[119] Usually called FOOs – Forward Observation Officers

The final use of ground based radar is in air defence – i.e. shooting down enemy aircraft. This is getting to the limit of Tommy's world, but we will consider it briefly in a later chapter.

RADIOS AND ELECTRONIC WARFARE

Although radios are traditionally considered part of the command and control system I'm going to include them here as they too are part of the electro-magnetic spectrum.

There are a whole range of radios available, with varying weights, sizes, antenna lengths and frequencies. Nowadays every soldier has a radio, and certainly every weapon system does That is an awful lot of people to be talking on a finite number of frequencies – and so there are strict protocols about who speaks when and how. Brevity and clarity is everything.

There are three bands[120] used in the military. High Frequency (HF) is used for speaking over long distances and as a standby. It is not particularly dependent on line of sight and indeed, with favourable atmospherics, can bounce signals a very long way – even across continents. HF tends to work on Amplitude Modulation (or AM) and signal quality is variable. Very High Frequency (VHF) is used for voice command nets, and passing data. It is very line of sight dependant. Most military VHF sets use Frequency Modulation, or FM. This gives a more robust signal. Ultra High Frequency is used for talking to aircraft.

Again, when one starts talking on a radio, you are blasting out electromagnetic radiation which is as receivable by the enemy as by whoever you were talking to. If he can hear Tommy, or more likely Rupert[121], the enemy has three options. Firstly he can intercept what is being said, and try to work out what is going on. Nowadays this is defeated by encrypting the signal automatically. Before encryption was common Tommy spent an awful amount of time manually encoding and decoding orders. This time delay slowed down command, and combat. Moving to encryption has made life

---

[120] Some armed forces also have their own, mobile, mobile phone system. This generally operates at higher levels of command and will not trouble us further.

[121] Officers notoriously tend to speak most on radios.

easier, although Tommy and Rupert both dread ever having to talk to Scots and Geordies on the radio, as their accent can be impenetrable.

The enemy's second option is to jam the signal – blasting out a more powerful signal on the same frequency. This used to be devastating, but the advent of frequency hopping[122] radios has made it much harder. If Tommy doesn't have frequency hopping, he changes to another frequency while hoping that someone knocks out the jammer.

Finally the enemy can triangulate where Tommy is, and either use this information to deduce what Tommy is up to or he can pass the location to his artillery and arrange for a bombardment. The defence against this is to use burst transmissions, which compress a long conversation into a short broadcast – thereby making it much harder for the enemy to triangulate the signal and deduce its source.

Anything that emits or receives electromagnetic radiation is vulnerable to jamming. As well as all the radars and radios that we have been discussing, there are a couple of others that might not be so obvious.

The first is some anti-tank guided missiles. Some of these track a flare at the back of the missile. If we broadcast a stronger signal from the target in the same frequency range as the flare, the tracker will not be able to distinguish the missile from its background – thus the guidance will fail and the missile miss. Some Russian tanks now have such a system fitted.

The other one is GPS. This system has now become part of the fabric of many military systems, including some bombs and projectiles. A GPS sensor relies on receiving a radio time signals from the constellation of GPS satellites, which are around 30,000Km away in a geosynchronous orbit. If we had a transmitter on that frequency at the target end it could interfere with that signal, with

---

[122] Frequency hopping radios change frequency frequently (several times a second or more) during a transmission. The clever (and secret) bit is making sure that every other radio listening to the conversation knows which frequency to go to next.

the net result that the projectile would no longer know where it was, and therefore miss. Some sources claim that GPS jammers were found on Iraqi positions in the First Gulf War. While destroying such a jammer is relatively straightforward, with an anti-radiation missile, it's yet one more thing that is making the electronic side of warfare more complicated at the sharp end.

REMOTE SENSORS

Most of the sensors that we have discussed still require a line of sight to the target. As we have seen from Chapter One onwards, that puts Tommy, Rupert and Gary in the firing line. One way of solving this is to use remote sensors.

The simplest remote sensors are static and are laid in a position of interest at a time when it is safe. Thereafter the sensor monitors the area, and sends data by radio link when it detects something. Typically remote sensors detect acoustically, magnetically, thermally or seismically. They have logic that enables them to count say the number of (magnetic) vehicles that pass through their detection array. They then send this information in a short burst. Generally these sensors are small, with limited battery life, so they don't send constant pictures or deliver high band-with information, such as a TV or thermal image. Some remote sensors can be deployed from artillery shells.

The second type, which is increasingly common, is Unmanned Aerial Vehicles, or UAVs.[123] These have varying degrees of autonomy, the most sophisticated being able to fly themselves to a specific point and then orbit that point. They generally carry a thermal camera, and increasingly a laser designator. The image is broadcast to a ground station, where Tommy can see it. Some UAV's are now armed, and can identify a target, designate it with a laser and then launch a guided weapon. At quite what point human control is removed is a matter of debate – the technology is perfectly capable of finding and engaging a target autonomously.

---

[123] Jargon Alert! Drones are pre-programmed to fly a certain course and take photos. UAVs are flown by an operator and can have their course changed. UCAV (Unmanned Combat Aerial Vehicles) carry weapons. The US Predator is a UCAV.

The technology is improving and "man portable" UAVs are now available. Don't forget that someone has to carry it, someone has to control it and someone else has to have a receiver to see the output. As well as further increasing Tommy's workload and burden there are also complexities in ensuring that the picture gets to the right man at the correct time. As a tired, hot and frightened Tommy already has plenty to worry about, adding a further information stream increases the risk of information overload. As is often the case with new technologies on the battlefield, fine tuning the existing organisations to reap the benefit of the technology is more complicated that the implementing technology itself.

In the meantime, we now understand how Tommy and his enemies acquire targets. We know that Tommy now has technology that enables him to turn night into day, see the other side of the hill and to interfere with the enemy's efforts to do the same.

We have just touched upon aerial vehicles, so while we're in the mood let's look at the whole world of aviation.

Chapter 8 Tommy Reaches for the Sky; Air, Aviation and Air Defence

Jargon first; "Aviation" refers to army aircraft, predominantly helicopters: "Air" refers to aircraft operated by the air forces, typically fast attack jets and large transport aircraft. You should not be surprised to discover that there is an anomaly in the British forces, as the RAF flies medium lift helicopters like the Chinook which in many other armies would be flown by the army. Another exception is the US Marine Corps, which operates its own fast jets.

While Tommy is vaguely aware of air superiority fighters, his interest is limited to those aircraft that are either going to attack him or smite his enemies. We shall therefore only look at fighter ground attack, or FGA.

FIGHTER GROUND ATTACK

Most modern fighter aircraft have some ability to attack ground targets, although there are a few like the American A-10 and the Russian SU-25 "Frogfoot" which have been specially designed for it. They are more rugged, with bigger guns and a slower attack speed. However, as this book is about Tommy, not Biggles, we'll leave the aerodynamics there and get to the weaponry.

Cannon

Most FGA aircraft have cannon, varying in calibre from 20 mm to 30 mm and rates of fire from 600 rounds per minute to over 6,000. Without doubt the most feared cannon is the GAU-8 30 mm cannon, a seven barrelled Gatling gun fitted to the A-10. This fires 50 30 mm rounds per second. It is optimised to fire in a 30° dive, so these projectiles are likely to hit the thinner top armour of any tank.

Although they have no explosive content,[124] a burst will demolish a building.

Most other jets have less specialised 20 mm cannon. These fire rounds with less armour penetration, some of which may have HE or incendiary content. Again, they're fired in a dive, increasing their lethality, and at a high rate of fire, increasing their chance of a hit.

Rockets

Air to ground rockets have the advantage of carrying more explosive and creating more fragments. A typical rocket is the Hydra, which can trace its design back to World War Two. With a 70 mm diameter and a length of about 1.75m and a rocket motor, warheads vary in the 5kg to 10kg range, and they may have anti-armour flechettes[125]. They are carried in pods of 15 to 20 and are a very potent direct fire weapon. The can also be carried by attack helicopters, of which more later. They are a direct fire weapon, which means that they can be aimed at a specific target, and of course they come from above, so avoid the challenge of having to penetrate frontal armour. Using FGA is a complex and expensive way of getting explosive onto the target when compared to artillery, but the accuracy makes the impact devastating.

Iron Bombs

These are unguided bombs, and the standard sizes[126] are 250lb, 500lb, 1,000lb and 2,000lb. Note that although the bomb is unguided and therefore follows a ballistic trajectory, aircraft have sophisticated fire control systems that deliver bombs accurately. FGA supporting Tommy are likely to use smaller munitions, although if pressed and the only bomb available is a 2,000 pounder that is what will be dropped. One 2,000 pound bomb is equivalent to

---

[124] The 30mm rounds are optimised for piercing armour. A depleted Uranium (DU) round is standard. DU is pyrophoric, which means that it ignites as it penetrates armour plate. Nice for Biggles, lousy for the tank crew.

[125] A flechette is a small dart like projectile – a little like a mini Sabot round.

[126] For the US M80 series

about 100 155mm HE rounds landing simultaneously at the same location. The effect is devastating[127].

Collateral damage, (a euphemism for killing civilians and/or demolishing their houses), is an increasing problem as bomb sizes increase. There is work now being done on producing smaller bombs to try and reduce collateral damage. Most of the current bomb inventory evolved during The Cold War, when military necessity ranked far above landscape preservation. Using them in counter insurgency scenarios is not always possible, and the rules of engagement are complex. It is not uncommon for targets to be identified but not engaged with a bomb as the potential for collateral damage is too high.

Napalm[128]

Sometimes known as *"bake and shake"*, Napalm combines an explosive burster charge and petroleum jelly to create a wall of flame. It is highly effective against almost any military force, including well entrenched infantry and those in caves. It is a truly terrifying weapon, as footage from the Vietnam War shows. Those whom it does not incinerate it may well asphyxiate, as when the petroleum jelly ignites it removes substantial amounts of oxygen from the air.

Guided Bombs

There are two common ways of guiding a bomb onto a target. The first is to use a laser. Tommy, Biggles or one of Biggles' colleagues in another aircraft, shines a laser at the target which reflects the beam into the sky. Biggles flies along in his jet, drops the bomb and the seeker on the front of the bomb flies down the laser beam,

---

[127] There is the same overkill problem with bombs as there is with artillery shells. This was solved by using cluster bombs, although these have now been banned by international convention. The armed forces of signatory countries are therefore less capable than they were before the treaty. But they're wonderfully politically correct!

[128] Pedant's Corner. Napalm specifically refers to NAPthenic and PALMitic acids, which were the thickeners first used. Nowadays different chemicals are used, which enables officials to deny dropping Napalm in spite of delivering a weapon with the same effect. This happened in the invasion of Iraq.

controlling its trajectory by moving fins attached to the back of the bomb.

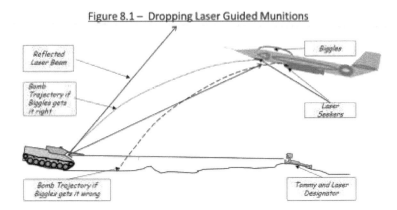

Figure 8.1 – Dropping Laser Guided Munitions

If Biggles drops the bomb too early he risks it falling out of the beam. The bomb is unlikely to have sufficient energy to be able to recapture the trajectory so it will miss. Similar problems arise if he drops too late. Moving targets are a challenge, as they will inevitably generate lots of fin movement, which in turn generates air friction, slowing the bomb and reducing its ability to follow the target.

The other common method of guiding a bomb is to use GPS – the most common example being the JDAM. This is a bolt-on guidance system for the iron bomb. Compared to laser guidance, GPS has the advantages of not needing line of sight, being immune to dust and weather, and not having to stay in the reflected beam. This makes it easier for Biggles to drop, and once released the bomb takes over – it is fire and forget. Note that the accuracy is still not 100%. The manufacturers claim that 95% of JDAMs dropped land within 5m of their target[129] – but that is enough to miss a bunker window. The latest Paveway IV combines GPS and laser guidance

But a JDAM is not the answer to all problems. Human error plays a part, most famously in Afghanistan when a special forces soldier changed the battery on one of the devices he was using to control

---

[129] i.e. within a circle of diameter 10m with its centre on the target. This is called the CEP, or the Circular Error Probable.

fire. This made it broadcast its own location, rather than the target one. The JDAM was dropped before the error was recognised, and there was no way of reprogramming it and the consequences were almost catastrophic. Never, ever forget that in combat Tommy is usually tired, stressed, full of adrenaline and frightened. Giving him more firepower increases the consequences of his mistakes.

Guided Missiles

The final FGA weapon is the air to ground guided missile. The most common is the American AGM-65 Maverick. This missile has a seeker head, which may be laser-seeking or passive imaging infra-red. The launching aircraft also has a stabilised laser designator and / or a view through the weapon's sight. He locks the missile or laser designator onto the target, fires and the missile does the rest.

In many ways Tommy uses FGA as another form of indirect fire, in as much as it delivers death and destruction to a target without Tommy having to engage it himself. In the same way that artillery is directed by a FOO, FGA is controlled by a Forward Air Controller or FAC. Many FOOs are also FACs. The FAC's job is to ensure that Biggles engages the right target. This is quite hard work; Biggles may well be travelling at 450 Knots at less than 1,000 feet above the ground, dodging his way past trees and hills while keeping at least half an eye out for enemy jets and trying to avoid anti-aircraft guns and missiles. He's likely to be pulling fair amounts of g, and in every minute he is covering almost 10 miles.

Most aircraft on FGA tasks have laser seekers so, provided the FAC can get a laser beam on the target and Biggles can detect it in time, it should be relatively straightforward. If not, then Biggles is going to have to use his eyes. This can cause problems, as Biggles is a busy chap and it's not always easy to distinguish vehicle types while trying not to fly into the ground or get shot down. One way to help is to paint identification marks on vehicles. In Normandy in World War Two most Allied vehicles had a large white star painted on their bonnet, roof or turret top. In the First Gulf War a black inverted chevron was supposed to perform the same task. Tommy wryly refers to them as "American aiming marks", reflecting the unfortunate US Air Force's history of shooting British vehicles.

HELICOPTERS

One of the joys of soldiering is the availability of quite cool toys – how many civilians routinely get free helicopter rides? Tommy generally quite likes riding in helicopters, with two caveats. The first is that he doesn't know why the helicopter flies; common sense says it should screw itself into the ground. The second is a deep suspicion that if the country is treating him like a celebrity there is likely to be something unpleasant at the end of the journey.

There are broadly three sorts of helicopters in Tommy's world, the first of which are attack helicopters such as the AH-64 Apache or the Russian Mil-24 Hind.

Attack Helicopters

Attack helicopters are variously armed with guided missiles, rockets, cannon and chain guns, all of which we know about. They are usually well armoured and able to survive hits from anything up to 23mm calibre. They have two broad roles.

In an armoured war they are intended to engage tanks, particularly where there is an enemy break through. They are well suited to this as they can cross the battlefield quickly and use ground for protection by flying "nap of the earth." Flying nap of the earth is exciting, bordering on the terrifying. The helicopter is rarely above treetop height, travelling at 30 to 100 knots. Flying this low has two advantages. Firstly it keeps the helicopter out of the way of fast jets engaging in FGA, who generally fly (just) above treetop height. Secondly it keeps their rotors screened from enemy radar. The downside is that it's dangerous, bird strikes and telephone lines being a particular concern, as well of course as any soldier with a machine gun.

Given the long range of their missiles, typically 4,000 metres plus, they are able to engage tanks from a variety of positions. It is astonishingly difficult to see a well flown helicopter, particularly if it has a mast-mounted sight, as Figure 8.2 shows. The target has almost no chance of seeing either the sight above the trees or the launch of the missile, which is screened by the trees. The missile needs some clever programming to get it to climb and Katie, the

Apache pilot, needs to leave room between the trees and her chopper for the missile to manoeuvre.

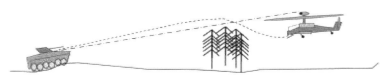
Figure 8.2 – The Benefit of a Mast Mounted Sight

The second role is to act as flying fire support. Generally the helicopter will fly higher, and be able to use its sensors and weapons to support Tommy's efforts. Because a helicopter can hover and fly slowly, target acquisition is far less of a challenge that it is for FGA. It is also easier than for Tommy, as Katie has a bird's eye view into Tommy's dead ground. This often means that as well as flying the aircraft and working the weapons and sensors, Katie is also a primary information source for the ground commanders. As with Rupert, the ability to multi-task is fundamental[130].

The risk of flying slowly is that the helicopter becomes an easy target. Katie tries to fly above the effective range of enemy weaponry, although this is not always possible. The other option is for pairs of helicopters to fly figure of eight patterns to provide mutual support – if an enemy tries to engage one helicopter the other one will kill him. This is much easier now that stabilised sensors and cannon are available.

Scout / Utility Helicopters

Small helicopters such as the Gazelle and Kiowa are used to perform reconnaissance, transport commanders, vital equipment and VIPs. They also have a limited capacity to provide casualty evacuation, although modern medical practice requires larger helicopters. In non-hostile environments, where the anti-aircraft threat is low, light helicopters can be used for surveillance and providing white light to illuminate the ground at night. Generally though, the roles are now met by larger machines which carry more fuel and heavier sensors.

---

[130] This is why almost all attack helicopters have two crew. FGA jets tend to be single-seaters.

Transport Helicopters

At the risk of stating the obvious, transport helicopters carry men and equipment about the battlefield. They are generally unarmed, or armed with door machine guns only. They are unarmoured – except perhaps for the pilots seats, fuel tanks and rotors, for the simple reason that if they were well armoured they would not be able to fly and carry a useful payload.

Typically they range from the light, like the Lynx or Blackhawk, able to carry 8 to 12 men, through to the heavy such as the Chinook, capable of lifting 50 plus troops. Carrying men and materiel in the air is expensive, but has two crucial benefits - speed and invulnerability to mines and improvised explosive devices.

Speed of deployment can create initiative and transform battles. There are generally two scenarios where helicopters provide this speed. The first is to counter an enemy penetration of our line. While there will be local, ground-based counter-attacks from whatever reserves are available, they are constrained by how quickly they can move. If things are going badly, which they will be, the reserves may be delayed by already being on contact or a key bridge being demolished. Being able to land a fresh force ahead of the enemy penetration, unconstrained by the situation on the ground, is hugely useful.

The second scenario is offensive – typically capturing a bridge or piece of key terrain behind the enemy's main force to interfere with his logistics and the ability of his reserves to deploy while securing passage through a major obstacle for our own ground forces.

Neither scenario is easy, but the offensive one is particularly difficult. Helicopters, particularly transport ones, are very vulnerable to air defence and jet fighters. To land a force in the enemy's rear requires huge effort to suppress the enemy air defence, shoot down enemy fighters and then provide fire support while the position is taken and held. And don't forget logistics; we need to fly ammunition in and casualties out. Every flight requires the same level of support to get through. The simple truth is that once Tommy is deposited behind enemy lines, he also has the entire enemy behind his lines.

This sort of operation is variously called air assault or descant. It requires a vast investment in helicopters, and huge amounts of training. The soldiers who land are effectively going to have to stand and fight, pretty much by themselves, until relief comes. Two classic examples from history stand out; Operation Market Garden in the Second World War and $1^{st}/7^{th}$ Air Cavalry's action in the Ia Drang Valley[131] in the Vietnam War. Both of these were performed with air supremacy, the Luftwaffe having more or less been destroyed and the North Vietnamese Air Force was entirely occupied with the air defence of the north. Market Garden failed, $1^{st}/7^{th}$ succeeded, but at a high cost. Air assault operations are high risk.

It is in counter-insurgency operations that helicopters are at their most powerful. Being able to move fast to raid known insurgent positions and secure vulnerable targets makes the life of the insurgent tricky. They never know what is in a helicopter, where it is going or what sensors it carries. It also deprives them of one of their most effective weapons, the roadside bomb. Surface to air missiles are available to some insurgents, but they are far more complicated to use and bring the insurgent into a direct fire battle with Katie and Tommy – which is dangerous. We'll return to this in the chapter on counter-insurgency.

Now that we have seen how useful and effective air and aviation can be, we had better consider what Tommy can do to reduce the effect that the enemy's air and aviation can have upon him.

ANTI-AIRCRAFT WEAPONRY

Now, this is a book about Tommy, not Biggles, and shooting down aircraft is the core expertise of the air force. While we discuss the kit available to Tommy and his pals it is important to bear in mind that most of the responsibility for knocking down enemy aircraft lies outside Tommy's realm, and even those bits that are his responsibility have to be coordinated within the overall air war, which is run by Biggles. Tommy is concerned only with providing

---

[131] These are described in the books "A Bridge Too Far" and "We Were Warriors Once, and Young." Unusually, both have been made into good films that are reasonably accurate.

defence of the area he is defending, called point defence. Tommy's solution to enemy air is characteristically direct - blast it out of the sky.

Compared to a tank, an aircraft is less armoured and much faster. The former means that a hit is likely to kill; the latter means it's going to be hard to get a hit. In a perfect world we want to hit the aircraft before it releases its weapons. This increases the engagement range and thus reduces the time available to acquire the target.

Let's start with shooting down FGA. The target is traveling at 10 miles a minute at a height of 0 to 1,000 metres. The higher it is, the more time we have. Problem number one is getting some warning so that we can have our weapon ready and pointing the right way the moment the target comes into range.

Nowadays, the best early warning will come from AWACS – a converted passenger jet carrying a huge radar. This is operated by Biggles and is very complicated. All we need to know is that its output – for example "Four fast jets at grid 123456, height 1000 metres, speed 450 Knots, heading 340" - can be passed immediately to everyone involved in air defence via electronics. Having detected a threat, we then need to establish its identity. There is an electronic system to do this called IFF[132]. The launcher electronically interrogates the target; if the target fails the challenge the engagement process starts. These air defenders will have one (or more) of three types of weapon available to them.

The first are actively guided missiles[133] – typically radar-guided although there are some laser beam riders. The radar may also have a search function, which augments and can replace the information produced from AWACS. A typical example is the British Starstreak (a laser beam rider). Actively guided missiles require the

---

[132] IFF ="Identify Friend of Foe"

[133] Many small antiaircraft missiles, the Starstreak included, are actually "hitiles", in as much as they only detonate on impact. To kill an aircraft if they miss requires a proximity fuse and some impressive computer logic, as well as a bigger explosive charge – which means that they will be too heavy to be man portable.

target to be tracked (optically or electronically) from the moment of launch to the moment of impact.

Passively guided missiles are usually Infra-red seekers. They home in on the hot bits of a jet. The most famous is the American Stinger. The upside of these is that they are fire and forget. The downside is that the heat seeker needs several seconds to lock onto the target before launch. During this time Gary[134] is standing in the open aiming at a jet approaching at something over 150 metres per second.

Finally there are guns, which may or may not be radar guided. Calibres range from 40 mm to 20 mm, and rates of fire from hundreds to thousands of rounds per minute. They are brutally effective, and have a useful secondary role in shooting at ground targets.

Tommy's last resort air defence weapon is a simple machine gun, usually of 7.62mm calibre or higher. These have the advantage that they are on the battlefield anyway, being carried by Tommy or mounted in a tank. The problems are sighting, a lack of IFF, a limited effective range (which means they are unlikely to kill the aircraft before weapons release) and the need to fire a large number of bullets into the air. As Sir Isaac Newton didn't say, "What goes up must come down" and most of the rounds fired will miss and thus have to land somewhere. There were incidents in the Falklands War of bullets from one position fired at a passing Argentine jet, landing on another, leading to some very full and frank exchanges of view. Because of these limitations, anti-aircraft shooting by Tommy is tightly controlled and usually forbidden.

Shooting down helicopters is slightly different as generally they're lower and slower. Low makes it harder for radar to acquire them as they tend to get lost in ground clutter. Most military helicopters are now fitted with IR suppression systems, which diffuse their exhausts, making them a harder target for IR seeking missiles. Of course this does not make them immune, as the large number of Russian Hinds shot down by the Stinger-equipped Mujahedin testifies. Being low also brings them into range of most ground

---

[134] In most armies, including the British, air defence is part of the role of artillery troops.

weapons, and being slow means that tank gun systems are good enough to track them; some tank guns have an anti-helicopter round (others rely on hitting with a sabot round – if it can destroy 70 tons of armour it will make mincemeat of a helicopter – if it hits). Again, machine guns, particularly .50" ones, have a reasonable chance of a hit, which in turn should bring a kill.

In summary, aircraft potentially provide Tommy with additional means of striking the enemy at long range and from cover. Their height above the ground means that sensors on them will have a far better view than Tommy can have from his place on the earth's surface. They also provide him with a fast form of transport that is immune to the effects of terrain, particularly broken bridges, land mines and IEDs.

Unfortunately all aircraft are very expensive, complicated and need much maintenance. There are therefore relatively few available. They are also vulnerable, as it is not generally possible to provide them with sufficient armour plate to protect anything but vital areas. Tommy also tends to forget that Biggles has to run the gauntlet of enemy air defence (and enemy aircraft) on the way to the target, at the target and on the way home. This is not a job for the faint-hearted.

Now, we've been flirting with the air for far too long in a book about land warfare. Let's get back to the basics of ground and see how we can manipulate it to our advantage. This is the job of engineers, or "sappers."

Chapter 9 Tommy Plays Mud Pies; Engineers and Sappery

As we know from Chapter Two, ground is the playing field for soldiering. However, this is war; Tommy's life is at risk and there is no benefit in having a level playing field. Altering the ground to our advantage is what sappers[135] do, although they also perform other civil engineering jobs like drilling for water. Most of their work can be classed as either mobility or counter-mobility. Let's consider a few of the challenges and opportunities that ground throws at us, and see how sappers can make Tommy's life longer and the enemy's shorter.

RIVERS, CUTTINGS, CANALS AND DITCHES

There are few obstacles that cause more military hassle than rivers. Even the few vehicles that can swim require the preparation of entry and exit points. Given the large volume and mass of materiel that is necessary to conduct land warfare, permanent crossings are vital. Bridges are magnets for combat, and much military effort is devoted to capturing them, defending them, blowing them up and rebuilding them.

Demolishing bridges is simpler, so let's look at that first. Figure 9.1 shows a typical bridge.

---

[135] A "sap" is a type of trench. In the First World War the Royal Engineers spent much of their time digging trenches, including saps. The name stuck.

Figure 9.1 – A Generic Bridge

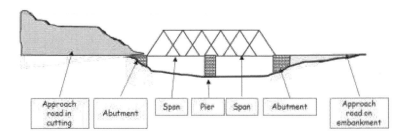

Not all bridges have piers. All of these parts are necessary for the bridge to function, which gives the Sapper plenty of opportunities to attack. Bridges can be made of wood, masonry (brick or stone), steel or reinforced concrete. All of these can be destroyed with explosives by sappers, or indeed Biggles with a big, accurate bomb.

If we knock out a span we have stopped the bridge being usable for as long as it takes the enemy to replace the missing span. While this is a considerable engineering challenge, as we shall see sappers have tools that can actually do this quite quickly for reasonable lengths. If we really want to take the bridge out of service the abutments have to go too.

Demolishing masonry requires the sappers to drill lots of holes into it, fill them with explosive and then pack the back of the hole with concrete or something similar. This is called tamping – it is necessary to ensure that the blast energy from the explosive goes into the masonry, causing it to crack. Without tamping the effect of the explosive is much reduced. All this drilling takes time, and can require a fair amount of scaffolding and the like[136]. Demolishing masonry is also very hard for Biggles. If his bomb detonates on the surface of the masonry it is unlikely to do much damage. He therefore has to use a specialist penetrating bomb. These do exist but are expensive, heavy and have to be delivered with great precision. Generally, while air power can drop individual spans of

---

[136] During The Cold War all the bridges built in West Germany actually had explosives chambers accessible by manholes built into them. All the sappers had to do was open the manhole and place the explosives in the chamber. The explosives were often stored close by.

multi-span bridges quite easily, damaging the piers and abutments is a Sapper job.

If the bridge is made of steel dropping a span is straightforward. Sappers use shaped charges to cut through steel in the same way that a HEAT round cleaves through armour plate. Clever sappers use the mass of the bridge to help them, and on a good (or lucky) day can arrange for the mass of the span to twist and damage piers and abutments. If the bridge is of reinforced concrete then they may have to perform a two stage demolition. Firstly they have to clear the concrete from the reinforcing steel - effectively a masonry demolition. Then they cut the steel with shaped charges. This obviously takes longer and uses more explosive.

Once the sapper has dropped the span and destroyed the abutments, there is still no need to make it easy for the enemy sappers to come and repair the bridge. If time and resources are available the approaching embankments can be weakened or collapsed, and the whole area sown with mines to cool the enthusiasm of the enemy engineers, who will at some stage have to attempt to rebuild it.

In defence, sapper time is at a premium as the local countryside has to be transformed into a defensive belt. If there is a build-up to the war, then the sooner the sappers can be allowed to start demolishing stuff the better – although there are obviously serious political and economic implications. Provided sappers have enough time and explosives, there is nothing that they can't demolish.

If Tommy is advancing towards a river his preferred option is always to capture an existing bridge. Unfortunately any competent enemy will probably have anticipated this, and prepared a strong defence. The best option for capturing one intact is probably a helicopter-borne descent operation, although as we have seen these are expensive and high risk. Attacking on the ground involves having to fight the enemy in a well-prepared position and then (potentially) having a grandstand view as the enemy demolishes the bridge anyway. The final option is to go round, and get the sappers to build a bridge somewhere else. Fortunately the sappers have a number of pieces of kit that can do this.

The fastest is to use an Armoured Vehicle Launched Bridge, or AVLB. This is basically a tank chassis carrying a bridge where a normal tank would have a turret, along with hydraulic systems capable of laying the bridge on the ground. The bridges come in a variety of sizes, and are able to span a gap of about 22 metres. It is possible to lay one AVLB from another, which takes the span to around 30 metres or so.

Laying the AVLB span takes about five minutes, but as we know a bridge also needs abutments on both the home and far banks. On the home bank, at least initially, we have some opportunity to pick a place that will be OK for the first 20 or so vehicles (that's over 1,200 tons if they're tanks). On the far bank we will have less choice. Being resourceful chaps Sappers have tools and plant to fix this. These include bulldozers and track-way layers. The latter are the quick fix, providing instant road that protects the ground (i.e. the abutments) at either end of the bridge.

Crossing the bridge is exciting for the tank crew – and not in a good way. The key thing is to avoid turning on the approach (turning mashes up the ground and in extreme cases can destabilise the AVLB), avoid excess speed and, above all, to stay on the bridge. Rupert and his crew all know that if their tank falls off the bridge they have a good chance of drowning, particularly the driver, who sits lowest in the hull and is hard to extricate through the turret. The solution is training, and driving over an AVLB is part of a tank crewman's driving test. The driver often can't see the bridge, and has to rely on a sapper standing on the bridge for hand signals, as well as direction from the commander over the intercom (if the commander can see the bridge – which he often can't). Once the tank is lined up and crossing the bridge, the sapper jumps aside and starts guiding the next one. At night this can get pretty hairy.

Of course, if the enemy works out what we're trying to do he'll interfere. The AVLB becomes a bullet magnet. Given their height AVLBs are hard to hide, but it is not uncommon for them to be escorted to the laying position by several tanks, whose prime job is to block the enemy's line of fire to the AVLB. Gary is also likely to be firing huge amounts of artillery smoke onto likely enemy positions to block their view, and the operation may be done in darkness (which makes it harder for the Sappers to get the bridge in the right place and for Rupert's driver to stay on the bridge). Often Tommy and some of his fellow infantrymen will have swum or rowed[137] across the river to provide some security on the far bank.

As well as laying the bridge and track-way, the sappers will also have put out a whole series of markers so that the tanks and IFVs can find the bridge. Although tank bridges look enormous when they're on the AVLB in daylight they are jolly hard to find in the dark.

Once the first wave of vehicles is over the sappers will get on and build more bridges. It is likely that this will be made harder by the enemy, who will at the least hammer the crossing site with artillery. Sappers are vulnerable to this as, in spite of having a range or armoured vehicles that give them reasonable protection against artillery splinters, some jobs they simply have to perform on their feet.

Sappers have a range of other bridges that can be built quickly, but nowhere near as fast as an AVLB. Typically, without enemy interference, they can span up to 40 metres and be built in a matter of hours. Some countries, including the UK and Germany also have self-propelled pontoon bridges, the current version known as the M3. These are large trucks that drive into the river, use inboard motors to become a boat and then unfold their body panels and join together to become either ferries or a long bridge. Eight rigs can form a bridge 100 metres long, capable of carrying tanks[138]. For small rivers and ditches, sappers can lay a bundle of pipes called a fascine. While these are not passable by wheeled vehicles they can quickly fill ditches, up to around 6 metres wide and 2 metres deep, well enough for tracked vehicles to cross.

The key points about assault bridging are that while an AVLB or fascine can be laid in a matter of minutes it takes significantly more effort to actually get the crossing prepared, the AVLB laid and Rupert over the bridge. Preventing the enemy from anticipating the

---

[137] Sappers provide assault boats too.

[138] One other approach to non-assault bridging is to use a ribbon bridge. These are usually truck mounted and can span long distances, provided that river depth is not greater than about 5m. The best example is the Russian TMM.

crossing site and limiting his ability to interfere with it are crucial. Deception and guile are fundamental, as is the efficient execution of a complicated plan.

ROADS AND TRACKS

While tanks and other tracked vehicles are able to move across country, the trucks that keep the fighting vehicles supplied with fuel and ammunition have a very limited ability to do the same.[139] Sappers therefore need to be able to mend roads. And, of course, sappers must be able to break them to make the enemy's life miserable.

Repairing roads is relatively straightforward, and armies have a range of standard civilian construction equipment such as diggers, bulldozers and graders to make it possible. The only real difference is that they will be painted green. Sappers also carry metal track-way, or instant road. You have probably driven on this at outdoor car parks for large events. Its heavy and expensive, but fast to lay and effective.

One special sort of road is a runway. While it is very hard to find and destroy Biggles in his fighter jet, knocking a hole in the two mile long runway that he needs to get airborne (or to land) is relatively straightforward[140]. Fighters are delicate things[141], and runway repairs need to be smooth. In Britain the job of airfield damage repair is another sapper task, and specialist sapper regiments exist to do it.

Breaking roads up is technically simple, although of course there is little point in breaking a road in flat hard ground where vehicles will be able to drive round the crater. Better to block a road on an embankment over bog, or in a cutting through hills. The best way to make the crater is to use explosives, and the Rapid Cratering Kit

---

[139] An alternative is to use tracked logistic vehicles. While this is sometimes done close to the sharp end, it adds to the logistic burden and is expensive.
[140] From the ground. In the Falklands war the RAF attempted to destroy the runway at Fort Stanley airfield in a hugely complicated operation. Only one crater was put into the tarmac, which the Argentines filled quickly.
[141] Except the Harrier, that lands vertically. But even it needs something firm to land on – a form of track way provided by sappers.

does exactly what it says on the tin. Having decided where the crater should be there are three steps. First a shaped charge blows a tubular hole vertically into the surface. This is likely to generate a hole over two metres deep, well into the ground underneath the road surface and foundations. Then sappers pack the bottom of the hole with explosives, and fill the hole in (tamping). Finally they move to a safe distance and detonate. The whole process takes less than half an hour and results in a satisfying crater several meters wide and deep. Making more than one crater produces a more formidable obstacle. Sappers then sow the area with mines to ensure the enemy engineers have a tough day. If cratering kits are not available or appropriate sappers, being resourceful chaps, can also block roads by felling trees to fall across them (using explosives rather than chainsaws they can do this quickly) or by blowing the sides of cuttings down.

It's now time to get a little controversial and consider mines.

MINES

In general, a mine is a buried explosive charge that detonates when the target steps on it or drives over it. They therefore have the ability to transform a piece of ground from being innocuous, or even pleasant, into lethal. Soldiering is about ground, and the ability to turn it from benign into lethal is of great interest and utility.

Mines come in two flavours, anti-personnel and anti-tank.

Anti-Personnel Mines

The Ottawa Treaty of 1997 banned anti-personnel mines, although as the US, USSR and Peoples Republic of China, who are major arms exporters, have not signed it's a reasonable bet that Tommy will encounter them. (Of course, the Taliban are not signatories to the treaty either. They have festooned Helmand with mines, although as they are homemade they are known as Improvised Explosive Devices or IEDs). There is also some scope for debate of what precisely is an anti-personnel mine (as opposed to, say, an anti-handling device), and of course, there are plenty of mines still laid. This book is about the world that Tommy works in, and the stark fact is that is contains anti-personnel mines.

Broadly there are two types of buried anti-personnel mine: those designed to kill the individual and those that aim to kill more than one person at a time. The former are simple. Once laid and armed, Tommy's foot detonates it by either activating a pressure switch or disturbing a trembler or trip wire. In either case the mine detonates and the blast will generally remove a limb. If that does not kill Tommy immediately, he then has to deal with the loss of blood. If he survives that he then has to deal with the infections that are likely to follow, as the mine will have blown all sorts of dirt into the wound. The only good news for Tommy is that at least his mates are alive to give him first aid. This might well not be the case if he had activated one of the more sophisticated ones.

Figure 9.2 – An Anti-Personnel Mine

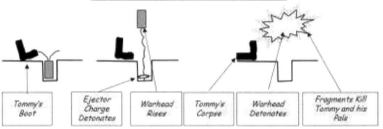

Tommy's Boot	Ejector Charge Detonates	Warhead Rises	Tommy's Corpse	Warhead Detonates	Fragments Kill Tommy and his Pals

Have a look at Figure 9.2. The mine is initiated by Tommy's boot. A small ejector charge then fires a canister into the air. This canister is packed with explosive and fragmentation material, and bursts at waist height. The effect is devastating. Depending upon the type, personnel up to 200 metres away can be injured

Chemical advances in the 1970s created a third type of anti-personnel mine, which was scatterable from aircraft and by artillery. The mine has a slow arming mechanism, which could take over 30 minutes – plenty of time for it to be fired and come back to earth. When over the target the projectile opens and scores of mines fall out. To ensure a good spread, they often have an aerodynamic shape, causing them to be referred to as butterfly or sycamore mines. Once they land and the arming is complete any deformation of the plastic mine case (caused by treading on it, or squeezing it to pick it up) detonates the explosive charge. Although the charge is relatively small, (around 30 grammes), it is enough to remove a limb.

Anti-Tank Mines

Anti-tank mines are similar in principle to simple anti-personnel mines. They have an explosive charge, typically 5 to 10Kg, are laid in or on the ground, have a pressure trigger and detonate when a sufficient weight is on them. Most anti-tank mines are set so that a man standing on them will not set them off,[142] but as Tommy says, *"After you!"* Some also have the option of setting multiple pressures; so, for example, it will blow up under the third tank to pass it – which means the two preceding ones are now stuck in a minefield.

There is limitation with mines that only detonate under direct pressure. Armoured vehicles have their wheels and / or running gear at the edges. While the explosion will certainly blow the wheel off or break the track, thereby stopping the vehicle, it will not usually harm the occupants and the vehicle may be straightforward to repair. The solution is a clever fuse which has a roller in the top of a sprung stalk. As the vehicle drives over the mine (missing it with its tracks) the roller which starts winding up the cord until it causes detonation. By that time the mine is under the middle of the vehicle, where the crew are, and the effect of the explosion will be devastating. A similar effect can be achieved with a magnetic fuse, although these are vulnerable to electronic spoofing.

USING MINES

Unlike most weapons, in conventional warfare the primary role of conventional mines is not to kill the enemy, but to delay or divert him. Tommy and Rupert, who are generally pretty brave chaps, have a visceral fear of mines. Most uses of mines play upon this fear. It makes sense to actually mark where the minefields are using barbed wire fencing festooned with warning signs. A soldier's natural reaction is to avoid these areas, in much the same way as he would avoid impassable terrain.

---

[142] Do NOT try this at home.

There are four types of minefield. Tactical minefields force the enemy to either move into a killing area[143] or slow him down once he is in it. They are generally planned at a high level of command, are marked and have varying densities of mine. They are large, covering tens of hectares. These are almost invariably laid by sappers. Next down the chain are protective minefields, sited relatively close to Tommy's position. Their role is to make the life of attacking enemy short, brutal and unpleasant. They are marked, but tend to be small and close to Tommy's position. Tommy often lays these as sappers generally have more important things to do.

Nuisance minefields are not marked (but are recorded) and are generally quite small. A few anti-tank mines on and near a track junction would constitute a nuisance minefield, as would a booby trap. They are there to cause casualties, but most importantly to raise the enemy's mine anxiety. These are usually laid by Tommy. The last type is the phoney minefield, which is almost identical to tactical and protective minefields. The one difference is that they have no mines in them whatsoever. Even if they have just one mine in them, they become a tactical or protective minefield. The effects of a phoney minefield are either to exploit the enemy's fear of mines while saving on the number of mines that are laid or to mess with his head, and encourage him to be reckless so that when he hits a real minefield he takes heavier casualties. Phoney minefields are also marked and recorded.

All minefield locations are recorded in detail for two reasons. The first one is to make sure Tommy and Rupert don't wander into their own minefields – there is no such thing as a friendly minefield if you're in it. The second is so that they can pick the mines up again if they're needed elsewhere, or indeed when we've won the war and are cleaning up. This fastidious, comprehensive record-keeping is one of the attributes of a first-rate army, as opposed to second rate

---

[143] When we lay out a defensive position, we identify killing areas. These are simply the piece of ground in which we anticipate killing the enemy, and therefore into which all our weapons can fire.

armies, militias, rabble or terrorist groups[144]. We'll return to this differentiation later.

CLEARING MINES

Unsurprisingly, the enemy will be deploying mines too. Depending upon his level of sophistication, training and discipline the fields may be well marked, or not[145]. Either way, once we have found a mine field we have two choices, go round or go through. The problem with going round is that is what the enemy wants us to do. The challenge with going through is that it's bloody dangerous, unless we can remove the mines. This is another job for the sappers.

First find your mine! If it has a metallic content, or like many NATO mines, a metallic strip, then we can find it using a mine detector, which is effectively a metal detector. Understandably, mine detectors tend to be set with a very high sensitivity, which can lead to a high rate of false positives. A more serious problem is that many mines are non-metallic, and therefore very hard to detect using conventional technologies. Although there are a range of research projects that have some potential they are a long way from field deployment.

Ignoring for a moment that there are some mines that we can't detect (easy for you and me, somewhat harder for Tommy and his sapper pals) having found one the next job is to unearth it. This is done, very carefully, by hand. A visual inspection is made, which should reveal the type of mine. It is then inspected for anti-handling devices and, assuming none are present, the fuse is removed and set to one side. The Sapper then continues his sweep.

If mine detectors are not available, perhaps because Tommy has wandered into a minefield himself, the other way of finding mines is by using a mine prodder or, in *extremis*, a bayonet. All soldiers are trained on how to do this. The prodder is pushed into the ground at

---

[144] The ban on anti-personnel mines would, arguably, have had more benefit if it banned incompetent armies from not recording where they had laid mines.

[145] Of course, if the enemy does not mark his real minefields he still has the opportunity to mark dummy minefields.

an angle of 45 degrees (the theory being that this will not detonate the mine). If nothing is touched the prodder is removed, the soldier advances (on his belly, of course) and the process repeated. If you're thinking that this sounds like hard work and very dangerous then, of course, you are right. But it is better than any of the available alternatives.

Now, all this takes time, which means that the minefield is already working because it is imposing delay. It's about to get worse for the breaching force, though. It is axiomatic that all minefields (except nuisance ones) are at the least "covered by view" and preferably "covered by fire." In plainer English, if we lay a minefield we make sure that there is someone watching it, and ideally someone (or more) with a direct fire weapon that can shoot into it. The breaching force, who are having a bad day anyway, should expect to be under direct fire and artillery bombardment throughout their operation. Unlike assault bridging, where there is a hope that the far bank won't be held, there is almost zero prospect of making an unopposed minefield breach. The armies of the world have therefore developed a range of equipment to speed the process up, and provide protection to the breaching force.

One alternative to hand breaching is to use a flail – which is a whole bunch of chains on a mechanically driven roller mounted in front of (originally) a tank. The flail beats the ground, detonating any mines. It works well, but has the problem of being a bullet magnet, and the flail gets in the way of the tank's gun. More modern versions, such as the Aardvark, are not assault vehicles, and are designed for follow up and peace support operations.

A better solution is to use a mine plough. This is attached to the front of a tank, or a specialist vehicle. These simply plough the ground ahead of where the tank tracks will fall. Generally they work well, and have the advantage that the tank can use its gun – remember we're doing all this under direct fire.

A variant on the plough is to use rollers. This was very popular with Soviet armour. The roller is mounted in front of the track and creates higher ground pressure – thereby detonating the mine before the tank gets there – although of course a double-impulse mine outwits this. The explosion will probably wreck the roller, so another roller equipped tank then has to lead. However up until that moment it was having a safe passage in the tracks of the lead tank. The merit of this approach is that a large number of breaching vehicles can be assembled, and the minefield breached quickly. The Soviets issued mine rollers in large numbers – as many as one tank in three was so equipped.

The final option that we will consider is to revert to the sapper's favourite approach, and use explosive. The British Python is one such device. A rocket is attached to a 200 metres long hose full of explosive. Sappers fire the rocket across the minefield, wait for the hose to land and then detonate the explosive. As there is some 1½ tons of TNT in the hose, this gives a satisfyingly large bang. The pressure wave is sufficient to detonate most of the mines, giving an instant safe lane over 7 metres wide. Usually the lane is then ploughed. Of course, if the minefield is more than 200 metres deep, we'll need another Python

Notice that none of these solutions is perfect, in as much as they do not destroy or disable all the mines. However they do substantially reduce the risk of hitting one. Manufacturers claim up to 90% reduction. This is of little comfort to Rupert, who is well aware that most military equipment is supplied by the lowest bidder, and less to the sappers – normal procedure is for them to drive a mine plough through the breach as the first vehicle to cross. Note also that this is likely to be as complicated an operation as assault bridging. And don't forget that at the end of it Tommy has to get on with his day job of actually seizing and holding the ground occupied by the enemy.

SCATTERABLE MINES

As we have seen, laying minefields is time consuming and hard work. There are some scenarios where we desperately want to lay a minefield, but don't have the time or the resources in the correct place. Let's look at two of them. Imagine that we are attacking, and we know that the enemy has a large reserve force 3,000 metres to his rear. We need to delay its arrival on the battlefield. On cheap and easy way to do this is to scatter mines (SM) all over the reserve's current location. This can be done by artillery. We don't have to hit the enemy, just surround him with mines – so one salvo[146] of an artillery regiment will suffice. The second is where the enemy has broken through, and we need to slow him down while we prepare our next line of defence. Landing a scatterable minefield in front of him will achieve this.

Scatterable minefields can't be marked, although they can be recorded. They are unlikely to be covered by view or fire, and are therefore really just large nuisance minefields. Anti-personnel SM are most common, although anti-vehicle scatterable mines exist. The latter are quite complicated as they have to be able to right themselves as they usually have a self-forging fragment[147] as their warhead.

Scatterable mines are particularly effective against vehicles in hides as they tend to get hooked up in camouflage nets. The entire net effectively becomes the fuse, and the crew have no easy way to get into their vehicle and join battle.

You may have formed the view that mines are barbaric, and should be banned. Few could argue with the first clause. However, mines are also of great military use. Banning them makes Tommy's life harder, and increases his chance of getting an equally barbaric bayonet in the guts. A better observation might be that war is barbaric, so ban that instead. Many have tried with an equal lack of success.

IEDs

Improvised Explosive Devices, or IEDs, are simply homemade mines. They can be very sophisticated, detonated by pressure plates (i.e. standing on them) or remote control. This latter can vary from using a mobile phone, laser, radio link or command wire.

IEDs are a prime weapon of insurgents, and they have a dramatic effect on operations – as has been witnessed in Afghanistan. The British Army has been particularly vulnerable to them, primarily due to its chronic shortage of helicopters. We will cover these in more detail in the chapter on counter-insurgency warfare.

---

[146] A salvo is when every gun fires one round.
[147] There is more detail on self-forging fragments in Appendix 2.

Other Engineering Tasks

Unsurprisingly, sappers are excellent at digging, and have a range of earthmoving equipment to create anti-tank ditches and the like. Occasionally they may have time to spare to help Tommy dig his trenches, but this is the exception. Sappers are particularly in demand when Tommy is fighting in towns, as their skill and equipment can be used to good effect – particularly if Tommy is defending.

Aside from conventional warfare, sappers build things and so are invaluable in peace support and humanitarian operations. (All sappers are also trained as construction workers, so they can build stuff). They are simply vital in counter-insurgency operations.

We have now come full circle, having started with ground, looked at all Tommy's tools and technology and just seen how that can be deployed to improve the ground. It's now time to move on and look at how an army is organised and where Tommy fits in the chain of command.

Chapter 10 Team Tommy; Who Does What

We already know that soldiering is a team game. This chapter will explain how the team is organised, who commands whom and how the team is adjusted to suit specific operations. There is going to be a fair bit of jargon and we're going to encounter some of the eccentricities of the British regimental system. This is unavoidable, so try to enjoy it.

Organisation is an important, indeed fundamental part of successful soldiering. As unsuccessful soldiering ends in funerals, soldiers spend much of their time thinking about it and trying to improve the system. This is unsurprising. Consider all the newspaper space given to football organisations, be it the benefit of 4-4-2 or how best to play a sweeper. All that effort is being expended so that 11 players have the best opportunity to win in a 90 minute game. A brigade in action has over 5,000 people variously shooting at the enemy that they can see, manoeuvring for an advantage, calling in air strikes over periods of days. As well as a plan for dealing with the enemy they also need food, water, ammunition and the ability to change the plan. Rather than being confined to one acre of football pitch they are spread over thousands of square kilometres. This is only possible if the troops are organised sensibly and commanded well. The first part of this is to ensure that the organisation is correct. The result of losing a football match is a drop in pay for the players, and prestige for the fans. The consequences of failure are death or dismemberment for the soldiers and loss of sovereignty or a vital national interest[148] for the country.

RANKS

The table below lists the ranks of the army from top to bottom. It is interesting that Tesco, which employs over 500,000 people and is therefore over five times the size of the British Army, has just six

---

[148] A cynic may ask where the vital national interest is in some recent wars. My answer is that it is a bit late to ask now — almost by definition once we're in a war it is in the national interest that we win.

grades of staff. They also fill a narrower range of roles than exists within an Army and don't have to cope with the probability (rather than remote possibility) of some of the management dying at work and needing to keep the chain of command intact. Rank structures in other, non-British armies are broadly similar.

Rank	Job	Comment
Field Marshall	Runs entire armed forces	Also called a five star general. British don't often have one
General	Runs an army	A four Star General
Lieutenant General	Commands a corps.	Usually knighted, so really is a Sir. A three star general
Major General	Commands a division.	Two star. This is the largest formation that the British Army is capable of fielding.
Brigadier	Commands a brigade.	One star. In the British army a brigadier is not really a general.
Colonel	A senior staff officer – he works in a headquarters but commands nothing directly himself.	Increasingly rare.
Lieutenant Colonel	Commands a Battalion

Also a staff rank. | The height of many officers' ambition. Lt Cols who have not commanded a battalion are very much a lesser breed, and much less likely to advance. |
| Major | Commands a company, a senior one might be 2IC of a | Sometimes referred to as a Field Officer |

	battalion. Many majors are staff officers	In many armies companies are commanded by captains.
Captain	A staff officer within a battalion and (occasionally) elsewhere, or second in command of a company	Captains and lieutenants are sometimes collectively known as subalterns
Lieutenant	Commands a Platoon	Theoretically more experienced than a Second Lieutenant BUT the anomalies of the British Army mean this is not always the case.
Second-Lieutenant	Also commands a platoon	This is the lowest form of commissioned life.
Warrant Officer Class One	Typically the Regimental Sergeant Major	Or God. The most senior soldier in a battalion.
Warrant Officer Class Two	A company sergeant major	There are also administrative jobs performed by WO2s
Colour Sergeant	Administrative head of a company	Might also command a specialist platoon. Everywhere but the infantry Colour Sergeants are called Staff Sergeants[149]
Sergeant	The administrative head of a platoon	May also command a platoon. Everyone of sergeant rank or higher is

---

[149] Well, almost everywhere. In the Household Cavalry they're called Staff Corporals, and in some cavalry regiment's they're called Sergeant Major (pronounced "sarnt major").

		called a Senior Non-Commissioned officer.
Corporal	Commands a Section	Or a tank. Corporals and Lance Corporals are Junior Non-Commissioned Officers
Lance Corporal	Commands a fire team	Or similar small group in non-infantry organisations.
Private	Kills Her Majesty's enemies	And never lacks for supervision

THE RIFLE COMPANY

Let's start at the bottom, and we'll focus on dismounted infantry. We know that Tommy never works alone, as that makes fire and manoeuvre impossible. In the British army the smallest infantry unit is the fire team of four men, commanded by a Lance Corporal. It comprises three riflemen, one of which is the commander, and a light machine gun. Take two fire teams and you have a section, commanded by a Corporal – who is also the commander of one fire team. Now look at Figure 10.1

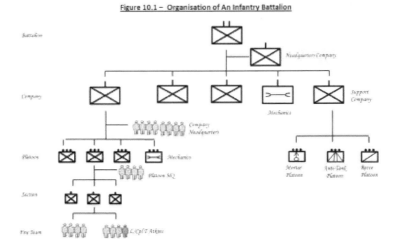

Figure 10.1 – Organisation of An Infantry Battalion

Take three sections; add a small headquarters and you have a platoon. This will be commanded by a junior officer, a Lieutenant or Second Lieutenant. He will be assisted by a Sergeant, who will take charge of discipline and logistics. The headquarters will usually have a radio operator and a 51mm mortar man. The radio operator is there as the platoon commander not only has to command his platoon but also report back up the line to his boss, the Company Commander.

Three platoons and a headquarters make a company. The headquarters includes the Company Commander (Major)[150], a Second in Command (Captain), a Company Sergeant Major (Warrant Officer Class 2), a Company Quarter Master Sergeant and about five soldiers who variously man radios and drive vehicles. The company will also have a company aid post, usually based on an ambulance and, if it is mechanised, a fitter platoon who mend (but don't service) the vehicles.

The Company Commander, (also known as the OC – short for Officer Commanding) commands the company, ensuring that it fulfils whatever missions and tasks that it is given. He has absolute responsibility for all its soldiers. The Company Sergeant Major or CSM is probably a little older than the Company Commander, who is in his mid-thirties. His role is to assist the Company Commander; however, he can and does take particular care of discipline.

The second in command (or 2IC) is there to take over from the Company Commander if he becomes a casualty or is not there. On operations his role is to provide information to the higher command, thereby leaving the Company Commander free to fight the immediate battle. He is probably ten years younger than the Company Commander, and has no idea how anyone can live as long as the CSM obviously has.

---

[150] In many armies, notably the US Army, companies are commanded by Captains. The debate about what level of experience is necessary to command a company really hinges on what level of autonomy they will have. The British history of a huge empire policed by a small army means that Company Commanders may operate with a level of independence and political sensitivity that require a rank higher than Captain. Examples include the Lebanon (1983-4), and Northern Ireland throughout "The Troubles"

The Company Quarter Master Sergeant, or CQMS, is there to make sure that all the combat supplies[151] required by all the men in the company are available. His rank is Colour Sergeant, which lies between Sergeant and Warrant Officer Class 2. We'll look at his role in detail in the chapter on logistics. The CQMS hopes that his next job will be CSM. Unfortunately for him, there are many things that can make a CQMS's life difficult and soldiers are pretty unimpressed if they run out of food. On the upside, everyone is grateful for an extra drink when the going gets tough, so the CQMS has plenty of opportunities to excel.

A company is the basic unit of warfare. It is rare to ever deploy less than a company to one place. It is also rare to break a company up for operations. In the overwhelming majority of cases, all the members of the company will always fight together. The total strength of a company is 100 to 150 men, all of whom know each other well.

THE BATTALION

The next level of command is the battalion. This comprises three rifle companies, a support company and a headquarters company. It will also have a number of mechanics, fitters and armourers; the precise quantity depends on whether the battalion is mechanised.

The battalion is commanded by a Lieutenant Colonel, referred to as the Commanding Officer (or "CO")[152] who is assisted by a Regimental Sergeant Major, who is a Warrant Officer, Class One. Both men have huge powers. The Commanding Officer, for example, can imprison Tommy for 28 days, reduce him in rank or promote him to the rank of Sergeant. The RSM has less formal power, but can freeze water at 100 paces just by looking at it. His role is to ensure that all parts of the battalion, which numbers some 600 to 800 men and women, are all dancing to the CO's tune, all the time. He is likely to be 5 or so years older than the 40 year-old Commanding Officer, and will have wide experience of soldiering.

---

[151] Combat supplies always include food, water, ammunition and fuel.

[152] The difference in implicit meaning between OC and CO is huge. Lieutenant Colonels hold much more power, for example in discipline. A CO can jail soldiers under the Army Acts, a (mere) OC can't.

He will actually be one of the happiest men on earth, as to become RSM is the ambition of almost every soldier when they embark upon their careers – including Tommy. However the RSM is likely to keep his joy well hidden as he seeks out the slovenly, lazy, scruffy and idle.

Falling foul of the RSM is not a path to happiness, and junior officers (particularly platoon commanders) and most soldiers find that their life runs most easily by giving him a wide berth. This should not be mistaken for fear, but respect. The RSM is one of the best soldiers in the battalion, and better than many will ever be. He has high standards, and does not accept second best. This does not mean that he is not compassionate, nor does it make him a caricature. The RSM is a very wise and experienced man, with a profound understanding of human nature.

SUPPORT COMPANY

The support company is an odd one. It usually comprises a mortar platoon, an anti-tank platoon and a reconnaissance platoon. The first two are fairly autonomous, providing indirect fire support and anti-tank capability respectively. The latter, which may or may not include snipers, generally consists of more senior soldiers and NCOs. It does work by itself, and in war is used by the commander to find the enemy. In barracks it generally exists in a happy state of conflict with the RSM. Hair length, quality of ironing and foot drill are usually the running sores.

The anti-tank platoon comprises a headquarters and three or four sections, each of which might have two to four anti-tank missile launchers. On operations the sections get sent to rifle companies as required, and are commanded by the rifle company commander. As operations ebb and flow they are likely to move from rifle company to rifle company.

The mortar platoon operates as an entity, although it can subdivide. Its headquarters becomes the mortar Fire Direction Centre. It sends out senior corporals as Mortar Fire Controllers ("MFCs") to the rifle companies. As operations ebb and flow the MFCs will be sent to the companies that need them most.

On operations the support company commander therefore does not have much to command, and he will usually be attached to the battalion headquarters.

HEADQUARTERS COMPANY

This is an amorphous group of officers, NCOs and soldiers who between them keep the battalion running. It includes all the bureaucratic side, led by the Chief Clerk and the Adjutant (a thrusting captain), a training and planning department, led by the Operations Officer (another thrusting captain, often a contemporary[153] of the Adjutant and usually slightly miffed that he is in the more junior position). Lower in the food chain are the Intelligence Officer (a more junior captain), who will have a sergeant to assist, and the Signals Officer (another junior captain) who generally runs the headquarters when it deploys. There is also, of course, a Second in Command, who is a major, usually about to be promoted. Together all these officers form the Battalion's headquarters when they are in the field.

There is more. A medical platoon, headed by a doctor and supported by a dentist forms the basis of the Battalion Aid Post, and provides medical care when in camp. A transport platoon provides the vehicles used to transport combat supplies. Chefs produce three meals a day, a Battalion Provost man the gate and guardroom[154] in peace and look after prisoners of war in the field.

There are also two quartermaster departments, each of which are headed by a captain Quartermaster supported by a Regimental Quartermaster Sergeant (who is a WO2) In the British Army quartermasters are usually commissioned warrant officers. The Regimental Quarter Master Sergeants are Warrant Officers, who perform at Battalion level broadly similar but larger functions to the Company Quarter Master Sergeants.

---

[153] As Rupert progresses though his career and the pyramidal structure of the Army asserts itself he starts to realises that his closest contemporaries are also his fiercest rivals.

[154] The guardroom is a combination of gatehouse, guard accommodation and prison. It is run by the Provost Sergeant, who reports directly to the RSM.

The Quartermaster (Technical) and his department supply spare parts for every machine and piece of equipment in the Battalion. In a mechanised battalion this involves holding a huge inventory of spare parts, and being able to find the part immediately. The stores are actually held on the back of lorries, so that they can leave camp complete. Even in these days of bar codes and computerised logistics, technical storemen need to be able to find and recognise everything.

Everything else, from boots and socks through combat supplies to the barracks buildings themselves falls into the purview of the Quartermaster. The process of issuing and receiving kit, inspecting its condition and making sure the correct amount is in place is a huge and complicated process.

This has been a little dry and complicated, but we need to get it straight. Taking it from the top:

A battalion is commanded by a Lieutenant Colonel, supported by a Warrant Officer (the RSM) and has 600 to 800 men in it. It is organised into:

- A headquarters company, which provides all the administration.
- A support company, which provides reconnaissance and specialist weapons
- Three rifle companies, each commanded by a Major, supported by a Warrant Officer (the CSM) and with 100 to 150 men in it. The rifle company comprises:
  - A small headquarters
  - Three rifle platoons, each commanded by a Lieutenant, supported by a Sergeant and has about 30 men in it. It comprises
    - A very small headquarters
    - Three rifle sections, each commanded by a corporal. A section comprises
      - One Fire team of four men commanded by the corporal
      - The other fire team, commanded by a lance corporal.

You will notice that there seems to be a love of having three parts to any organisation. In general this allows one to be firing, one to be moving and one to be in reserve. Some armies also have three teams in a section, although the need to be able to fit a section into a single vehicle limits this, unless the fire team size is reduced to three[155]. Other armies have four sections to a platoon, and four platoons to a company, arguing (with compelling evidence) that this is a more resilient and flexible structure. It is, of course, also more expensive.

Note also that at every level an officer has a sergeant or warrant officer alongside him. Mutual trust and respect between sergeants and officers is fundamental to the practice of warfare. If it breaks down, as for instance it did in many US Army units in Vietnam, the chances of winning a war are slim indeed. This is drilled into British Army officers from day one of their training. Rupert, our young second lieutenant is acutely aware of two things. Firstly he outranks his Sergeant, who calls him "Sir" and expects orders from him. Secondly, the Sergeant is paid more, and has taken a decade to produce, is better known to the Commanding Officer and is, frankly, more valuable. If Rupert gave an order that the Sergeant chose not to obey The Army Act might in theory back Rupert, but in practice officers do not exist to give bad orders. If he is to succeed, Rupert urgently needs to learn how to invite and take advice without losing authority.

Organisations change as new weapons are introduced and, a cynic would say, as funding gets tight. There is little doubt that most commanders would prefer to have four companies, each of four platoons comprising four sections. The corollary of that would be that each battalion had larger areas to cover, and so needed more powerful mortars etc. etc. There is no right organisation, although there are definitely some wrong ones.

---

[155] This is another of the great military debates. Some armies do have three fire teams in a section, and bigger vehicles. The author worked extensively on this in the past, but lost the will to live as the question kept changing. His recollection is that the least effective organisation was the British one, of two teams of four.

It is instructive to look at "bayonet strength," or fighting strength. Each platoon has 28 fighting men in it, which makes a rifle company have 84, as the company headquarters is not intended to fight. It does, frequently, but that is not the plan. The three rifle companies therefore produce 252 bayonets, which is around 40% of the strength of a 600 man battalion. This is neither a good thing nor a bad thing; it is just the way that it is. Keeping Tommy in the field and combat effective consumes manpower. Next time you hear on the news that another 1,000 soldiers are being sent to war do remember that most of them are not in the front line.

ANOMALIES AND SYNONYMS

Now, before we continue our ascent of the chain of command, and start reaching the dizzy heights of brigades and divisions, we need to understand a few historical anomalies. These are common in most armies, but have been elevated to an art form in the British.

We know that a battalion of infantry is commanded by a Lieutenant Colonel. The equivalent size organisation would be called a regiment if it had tanks, artillery pieces or indeed was full of sappers. A company is equivalent to a battery or squadron. A platoon is equivalent to a troop. The table below explains. The difference between cavalry and tanks is historic – the tank regiments were invented in 1917 with the tank[156], whereas cavalry regiments had existed for hundreds of years before that, and many kept their horses for a couple of decades afterwards.

Infantry	Cavalry/Tanks	Artillery	Engineers	Royal Marines	Logistics
Battalion	Regiment	Regiment	Regiment	Commando	Battalion
Company	Squadron	Battery	Squadron	Company	Company
Platoon	Troop	Troop	Troop	Troop	Platoon
Section	Tank	Gun	Section	Section	Section

I have included the Royal Marines for your information; they are actually part of the Royal Navy which explains their endearing habit

---

[156] The Royal Tank Regiment actually started as part of the Machine Gun Corps – but let's not go there.

of referring to the ground as "the deck", drinks as "wets" and myriad other linguistic eccentricities.

REGIMENTS AND THE BRITISH REGIMENTAL SYSTEM

In some armies the regiment is a level of command roughly equal to a brigade. In some armies it's a level equivalent to battalion. In the British army it is partly the latter and partly something else entirely. Now, this book has not the space to explain the entire organisation of the British Army, which has been better done by others. However, you do need to understand a bit.

The first piece is simple, for non-infantry combat arms a Regiment is the same as a Battalion, as shown in the table above. Now for the harder bit; the British Infantry also has Regiments, although these are not a combat organisation. Regiments have one or more battalions. So for example, you may have heard of

3rd Battalion, The Rifles,

2nd Battalion, The Royal Anglian Regiment

1st Battalion, The Yorkshire Regiment.

Now on any one day, 1st Battalion, The Rifles may be in Afghanistan, 2nd Battalion, The Rifles in Belfast and 3rd Battalion, The Rifles in Germany. There is no tactical significance in the fact that they are battalions of the same Regiment. However if Tommy is a Rifleman he will spend his entire career in Battalions of the Rifles, possibly the same battalion. He is most unlikely to serve in the Royal Anglians, or any other Regiment. This produces a sense of shared identity, which increases in those Regiments that chose to minimise posting between battalions. This bond reaches its strongest in single battalion infantry regiments, such as the foot guards, and the cavalry and tank regiments, who operate in the same way. In these regiments the regiment is a family - everyone knows everyone else, well. The relationships between officers and senior NCOs are strong, long and based on mutual respect. Family traditions of service in the regiment are common over several generations. The soldiers will all come from the same geographic part of the UK. Attempts to amalgamate or disband regiments cause great emotional reactions.

Artillery[157], engineer and other sorts of regiment tend to post officers around every couple of years, and soldiers as needed.

Let's continue our ascent of the military scale.

BRIGADES

A brigade is commanded by a Brigadier – who in any army but the British is a general. It comprises a headquarters of about 150[158], commanding a number of Regiments and Battalions. It will also have artillery, engineers and logistics. If it is an air assault brigade it will have some helicopters. If it's a (or rather, the) British Air Assault brigade these will only be attack helicopters as the RAF owns all the transport helicopters[159]. It is important to understand that the composition of a brigade is driven by operations and is flexible – some might have three armoured regiments and just one infantry battalion – and it can change quickly. The inherent feature of the structure of the army is that it is strong, but flexible.

Let's consider a "square" mechanised brigade, comprising two mechanised infantry battalions and two armoured regiments. These will form four battle groups, each based on the battalion or regimental headquarters of the mechanised battalions and armoured regiments.

They are battle groups because they are now all arms organisations. At the brigadier's direction, each armoured regiment will swap one or more of its squadrons for a mechanised company from one of the infantry battalions. This regrouping is also driven by the tactical objectives, and is flexible. Each battle group will also receive a battery commander (BC) from the artillery regiment to assist with fire planning. The BC will bring a selection of FOOs with him.

---

[157] It gets worse with the artillery. Every British artilleryman is actually a member of the "Royal Regiment of Artillery" including those who serve in the Royal Horse Artillery. For a long lime there was a Royal Horse Artillery regiment that was actually parachute trained. This is not as absurd as it sounds as there is no difference in equipment between a RHA regiment and a normal regiment. But there are hundreds of years of history...

[158] Based upon a Royal Signals squadron.

[159] This is not a quaint historical anomaly, merely an example of how inter-service rivalry within the UK ministry of Defence rarely produces efficient, rational organisations.

Similarly the sappers will send a captain to each battle group to coordinate the supply of sappery.

Let's look at the bayonet strength: the infantry bring 252, plus each battalion has 48 Warriors with a crew of three, making a total of 396 from each infantry battalions. The tank regiments have 50 tanks each, with 4 man crews so that is a total of 400 from them both. The total fighting element is therefore 1,192. The total manpower of the brigade is 750 for each infantry regiment, 600 each for the armoured, artillery, engineer and logistic regiments plus 150 for the headquarters giving a total of 4,650. Just 25% of the manpower is intimately involved in the direct fire battle.

DIVISIONS

A division is commanded by a Major-General. Its composition will vary but is typically two to four brigades, a reconnaissance regiment, one or more artillery regiments, which may include missiles, an air defence regiment, one or more engineer regiments, an attack helicopter regiment, a signals regiment, which also provides the headquarters, a military police company and a whole bunch of logistics including a hospital and a field workshop.

The total strength is likely to be around 18,000 men if it has three brigades. Of these around 20% [the brigades' fighting element] will be involved in the direct fire battle.

We have come a long way from Tommy and his fire team, who we now see are very much the sharp end of a large wedge. We have also reached about the limit of what the British Army is capable of deploying – a force of about this composition was sent to both the First and Second Gulf Wars.

CORPS

The next level of command, which is included for completeness, is a Corps, commanded by a Lieutenant General. It comprises two to five divisions plus a whole bunch of support. Its artillery may well have tactical nuclear weapons (as they did in The Cold War) – however using these is not the Corps Commanders decision.

Throughout The Cold War the British maintained a corps in (West) Germany. Its strength was around 55,000 men – which would have been increased on mobilisation[160]. Levels of command above Corps do exist; Army and Army Group. However, their composition and level of commander varies widely. At the moment the British Army would struggle to field an entire division, let alone a corps.

PEACETIME AND WARTIME ESTABLISHMENTS

A battalion needs more soldiers when it is at war than in peacetime. For example, a provost staff of five is perfectly adequate to police a battalion's barracks. However operating a prisoner of war (PW) cage in wartime requires more men, probably at least 30. Although Tommy is not particularly well paid, he is also fed and housed. He is equipped, and trains almost continuously. Training involves some very expensive toys, which means that Tommy is not cheap to run.

While in the perfect world the 30 men to run the PW cage would be with the battalion all the time, it is not cost effective to keep them there. In war, the theory goes, the battalion can be augmented by reservists who have either completed their military service or who volunteered to join a reserve force. Saving the cost of the PW cage for each of 20 battalions actually produces enough headcount to create another battalion, albeit one that is understrength compared to its wartime needs.

As with POW cages, so with many other small parts of a battalion. The net result is that you end up with a larger number of battalions, but that they are understrength by 30 to 100 men. This is acceptable provided a good reserve recall system exists, so that on the first signs of war the reservists can get to their battalions before the fighting starts. The problem arises when the battalion gets involved in a war that does not trigger calling up the reserves. The only option is for the battalion to "borrow" soldiers from another battalion. This happened in the Northern Ireland troubles, both Gulf Wars and it is happening in Afghanistan now. While its impact can be reduced by sufficient pre-deployment training, it is not ideal. It

---

[160] Mobilisation is the term used to switch the entire economy to a war footing. It involves many procedures, one of which is the summoning of all members of the reserve (ex-soldiers) and Territorial Army (reserve soldiers) to report for duty. It is possible for TA soldiers to deploy on operations without mobilisation, indeed the TA form a large part of the deployment to Afghanistan.

also, inevitably, produces some soldiers who are doing more than their fair share of tours. Not a problem in the short term, but nowhere near ideal[161].

The good news is that we have now covered everything we need to know about organisations and equipment to go to war and put it all in context. It's time to drag Rupert, Tommy and the rest from in front of their X-boxes and kick them into action.

---

[161] The British Army is now attempting to integrate more closely with the reserves (known in the UK as the Territorial Army, or TA). These are civilians, who undergo military training at the weekend. Some employers, particularly the small companies that make up 70% of the British economy, are distinctly underwhelmed at the prospect of losing a key employee (in small firms all employees are key) for one year and having to hold a job open for him (or her). This problem is a surprise to no one outside the government.

Chapter 11 Tommy Gets Intense; High-Intensity War

Let's have a war!

We'll leave Tommy, Rupert and the gang rushing about, packing their kit and deploying to the battlefield and consider types of war. Many academics and theoreticians have devised plenty of jargon – most of which we're going to avoid. For our purposes there are two sorts of war.

Firstly there is "General War", where we have an enemy, a battle field, no constraints on the weapons that we can use and no great concern about the condition that we leave the pitch in. We can use everything that is in this book – including nuclear and chemical weapons. General war comes in two flavours, "High Intensity" where there is armoured conflict with lots of firepower being deployed. High intensity wars include the First Gulf War, The Yom Kippur and Six-Day Wars in Israel, the Korean War, and both world wars. The combatants are national armies, with broadly similar equipment. The politics are simple and we are seeking a decisive outcome on the battlefield[162].

The other flavour, "low intensity war," describes wars where less firepower is available or deployed. The Falklands War of 1982 was low intensity, largely due to the constraints on equipment deployed. So was most of the Vietnamese War. Many wars between second and third rate military powers are low intensity, simply because their armies are not equipped or trained for high intensity warfare. Do not make the mistake of thinking that there are no intense moments in low intensity war - there are plenty.

The other sort of war, which we'll cover in Chapter 13, is counter-insurgency warfare. The enemy is not a conventional army, there are constraints on the use of firepower and some form of hearts and minds campaign will be running alongside the military fight. Classic

---

[162] I accept that the Korean War was fought to a standstill, and is technically still in a ceasefire rather than a peace. Perhaps the decisive conclusion was that the protagonists and their backers did NOT want to pay the cost of winning the war.

counter insurgent wars are Afghanistan, Malaya and the "troubles" in Northern Ireland. Note that counter insurgent wars can also be pretty intense when Tommy gets into contact.

High intensity warfare is likely to involve armour, and is likely to be significantly about the possession of ground. For at least one side, winning or losing is a probably matter of national survival. Now, in any general war there are broadly four things that Tommy and Rupert can do: they can advance, meaning that they cross ground towards the enemy until they find him; they can attack the enemy, if they know where he is; they can defend, holding important ground and violently and implacably resist the enemy's attempts to seize it; or they can withdraw, usually to move to a better more defensible position. Notice please that only the enemy "retreats."

At any one time some of our forces can be performing all of these tasks. However, for any one commander, it's one at time. Remember also that if the enemy is attacking, we are defending. It takes two to fight and, generally, only one side can have the initiative at any one time; usually the one that has concentrated most combat power available and is advancing and attacking. There is a useful analogy that helps explain how both sides interact.

Imagine a rapist breaking into a dark house, at night. He knows that the only occupant is a female, but he doesn't know where she is. He needs to feel his way through the house until he finds her. Then he needs to fix her in position so that he can fornicate[163] (with or without her consent). At the same time, she needs to blind him, by turning out lights and removing the fuse. She can then block him by tipping over a book case. As she retreats up the stairs she needs to bash him with a frying pan or similar blunt object. When he eventually gets to the top of the stairs she can then obliterate him by hitting him over the head with a fire extinguisher.

If you can remember the four Fs and the four Bs you're well on the way to becoming a convincing armchair general. Now let's look at each phase in a little more detail.

---

[163] In military circles a shorter word is more commonly used.

ADVANCE

Advancing is how wars are won, provided you don't get over-extended. Tommy will tell you of an old adage, which states that *"If your advance is going really well you're walking into an ambush!"*[164] At the same time, the faster we can advance, the less time the enemy has to prepare and the less resistance he will be able to put up. Eventually his withdrawal (or retreat) will become a rout. If you are going to win a high intensity war, you need a strong, prolonged advance. Examples abound, but think of the Russian Vistula-Oder offensive in 1944, The British March across the Falklands in 1982, the one hundred hours of the First Gulf War 1990 and the final British advances in 1918. It is easy for the ignorant to mock the craving for "The Big Push" of the First World War; it is harder to explain how the war would have been won without it.

Advances are usually led and flanked by reconnaissance forces, which will be in light armour[165]. They have to use the ground, guile and mobility to stay alive and are generally quite cautious. When they come onto a bound they have to establish that it is clear before they move forward. A bound is a piece of ground of tactical significance that can be defended, which is a lot of jargon for a hill or ridge. Have a look at the Figure 11.1 below.

Figure 11.1 – Tactical Bounds

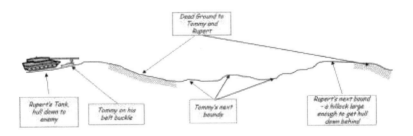

---

[164] This is one of Murphy's Laws of Combat.

[165] Some Armies, notably the Russians, augment reconnaissance forces with tanks. If you have the tanks to spare this can make sense, although it inevitably leads to the (heated) topic of whether (and how) reconnaissance forces should "fight for information." Heinz Guderian, the inventor of armoured warfare, was generally convinced that they should not.

Note that the hardest thing for the recce commanders to see is enemy on the reverse slope immediately to their front. As they move forward they will see more, but become more exposed.

This invariably involves the reconnaissance force stopping, looking, looking again, manoeuvring to a better position and looking yet again. Only when they are satisfied that there are no enemy and they can't see any minefields about will they move onto the next bound. While one vehicle moves, its partner watches. The purpose of watching is to see if any enemy appear while the partner is vulnerable. If the enemy does emerge the stationary vehicle kills them, ideally before the enemy engages the advancing friendly vehicle. If it can't kill them then it is still alive to pass information to higher command. The brutal reality is that if the enemy is there and is any good, the first that the recce troops will know about it is when one of their lead vehicles gets hit. Of course, to the thrusting commanders of the heavily armoured tanks behind, this is just recce being "wet" and "lacking drive". This can lead to some fairly full and frank discussions between recce commanders and those who follow in their footsteps.

Nowadays, reconnaissance is likely to be supported by UAVs and possibly Katie in her attack helicopter, who may have a better view and may produce additional information. However, the problem remains the age old one of finding out what is on the other side of the hill.

Generally we'll start off advancing to contact – we know that there is some enemy about, but we haven't found them yet; we're feeling and finding our way to them. Of course, we'll know when we've found them as they'll start shooting and, hey presto, we're now in contact. The next job is to fix the enemy – which means keeping him static while we manoeuvre to destroy him or bypass him.

It should be clear that the moment of making contact is when plans start to unravel. Recce will be taking casualties, and if the enemy manages to kill them too quickly then we'll be blind. If our recce can get a location and estimate of the enemy strength and equipment then we are making progress. Crucially, if he can land some artillery accurately on target, include some smoke and move to a flank, we may be in a position to make a quick attack and maintain both the advance and the initiative.

As we know, even self-propelled artillery with full inertial navigation systems can't come into action immediately. Gary therefore has to keep least one battery[166] ready to fire, tracking the advance while the other batteries in the regiment will be moving forward to the next gun position. Once they're established the first battery can move. Having longer range artillery makes this process easier, but don't forget the point that at the moment of contact, and for a few minutes thereafter, not all artillery fire support will be available.

ATTACK

There are two types of attack. The quick attack is the natural successor to the advance to contact, and occurs once we have found the enemy. Indeed, an advance in contact can sometimes look like a succession of quick attacks. The key point about a quick attack is that we know little in detail about the enemy's location and strength until we engage. This implies that no-one has detailed orders on performing the attack before it starts. Moreover, commanders, at all levels, have not conducted a detailed study of the enemy to produce a cunning plan and not all the available fire support will be in range, or will have registered targets. In a quick attack we're trading the benefits of detailed planning for the benefits of surprise and momentum.

And, of course, the enemy is shooting at us. This is not the best of situations to start an attack from, but it is the one that we have. The alternative of withdrawing quickly if we're outnumbered is equally difficult. Quick attacks are endemic in armoured warfare, where the drive to advance means that we will soon get ahead of the intelligence picture. The secret of success is teamwork[167], speed, determination and plentiful firepower.

The other sort of attack is the deliberate[168] attack. These happen when we know where the enemy position is and there has been sufficient time for detailed reconnaissance and planning. This will have included rehearsals, some preliminary bombardment,

---

[166] 6 to 8 guns in most armies.

[167] Teamwork requires training – and lots of it.

[168] "Deliberate" as in planned – not the opposite of accidental. That said, considering a quick attack as an accidental one is not a bad starting point – although of course it does not look good in the manuals and pamphlets.

deception plans and the full panoply of military activity. Inevitably, deliberate attacks tend to occur at the start of campaigns, and after lulls in battle. A well-executed deliberate attack should give the attacker the best chance of defeating a well prepared enemy in a defensive position, provided surprise is maintained. However, remember that no plan survives contact with the enemy, and therefore flexibility should be built in. The enemy will be doing his utmost to defeat us and the defender generally has the advantage (not least because he chose the ground).

WITHDRAWING

The difference between a withdrawal and a retreat is partly semantic – a withdrawal implies a level of intention whereas a retreat is a passive response to being attacked by a superior enemy. Most armies force their enemies to "retreat", although if the situation is reversed they prefer to "withdraw". In many ways it is the most perilous phase of war – almost by definition one is outnumbered, the enemy is advancing and (usually) getting closer and inflicting casualties. Advancing is hard work, but exhilarating as we're winning. Withdrawing is even harder work and depressing. The absolute priority in a withdrawal is to prevent it becoming a rout. This requires strong, tough and brave leadership at every level.

On the ground, withdrawing looks like an advance in reverse – we move from bound to bound, killing as many enemy as we can from each bound. Ideally we want to stay at least one bound ahead of the enemy. In practice this is hard to maintain; the numerically superior enemy will press forward and seek to outflank at every opportunity. We also have to travel further, and set up those weapons that can't fire on the move – which is anything that isn't on a top of the range armoured vehicle – dismantle them again, and then remount vehicles and continue to withdraw.

Eventually we need to come to either a strongly defended location, where we can pass through and leave the enemy to grind himself against superior forces, or we need to break clean. This means switching from withdrawing in contact, where we fight the enemy bound by bound, to withdrawing out of contact, where we are out of sight of the enemy and can thus move quickly to establish a new defensive position. Breaking clean therefore requires getting rid of the enemy advance, which in turn needs direct fire. This is one of the occasions when attack helicopters are a real bonus. As we withdraw they can move quickly to a bound behind, undetected by the enemy. When we reach the break clean line we can then have a bit of a turkey shoot with the advancing enemy, and then withdraw with the attack helicopters able to provide some cover[169].

DEFENCE

A defensive position is a piece of ground that we are going to hold. This is a word with a specific military meaning, which is to occupy the ground and stay there in spite of the enemy's best efforts to remove us. Holding ground is one of the prime roles of infantry, who can dig in. It is a ground based phase of war – there are some pieces of ground that are almost indefensible[170] and wherever we are, if we can get hold of some Sappers we can exploit the ground to our advantage.

Soldiers sometimes refer to hasty defences and deliberate defence, but the difference is really in how much time and resource is available and invested. Wherever Tommy is, he will dig a shell scrape, which is about six inches deep and lowers most of his body below ground level. This might happen in a patrol base, any overnight location or hide and on a break clean line. We also saw it in Chapter four, after the reorganisation. If he is to stay in the location for much longer he will start to dig a trench.

There is more to defence than digging. We have to coordinate arcs of fire, artillery targets, tank routes, obstacles and minefields, logistics, air defence, food and latrines - to name but a few. But the key joy of defence is that we have chosen the ground to best suit our weapons. The enemy's choice is stark – go round (known as

---

[169] Not all armies are content for attack helicopters to operate ahead of their own troops.

[170] Possibly the entire Somme in World War 1, as it was overlooked by German positions, who were able to snipe and shell accurately from the luxury of well dug trenches in chalk. Tommy meantime could not dig deep due to the low water table. Withdrawing the line further west was politically unacceptable, hence the repeated attempts throughout the War to capture higher ground to the East

bypassing), which leaves us alive to attack him in his rear[171], or take us on where we have stacked the deck in our favour.

ENCOUNTER BATTLE

There is one final sort of battle that you might hear about, which is the encounter battle. This happens when two forces are advancing to contact, and then meet. Both then try to perform a quick attack, and then it gets messy and (usually) degenerates as each side manoeuvres for advantage while thoroughly confused. The Cold War Soviet army was a master at these – or at least it practiced them a lot. The force that is slowest to work out that it is in an encounter battle is unlikely to survive.

COUNTER MOVES

You may also hear of counter-attacks, counter-penetrations and counter-strokes. Counter-attacks are an integral part of any defence. Their objective is to recapture lost ground, and to continue holding it. A well timed counter-attack will catch the attacking force just as they are reorganising on their objective. It you think back to Chapter Four, there was a moment when there were only two people (Tommy's section commander and one man) able to defend the position, with the other four moving to join them. If the enemy had counter-attacked then it would have been hard to hold onto the position.

The other two manoeuvres are usually brigade or divisional level actions, so a little above Tommy's pay grade. A counter-penetration is intended to destroy an advancing force that has broken through a defensive position. It is effectively a pre-planned defence which is rapidly occupied, frequently by heliborne infantry. A counter-stroke is an armoured attack into the flanks of an advancing enemy. The aim is the destruction of enemy combat power, rather than taking ground. The counter-stroke usually comes in behind (i.e. on the enemy side of) the leading enemy units, which usually presents a rich array of targets like headquarters, artillery units and logistic

---

[171] Another of Murphy's Laws of combat is "remember that whenever you have got behind the enemy's lines, you have also put the enemy behind your lines."

units. The tricky bit is in sneaking an armoured brigade or more into a position from which it can launch.

Right, that is a lot of theory. Let's now go and watch Tommy, Rupert and the gang putting it into practice.

A High Intensity Defensive Battle

The scenario is simple. The enemy is thought to be about to attack, and Tommy's battle group has deployed to hold a piece of important ground. Rupert's squadron has joined Tommy's battle group, although the rest of Rupert's regiment has deployed forward to delay the enemy[172].

Tommy's battle group mission is simple, to hold the ground in order to halt the enemy advance. Sappers are out laying minefields and blowing up bridges. Gary is registering targets, although the guns are primarily concerned with supporting Rupert's battle-group.

Day One

The Battle Group Commander has had sufficient time to look at the ground, and with his company commanders has sited every trench, and marked them. His aim is to ensure that every trench's arcs of fire interlocks with ones on both sides and that the fire from machine guns overlaps. The diagrams below should make this clear.

---

[172] The jargon for this is a "covering force."

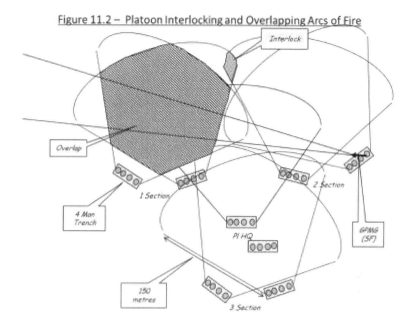

Figure 11.2 – Platoon Interlocking and Overlapping Arcs of Fire

We're in defence, so a GPMG (SF)[173] has been issued and we have a MFC[174] party attached, which is why the platoon headquarters has more men. Note that the arcs from each trench are only 150 metres long, although we know that rifle range is 300 metres. This is the effect of folds in the ground blocking lines of sight to the surface. A man on his feet will be visible further away. The interlock is where the right hand arc of 1 Section is between the left and right arcs of 2 Section. This is the minimum acceptable level of connection. Much better is the overlap, where most of the area covered by the left hand trench of 1 Section is also covered by its right hand trench.

Imagine for a moment that you are assaulting Tommy, who commands the left trench of 2 Section. To get to Tommy's trench you have to pass through the fire of at least three other trenches, and the GPMG (SF). It's actually worse than that, because 300 to 500 metres to the left is another platoon. They too have a GPMG (SF), sited so that its arc of fire covers the front of Tommy's trench

---

[173] GPMG(SF)= General Purpose Machine Gun (Sustained Fire). A 7.62mm machine gun mounted on a tripod. Range 1,100m + Rate of fire 600 rounds / minute. 2 spare barrels.
[174] MFC = Mortar Fire Controller, as you learnt in Chapter 5

too. Notice also that 3 Section is sited in depth. Even if the enemy gets into Tommy's trench he will stay under fire and be counter-attacked, either from the other 2 Section trench or Platoon Headquarters.

Note also that even if the enemy approaches from another direction he faces the same problem; it is impossible to attack one trench without being engaged from several other trenches.

Tommy and his pals are about to go into navvy mode to construct this position. Each trench will hold a fire team, and will have the approximate dimensions shown in Figure 11.3. The sides of the trench will be reinforced with corrugated iron, and this will also be used to construct the shelter bays and the overhead cover. The spoil from the trench will be spread out under the turf to provide a gentle slope up to the parapet and parados. Digging this out by hand is going to take two men around 12 hours, and building the overhead cover at least another eight.

Figure 11.3 - A Four-Man Slit Trench

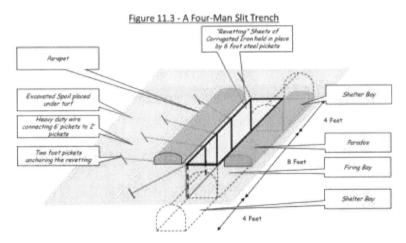

But what about the other two men in the fire team, you will ask. Well, there are other jobs that the platoon needs doing. Firstly, the platoon needs security, so it will send out a standing patrol of eight men 500 to 1,000 metres towards the enemy. If the enemy arrives before digging is complete the standing patrol will engage them.

The platoon also has to lay telephone[175] wire to the company headquarters, and from the platoon HQ trench to the fire trenches. The wire has to be buried, and this will take another two men most of the day.

The other platoon asset that could be employed is its four Warrior IFV[176]s. Their total of four 30 mm cannon and four 7.62mm chain guns would add hugely to the available firepower. The problem is concealing and protecting them. Digging a Warrior in is a huge amount of earthwork, and even then the IFV is obvious from above. As the battlegroup commander does not (yet) have the engineering resources to dig them in, his plan involves the Warriors using the ground for protection and forming the basis of his counter-attack plans. In the interim they are kept off the position, to the rear. They are also used for transporting defence stores like pickets, corrugated iron, wire and mines. Some might be sent forward to strengthen the standing patrol.

The company commander also has an obstacle plan involving mines and wire. There aren't any sappers available, so four men per platoon are being taken as a mine laying party.

The platoon commander is busy reconnoitring his counter-attack routes, checking arcs interlock and overlap and he has his runner with him. In total, 16 men from Tommy's platoon are doing other stuff, which leaves less than half to do the digging. Tommy is one of those on the position (his corporal is on the standing patrol), and he has several trenches to dig. It's a change from being a beast of burden, but it is still hard work.

The surrounding turf is rolled back and excavated earth spread out to give a gentle rise to the parapet. The turf is then laid back, which should make the earthwork hard to distinguish from the surrounding land. The sides of the trench are faced with corrugated iron sheets, which are held in place by 6 foot[177] pickets, themselves

---

[175] Military radios can also work as telephones, albeit without the complex dialling options. The advantage is that significantly less radiation is produced for the enemy to detect.

[176] IFV = Infantry Fighting Vehicle

[177] The length of these pickets was determined long before the UK went metric.

held in place by being windlassed to a 2 foot picket in the spoil. The shelter bays are formed from special arched sheets of corrugated iron, and then covered in and re-turfed. The final stage, which is not shown in the diagram, is to use sandbags and yet more corrugated iron and pickets to put a roof on the fire bay, which is then covered with 18 inches of soil. The result of this substantial construction is a fragment-proof trench from which Tommy's fire team can fight, and in which they can shelter during artillery barrages.

They remain vulnerable to a direct hit and to direct fire. In spite of Tommy's best efforts, the bulge and particularly the overhead cover make the trench relatively easy to spot. Wherever possible trenches are sited in shadow, under trees and close to hedges. While this makes them much better concealed, it makes digging still harder work as Tommy has to cut through roots - no fun at all.

The whole company position is shown in Figure 11.4 below. The enemy is advancing from the north. The company has two platoons forward, on the reverse slope of Hill 192, and one back on the forward slope of Hill 181. Note that the enemy can't see Hill 181 until he is on Hill 192. The company has a FOO[178], and has also been allocated eight anti-tank missile launchers. These are sited with the same principles of interlock and overlap, and of course pay special attention to the minefield.

---

[178] Forward Observation Officer –the man (or woman) who talks to Gary the gunner.

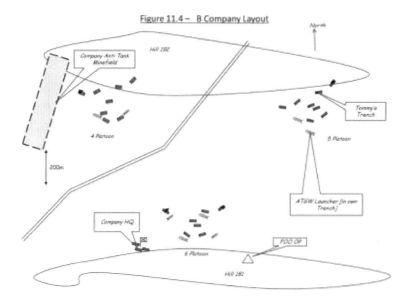

Figure 11.4 – B Company Layout

So we now have the company hard at work, digging in and laying mines and other defences. What of Rupert and his tank squadron? To understand what he's up to we need first of all to look at the whole battle group. The broad position is set out below in Figure 11.5.

Figure 11.5 – The Battle-Group Layout

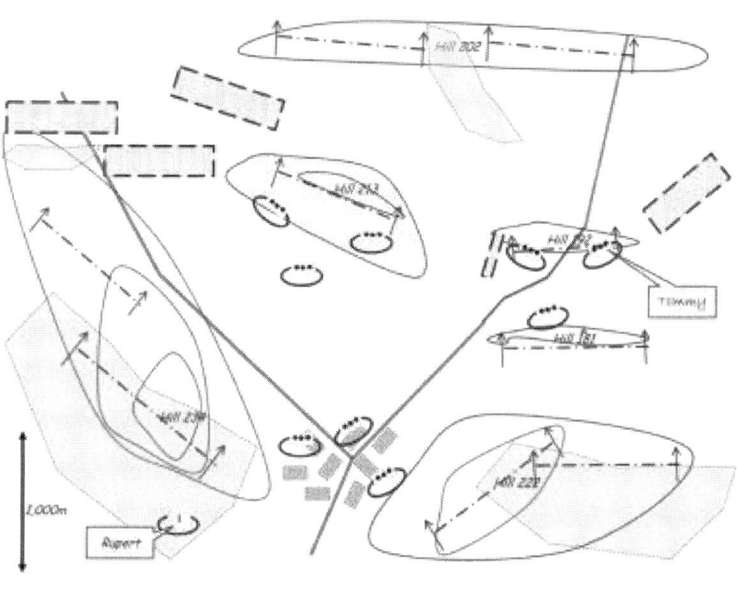

As the map shows, Rupert is with his entire squadron, 14 tanks, hidden in the woods behind Hill 234. Tommy's B Company is front right, on the reverse slope of Hill 192. A Company is front left, on the reverse slope of Hill 213 and C Company is in depth, dug in round the village. They are invisible to any enemy to the North of Hills 213 and 234. Battlegroup headquarters is in the village, with an alternate headquarters behind Hill 222. All of the hills have FOO parties digging in on them. The standing patrols from A and B Companies are forward, concealed on Hill 202. The mortar platoon is digging in behind Hill 222, whence it will be able to provide fire throughout the battlegroup area. The reconnaissance platoon is forward of Hill 202. The battlegroup deployment is broadly as deep as it is wide – the days of the Thin Red Line are long gone.

Further to the north, an armoured battlegroup is deployed, awaiting the enemy advance. Their role will be to impose delay and casualties on the enemy advance, while withdrawing in contact. They will break clean at Hill 202, having handed over contact to this battlegroup. The armour will then withdraws to the rear, rearm and be ready to counter-attack as required.

To the east and west, similar operations are underway. Sappers are laying mines and destroying bridges. Gunners are surveying in positions and the electronic warfare types are trying to identify early indications of enemy activity. Air defence chaps (and chapettes) are deploying to protect key defensive positions, like this one, and even the air force is busy, preparing to launch strikes and take on enemy airfields.

While Tommy is busy digging Rupert is working hard too. The 14 tanks have 56 crewmen, and the squadron headquarters has a further five, including the SSM[179] but excluding the SQMS[180], who is off collecting more combat supplies. As they drove into their hide their enterprising SSM had arranged a bore-sighting screen, so the crews are confident that the sights are pointing the same way as their guns.

---

[179] SSM = Squadron Sergeant Major, who is the equivalent of the Company Sergeant Major
[180] SQMS = Squadron Quartermaster Sergeant, who is the equivalent of the CQMS.

The tanks are in a hide, not a defensive position. If attacked, their defence is to move and their role in this battle will be to engage the enemy from various fire positions, marked by the dashed lines on Figure 11.5. While they wait they are busy. The first job is to put up thermal and visual camouflage, and to connect all the tanks via landline. Then they have to cover up the track marks that they made getting into their hide. Commanders are now with the squadron leader receiving orders; the crews are mending the gremlins whose spontaneous appearance is endemic in British tanks. They are helped in this by the Light Aid Detachment, which is a Staff Sergeant and eight or so men who travel in three armoured recovery vehicles.

Once their orders are complete, the commanders and drivers will walk key parts of the routes to the various engagement positions, to ensure that they can get there quickly day or night without running over Tommy or his pals - harder than it sounds. If there is time, the gunners will then be taken to the bounds so that they can get a view of the battlefield. It there isn't time, Rupert and the commanders will prepare range cards and panoramic sketches. The battlegroup Intelligence Officer[181] will take their estimates of the time to get to each engagement position and ensure that he has sited assets (primarily the Observation Positions of the recce platoon) which can provide the necessary amount of early warning to ensure the tanks get to their firing positions on time, by day or night.

The squadron leader will also have a good look at the detail siting of his tanks, and may decide to dig tank scrapes, to lower the tank's profile in a firing position. If so they'll use either a dozer tank[182] or one of the recovery vehicles, or both. A tank scrape will also work for an IFV, and they may dig extra ones. It takes around 30 minutes to dig one scrape, depending on soil conditions. It also creates large amounts of noise and smoke, and of course the scrapes can be seen from the air, which gives the enemy some warning of what to expect.

Once back, the troop leaders will brief all their troop and they will then settle into defensive routine. Of the 12 men in a troop, three

---

[181] A more junior captain, slightly senior to company 2ICs.
[182] Typically one tank per squadron has a bulldozer blade on the front.

are commanders. The other nine have to provide a radio watch, a ground sentry an air sentry and a chemical sentry if there is a threat of nuclear, biological or chemical weapons. The entire crew is therefore working two hours on, four hours off, even before they get into maintenance. When not "on stag" the crews work on the vehicles or catch up on sleep. The key thing to remember about a hide is that it is just that, a hide. Engines are rarely started and noise and movement kept to a minimum. If the enemy does attack, the plan is to move rather than stand and fight.

Day Two

After about 24 hours the battlegroup commander should have the overwhelming majority of his battlegroup dug in and prepared. He now has two conflicting priorities – concealment, and improving his defences. Concealment is crucial; if the enemy can locate the battlegroup positions then the commander risks receiving early and unpleasant attention from enemy artillery and air attacks.

Having completed digging there is much more that can be done to strengthen the position. As well as laying mines and barbed wire, the commander now has the resources to start building a deception plan. If he digs some trenches on the north slopes of Hills 192 and 213 the enemy might be persuaded that this is the main position, and assault that. This is sometimes known as a "false front"; with the help of Rupert and Gary, the enemy can sometimes be induced into attacking the wrong position. This will consume time and the enemy's combat supplies as well as presenting more targets for Rupert. It will also confuse the enemy commander and undermine his subordinate's confidence in him. It's a good return for a bit more of Tommy's sweat. It also gives Tommy and his men something to do - otherwise they will be spending all their time sitting in their trench, worrying.

By the same token, within the platoons' areas it is worth constructing dummy positions. Every round fired at them is one less being fired at Tommy. While dummy positions do not have to be fully dug, they do have to be coherent and credible. The more professional they look, the more the enemy will believe them.

Tommy's section is pretty tired by now. Like Rupert's troop, they too have to provide sentries, radio stags and the like. The mine laying party is back, but then another party is out building the false front and Tommy's platoon commander wants decoy trenches, while the sergeant is creating a barbed wire entanglement in front of the forward trenches. At the same time the Company Commander is running through counter-attack plans and rehearsals. These have to be repeated as everyone must know where to go, even if it is raining artillery. The battlegroup commander has sited the Warriors from Tommy's platoon in scrapes behind Hill 181. From the scrapes they can support A and C Companies, while they have the option of leaving the scrapes and supporting B Company from hull down positions behind the crest of Hill 181.

By the end of the second day most of the platoon are shattered – the people who have had the softest time are probably those on the standing patrol. Everyone's sleep is ruined by the announcement that the enemy has attacked and they're at war. The battlegroup ceases any further preparations and everyone is ordered back to their trench. The position is now complete so the standing patrols are recalled, and finally Tommy's platoon is at full strength in its position. After standing down, sleep is interrupted by the sounds of distant gunfire and the odd jet passing overhead.

The battlegroup commander's main worry at the moment is reserves. If his three rifle companies are attacked, or at least supressed simultaneously then he has no reserve other than his empty Warriors. While those provide plenty of firepower, he needs men in the back to reoccupy the trenches. In the perfect world he would have another rifle company or a smaller area to defend. In the imperfect world in which he lives his options are simple and stark. This is what colonels earn their pay for, so it's worth considering his options:

> He can thin out all the platoons, each providing him one fire team. The problem with that is that it makes it easier for the enemy to break into the battle group's position.

> He can take an entire platoon from C Company, although this will significantly weaken their positions

> He can take some of the Warrior crews and put them in the back of other Warriors. This renders many of his Warriors

unmanned, and he therefore loses their firepower and mobility.

He can go through the administrative elements of the battlegroup, extracting men, forming them into sections and getting them into the back of Warriors. The problem with this is that it undermines the administrative and logistic soundness of the battlegroup.

It the event he opts to convert some of his logisticians to foot soldiers. They can then undergo intense training and rehearsal; every soldier is trained as an infantryman first so at least he's not starting from scratch. The obvious place for him to raid for manpower is his Light Aid Detachment. This yields him the manpower for two platoons. Commanders come from the Warrior crews, a junior captain from the Battlegroup Headquarters and the headquarters company's CSM.

As the RSM says, "God is on the side of the big battalions[183].... And this one is getting bigger." The ability to find extra troops is a key skill, and it relies heavily upon all soldiers being fit and proficient with basic weaponry. The reserve platoons are located in the woods behind Hill 222.

Day Three

Rupert, Tommy and everyone else in the battlegroup "stands to" before dawn. "Stand to" means that every man is awake, at his post with his weapon and ready for the enemy to attack. Most armies routinely stand to at dawn and dusk as these are the optimum time for an enemy to attack[184]. This basic routine also provides the basis for the entire day and provides commanders at all levels with an

---

[183] It was actually Voltaire – who later modified it to god being on the side of big battalions that can shoot straight.

[184] The obvious option of attacking just before stand to or just after stand down is one beloved of cheeky cadets. The advantage of attacking at dawn is that one has the cover of night (such as it is) to get into position and all day to fight. The advantage of attacking at dusk is that you don't get lost on the approach in the day, and the enemy will have the challenge of organising counter-attacks in the dark. Attacking at noon is either the best of all worlds or the worst of all worlds. Attacking in the middle of the night is similarly effective, provided that you are proficient at night fighting.

opportunity to speak to their men and check that they are fit, well and alert. Without it, days merge into a constant blend of time on stag, performing fatigues and sleeping. Body clocks lose focus, fatigue increases and morale suffers.

The position is now complete. Men live in their trenches, with the minimum of movement and no light at night. Once the battlegroup stands down Tommy instructs one of his soldiers to "get a brew on" and two of them to clean their weapons. The same process is happening in every other trench. Platoon commanders and sergeants move from trench to trench to have a quick word – leadership involves legwork, and the Company Commander and CSM join the forward platoon commanders on their rounds. Tension is rising as the sounds of the battles to the north get louder. As he leaves the position the Company Commander tells the platoon commander that they expect probing attacks from about midday. He urges him to ensure that all his men get as much sleep as they possibly can[185]. Within an hour of standing down the position is still and quiet (apart from the odd snore).

Rupert's troop had a similar dawn. They are currently at 30 minutes' notice to move[186], which means that maintenance is continuing. As they are in a hide they do not run engines unless this is necessary to charge batteries, which they don't have to this morning. Most of the maintenance is complete, and as they received a full load of ammunition before they arrived there is no re-stowing to do. Weapon cleaning, food and sleep remain the priority. Movement is minimised, again with the exception of the

---

[185] Alexander the Great demonstrated the power of sleep at the battle of Gaugamela in 331BC. The Persians were defending a river line. When Alexander's army arrived close to dusk the Persians went onto full alert, fearing a night attack. Alexander declined to launch an attack that night, and had a good night's sleep. In the morning the attack was successful, not least because the Persians were exhausted from being up all night. A good soldier sleeps whenever and wherever possible.

[186] This means that if someone tells them to move, it will take 30 minutes to get packed up and moving. There are various notices to move, 30 typically the longest and immediate the shortest. Some staff officers forget that it actually takes 30minutes to get from 30 minutes' notice to immediate. Operating the notice system efficiently is a key skill for headquarters, and it comes only with practice.

squadron leader and SSM, who quietly move from troop to troop. Anxiety is rising, as they know that the rest of their Regiment is fighting to their north.

At 9am the B Company's CSM deploys forward to the dead ground behind Hill 202 in a vehicle. As the friendly forces to the north start to withdraw down the road they send liaison officers back. They meet the CSM, count their vehicles through and then depart. The CSM uses a landline connection to warn B Company that friendly forces are coming through their position. This prevents panic and "friendly fire[187]" incidents, also known as "blue on blue." There are over 500 friendly vehicles to the north, or at least there were when the war started, so the CSM is going to be busy. At the rear of the battlegroup area another Liaison Officer[188] checks them out. The last thing anyone wants is for friendly vehicles to be blundering about the place.

It is not only military vehicles on the road. There are refugees, both on foot and in cars, who have fled rather than be in the middle of a battle. The CSM, who in spite of his bark and bite, is a compassionate man, tries to organise them into some form of order and to escort them through the area with a couple of Warriors. The terrible fact is that the refugees are in the way and in mortal peril. And of course the CSM has no way of knowing whether they include saboteurs or enemy special forces. C Company, which has been converting the village into a death trap for the enemy, has found the civilians most wearing and has encouraged the inhabitants to either leave or get into a cellar. At this juncture in the battle the soldiers just wish the refugees would get out of the way.

The vehicle noise adds to the tension in Tommy's trench, although two of his soldiers manage to doze through it. The sight of the refugees does little to boost morale. Cigarette consumption increases and yet another brew is made.

---

[187] Another of Murphy's Laws of Combat states that no incoming fire is "friendly"

[188] A liaison officer is usually a Sergeant, Warrant Officer or Captain with a vehicle and a radio who knows what is going on. "Hello LO" is not one of the best military puns (although at least it's printable!)

By 10am it is clear that the battle is coming closer, probably only 5km to the north. Rupert's squadron's notice to move is reduced to 10 minutes. The thermal camouflage and any tents are packed away, although the visual camouflage remains as they are suspended from the trees, making a garage like structure whence the tank can drive out. The crews climb into their tanks, and busy themselves with minor tasks like checking storage bins are all shut, ensuring that the camouflage nets will not snag on antennae etc. Radios are turned on and commanders listen to the radio nets, which are still silent. As they have not yet started their engines the BVs aren't working; the better radio operators make tea from hot water stored in thermos flasks filled the night before when the engine was running. Books, cards and cigarettes help to while away the time for those who can't doze.

To the north the battlegroup's reconnaissance platoon sees the tanks of the forward battlegroup withdrawing in contact. They scan the horizon closely, looking for first sight of the enemy. The platoon commander is listening to that battlegroup's radio, and works out what is going on. In the battlegroup headquarters the Commanding Officer is also listening to that net when he is called to the brigade command radio net. The time has come for the northern battlegroup to break clean, which means that his battlegroup is next to fight. The brigadier sets the break clean time for 10.30 (it's now 10.10). The intelligence officer points out that with Rupert's squadron seven minutes motoring from the fire positions on Hill 202 and at 10 minutes' notice to move, they need to be brought to immediate notice. The message is passed by landline.

Back in his tank, the squadron leader hears the order at the same time as his other commanders because all the tanks are connected by landline. The 14 tanks start their engines, shut their drivers down and start warming up their thermal imagers and fire control computers. Actually only 13 start. The fourteenth, belonging to Rupert's sergeant, has a flat battery. Frantic activity enables them to jump start it in a couple of minutes. Commanders, who all know that the plan is for them to go to Hill 202, start revising the route and order over the intercom with their drivers. Loaders load fin and the co-axial chain gun and turn up the airflow on the ventilation pack. With a last look at the sky they shut their hatches. The commander keeps his open – he'll shut it once they're out of the woods. Rupert glances at his watch 10:15. Years of training have paid off and they're five minutes ahead of the game; time for a quick cigarette.

Day 3, 10:15

Back in the battlegroup headquarters the battery commander has an unmanned aerial vehicle (UAV) up, which is observing the battle, now under 5km away. The recce platoon has moved two of its four sections[189] back, one to a new OP on Hill 202, the other passes B Company CSM and heads for the woods on the north end of Hill 234. The recce platoon commander gives a situation report, known as a "SitRep". His section on Hill 202 confirms that it is in position and the rest of the recce platoon withdraws.

The northern battlegroup is now all past B company CSM, apart from two tank squadrons which are about to break clean from the enemy on the bound north of Hill 202. To help them, the brigade has sent Katie with four Apache attack helicopters that are now coming into fire positions hovering behind Hill 213 and Hill 192. The noise and downdraught don't add to Tommy's quality of life. His soldiers pack away unnecessary kit and, at Tommy's insistence, stay in the bottom of their trench and the shelter bays. Their weapons are loaded and cocked. Tommy wonders whether to order bayonets fixed...

Day 3, 10:20

The recce platoon races south, past the B Company CSM, who logs its passing. The battlegroup commander speaks on the command net;

"*T10 this is OA, Move now! Over.*"

Rupert's squadron leader replies "*T10A, moving now, out.*"

The squadron begins the tricky task of extricating itself in order from the woods. Again, training pays off and by 10:22 they are thundering towards the village occupied by C Company. Having shut his hatch, Rupert is peering through his episcopes; 100 metres

---

[189] A section of a recce platoon comprises two recce vehicles, usually one commanded by a sergeant (or higher) and the other by a corporal.

ahead on the road he can see his corporal's tank, his sergeant is 100 metres behind him. As they come out of the village they move off the road and head for the low ground between Hills 192 and 213. Gunners start scanning the ground, slowly traversing their turrets left and right. Rupert's troop is on the right, and as they shake out into line he desperately looks for the B Company minefield. It's 10:24 and his Challenger is now at near full speed as he swings right and then left, moving parallel to the road.

"What's that?" his gunner asks over the intercom. He has seen B Company's CSM and has laid the MBS mark on it.

"Looks like a couple of Land Rovers?" says Rupert. *"Must be a liaison bloke"* Rupert uses his gun controls to point the turret to the north. *"Well spotted, but that's where the enemy should be. Ease up a bit Jonah, and just crawl up the ridge to your front – that's our fire position"*

"OK Boss" replies his driver and the tank slows. It's 10:25 and Rupert's squadron is now turret down behind Hill 202. Rupert glances though his episcopes. His Corporal's Challenger 2 is 200 metres to his right, his Sergeant's 300 metres to his left. The leviathans are now crawling up the slope at walking pace and Rupert concentrates on his sight, waiting until he can just see over the ridge.

"Halt. OK, I can see over. Jonah, when I say advance crawl forward about another 20 metres."

"OK Boss"

"Smitty," (to his gunner), *"Check MRS[190]"*

"All good boss"

Day 3, 10:25

Tommy takes a call from the landline. It's his platoon commander, desperately trying to sound laconic. *"OK chaps, the donkey-wallopers[191] are about to earn their pay. Radios on, one man per trench up. Remember, cover your arcs. We still have friendly*

---

[190] The MRS is the Muzzle Reference System – it checks that the tank's gun is pointing the same way as the gun sight.

[191] An infantry term of respect and affection for cavalry soldiers.

armour in front of us." Tommy tells one of his men to prepare the MBT-LAW[192] for firing, and lay them on the trench floor, which is getting a bit cluttered. He has to shout, as the Apaches are still hovering overhead. He stands and peers over the parapet. *"I can see f--- all"* he announces, as the dust whipped up from the Apache's rotors swirls round the trench.

Day 3, 10:26

"BLOODY HELL!"

Katie launched a Hellfire missile while still hovering over Tommy. The flame and noise are impressive. The missile streaks over Tommy's trench, past Rupert's tank and on to the next ridge where it destroys a T-72, just out of sight to Tommy.

"I can see some Challengers withdrawing, and the Apaches are engaging. Can't see any targets yet." Rupert tells his crew.

"All stations, this is 0A, friendlies withdrawing past us in next couple of minutes, then we're on. Stay periscope up until my order. Out." Rupert's squadron leader orders.

Rupert glances through his right episcopes and sees three Challengers hurtling down the road, their turrets pointing north.

"Smitty, keep the turret facing North until I tell you otherwise. Otherwise the crunchies[193] will treat us as enemy"

"OK Boss."

Day 3, 10:30

"Jesus Wept!" Rupert mutters as he looks through his periscope.

"What, boss?" Jonah asks.

"Someone has just stonked that ridge with artillery."

Rupert is correct; as the final part of the break clean half[194] of the all the artillery pieces in range has just fired 3 rounds along the ridge.

---

[192] A one man operated light anti-tank weapon.

[193] A term of affection and respect used by armoured soldiers to describe infantrymen. It derives from the noise an infantryman makes when a tank runs him over.

In just 15 seconds over three tons of explosive has just detonated on the ridge. Tommy, still in the downdraft of the Apache, barely heard it, although he felt the ground shake.

"OA this is U22A; all my tanks are now to your rear"

"Roger, out.[195]" The second in command of the withdrawing squadron has just passed Rupert, and came onto Rupert's net to let him know. Rupert glances right, and sees U22A pass in his tank. He recognises the voice as one of his contemporaries, who has obviously been promoted. Before he can dwell on the implications of rapid battlefield promotion his squadron leader is on the air again

"All stations this is OA. Anything to our front is enemy. Remember to take command vehicles first. We'll fire one salvo together and then fire at will. Prepare to advance to hull down. Out."

"Jonah, prepare to advance 20 metres gently. Smitty, tell me when you can see over the crest"

"Right boss, I'll level the gun"

Day 3, 10:35

Rupert scans with his panoramic sight, relating the ground to his map. He sees three shapes familiar from training manuals emerging from the smoke and dust from the artillery barrage.

"OA this is T30. Sighting, 10:35 Grid 355 780. Three T72s moving south. Am observing, over." Rupert takes smug pride in producing a radio message straight from the textbooks. His crew and troop smile – maybe the boss knows his stuff after all.

"OA, roger. All stations prepare to engage on my order."

"Jonah advance now. Smitty, there's at least five of them. "

"Crest clear, Boss." Smitty the gunner confirms.

"Jonah, halt. Fin tank on!"

"On!" Smitty confirms he has identified the target and is laying the gun onto it.

---

[194] Only half, because of course they're then going to have to move to avoid counter battery fire. Rupert and Tommy will need the other half.

[195] "Roger" is military shorthand for "I understand and will act as required".

"Loaded!"

"Lasing!"

"Wait for the squadron leader." Rupert cautions, trying to reduce the tension.

Over the radio the squadron leader counts down: *"All stations this is 0A, three, two, one, Fire! Out"*

"Firing now" Smitty was listening – as was everyone else. The 14 Challengers fire together. One second later and one mile north eight T72s are hit, two exploding. Rupert's crew get busy shooting at the surviving tanks – Rupert lays the gun onto another one.

"Target – fin tank on"

"On"

"Loaded!"

"Fire!"

The rhythms of countless sessions in the gunnery simulators kick in as they hunt for targets and destroy them. It has not been entirely one way traffic – the surviving T72s are shooting back, although Rupert can't see who they have hit. At the target end, over 20 armoured vehicles have been destroyed. On the battlegroup net Katie states that she and her Apaches are leaving as planned. In Tommy's trench the noise diminishes as the rotor downwash abates. *"Peace at last"* mutters Private Evans, as he moves the LAW in a vain search for comfort in the bottom of Tommy's trench.

Day 3, 10:38

The enemy brigade commander is actually quite pleased. His job was to advance to find the defensive position. After a tiresome 24 hours of advancing in contact, which cost him 40 of his 95 tanks and took twice as long as planned, his lead battalion reports a stiffening of resistance, coming under fire from missiles and seeing trenches. He has at last found the enemy. His job now is to fix Tommy and Rupert while trying to work to the flanks. Another brigade comprising three infantry battalions is following him, and will be able to deliver an attack in about 30 minutes time. In the meantime he needs to get more fire to bear, and that means artillery. Ten kilometres to his rear a rocket launcher battalion swings into action. Meanwhile he urges his remaining tanks forward.

Day 3, 10:41

Rupert is starting to worry. The squadron has now been fighting off this ridge for five minutes. Two Challengers have been hit and another 15 T72s have just appeared. It will soon be time to move, but they have to stay as long as possible to give the impression of the false front. To his right he sees a pair of enemy recce vehicles at some 3,000 metres range. He slews the turret round – it's a long shot but Smitty is having a good day so far. As he is about to give the fire order the whole ridge erupts in a maelstrom of explosions. The enemy rockets have arrived.

"Reverse!"

Jonah needs no urging and the tank accelerates backwards, explosions continue all round it, and the crew can hear shell fragments bouncing off the turret. They can see nothing but smoke and debris as Jonah accelerates and the tank continues backwards down the slope. The top of Hill 202, an area 1,000 metres by 200 metres has just been hit by 720 122mm rockets. If they fell in a uniform pattern, that would be only 10 metres between rockets, or one rocket per 300 square metres. The Challenger is eight metres long and four wide, giving an area of 32 square metres, and therefore a one in ten chance of receiving a direct hit. Of course, near misses do damage too, and as Rupert looks out his episcopes to see where the rest of the squadron is he notices that some of them are broken and his radio antennae are missing.

"Smitty, how are your sights? Jonah, left stick...on." The driver has no rear vision, so Rupert has to direct him. *"Ease up a bit – I can't see that well."*

"Boss, we've lost the thermal sight, the day sight is OK – can't tell about MRS yet. Gun kit seems to be fine." Smitty reports.

Rupert is struggling to hear anything on the radio. His sergeant's and corporal's tanks are with him. His next position is behind Hill 192, so he continues to reverse, again cursing the B Company minefield, which he passes too close for comfort.

"OK Jonah, halt. Forward hard right, up the valley and then left at the end – it's the second bound. Stay low, take it steady and look out for the trenches. Banger, dig out the spare antenna."

"Boss, I can't see anything – looks like a clod of earth has landed on my sight," Jonah complains.

"OK, I'll talk you on. Forward, right stick, steady... that'll do. Smitty, keep the bloody gun pointing north!"

Behind him the other two tanks of his troop follow and behind them another two, which should include the Squadron 2IC.

Tommy looks left as he hears the tracks and engines. He recognises the Challengers and tells his team that the cavalry is coming. He keeps watching the tanks; the last thing he wants is to be in the trench with a tank driving over it. He notices the damage to the vehicles; bins have been torn off, episcopes shattered, paint chipped and scarred.

"Sooner you than me, stuck in that metal coffin," he mutters.

As he watches, the commander's hatch on the nearest tank opens. Rupert sticks in new antennae and then scrambles down the sloping armour at the front of his turret to clear the driver's sight and have a look at the thermal sight, the lens of which has been shattered. As he scampers back to his hatch he looks down and sees Tommy. He waves and, remembering the artillery that he has just escaped from, thinks

"Sooner you than me, standing in your pre-dug grave."

To the north, the top of Hill 202 reverberates as more and more artillery lands on it. Rupert drops into his seat, shuts his hatch and accepts a cup of coffee from his loader, who has been busy with the BV[196].

---

[196] The boiling vessel, which is an electric cooker operated by the loader. If the engine is running the crew should have near constant access to hot water.

"Right, check MRS and then let's re-stow ammunition[197]." He now has radio again, and he listens for more orders.

Day 3, 10:55

Back on Hill 202, deep in a trench, the recce section is watching as the enemy prepares to assault the hill. It seems that they have fallen for the false front, and are now enthusiastically pounding the hill with preparatory artillery. The dust and debris make it hard for the enemy to notice his error. The Recce Platoon OP on Hill 202 is about to have a ringside seat at an enemy brigade attack.

The enemy artillery shells are being tracked by gun-locating radar and a UAV has seen the smoke generated by the enemy rocket launcher battalion when it fired. In the Fire Direction Centre the target details are passed to an MLRS battery on the move as a high priority target. The six launchers of the MLRS battery halt and fire. Rupert and Tommy see the trails of the 72 missiles as they pass overhead, brilliant white against the sky.

"Someone is going to get a kicking!" says Rupert as he describes it to his crew. Sure enough, a minute later, out of sight to Tommy and Rupert, the enemy rocket launcher battalion ceases to exist in a maelstrom of high explosive. Meanwhile the enemy infantry brigade is making good progress, and its 130 or so IFVs are now 3,000 metres from Hill 202 and shaking out into assault formation.

One bound back, the nine functioning tanks of Rupert's squadron are again periscope up on Hills 213 and 192. Further back, on Hills 234 and 222, FOOs are watching hill 202 while the recce section provides a running commentary on events. The map below shows what is going on:

---

[197] Tank ammunition is stored all over the inside of the vehicle. Only some of it is immediately available to the loader (in the ready racks). It is therefore necessary to take advantages of pauses in battle to move ammunition from the more remote storage locations to the ready racks. This has to be accomplished without opening the hatches and can at times require black belt yoga skills.

Figure 11.6 – Situation Day 3, 11:00 hours

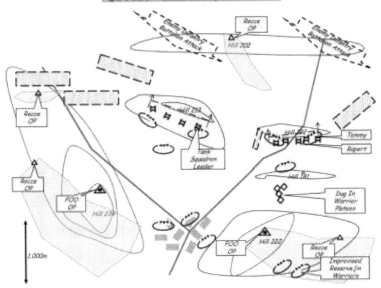

The enemy's plan is simple; attack and capture Hill 202 with two battalions, each of 45 IFVs and 12 tanks. Then the third battalion, plus whatever is left of the tank brigade mauled by Rupert and Katie, is to pass through to capture Hills 192 and 231. The battlegroup plan is simple too; let the enemy attack Hill 202 and hit him hard with artillery and tank gun fire. Then deal with the survivors as they attack Hills 192 and 213.

Let's just consider the defence of Hill 192, where Tommy and Rupert are, in more detail. The enemy is going to attack with some 60 vehicles, which have to drive for 1,000 metres, taking about two minutes. For the first minute they will be visible to the 5 tanks with Rupert, which gives 20 potential shots, say 15 kills if Smitty and the other gunners keep cool. Then Rupert is going to have to withdraw to Hill 181, which will take a further two to three minutes. As he withdraws the north side of the hill will be hit hard by artillery, but in the third minute the surviving 45 enemy vehicles will come over the crest, 200 metres north of Tommy.

They will then be engaged by ATGW from the depth platoons and maybe C Company as well - say 10 ATGW shots, of which 7 might kill. The forward trenches all have 2 LAW, 32 in the forward platoons. If 50% kill we're doing well, so that is another 16 kills.

This still leaves the enemy with 22 vehicles, each of which will be disgorging six infantrymen onto the front trenches, making a total of 132 against the 32 men in the front trenches. Clearly Tommy is in for a tough time. His survival will depend entirely upon the mutual support from the depth section and platoon, and of course, Rupert's tanks shooting straight.

Day 3, 11:00

It starts badly. As the enemy gets to within 700 metres of Hill 202 his artillery cover it in smoke. Rupert's tanks move to hull down and search for targets. His sergeant, whose thermal sights are working, fires at leading BMPs.[198] In total four are hit, all exploding as their light armour is completely inadequate to stop the fin rounds.

In their trench, Tommy's fire team are astounded at how loud a Challenger main gun is. Two trenches to the left and closer to Rupert's sergeant, the section commander's ear drum is burst.

On Hill 202 the right hand BMP company commander, who lost three of the four vehicles, assumes that he is in amongst the enemy and orders his infantry to dismount, which they do. As the smoke clears it becomes apparent that the trenches are empty or dummies. By 11:05 the Company Commander has told his battalion commander of the deception and ordered his men to remount their BMPs. Unfortunately for them, this is when Gary lands a regimental fire mission on them. Two tons of explosive, a mixture of air and ground burst, causes carnage. The remaining two companies accelerate over the crest of hill 202, accompanied by their ten remaining tanks.

Rupert tries to ignore the tanks, as he directs Smitty to engage the BMPs – which are the real threat to the battlegroup position. They get off three shots, with three hits and then the whole vehicle rocks. They must have been hit on the turret, but the Chobham armour saves them.

"*Reverse!*" Rupert shouts. Smitty fires once more, as Rupert tries to navigate through the trenches. As they leave the ground shudders and the sky turns black. An artillery barrage is landing on Hill 192.

---

[198] BMP-1 is a Russian designed infantry fighting vehicle. It has its faults, but there are lots of them.

Rupert can't see, so he tells Jonah to just go straight and not pull any sticks, as turning tracked vehicles fill trenches in. The occupants of the right hand trench of 6 Platoon owe their lives to this order, but they don't see it that way as Rupert's tank passes over their shelter bay. As they're caught up in the artillery barrage it's just one more bad thing in a day that is deteriorating fast.

As he emerges from the barrage, Rupert sees that he is on the forward slope of Hill 181 – not the best use of ground. In desperation he fires his smoke grenade dischargers, hoping that Tommy is not too close to the white phosphorous as it ignites.

"Speed up and make smoke. Once you're over the crest get into the low ground and come back up to the right of where we crossed. We'll go straight to hull down."

This time the artillery has not hurt his radios, and Rupert can still hear what is going on. He is about three minutes ahead of the rest of his squadron, who are only now emerging from the barrage. Once again, the barrage turns to smoke.

Day 3, 11:20

Tommy is getting his first taste of being hit by artillery, and is not enjoying the experience. Altogether 36 guns are firing on Hill 192 pouring around 200 rounds a minute into the 500 metres by 500 metres area occupied by B Company. The good news is that they are only 122mm calibre, but even so that is about a ton of HE arriving every minute. The bad news is that it is ground bursting - in his trench Tommy is pretty much immune to airburst fragmentation. If a ground bursting round lands in or close to his trench, Tommy will die. After three minutes the HE is replaced with white phosphorous smoke. The overhead cover saves Tommy's team from being burnt, although the grass round their trench catches fire. Although his ears are ringing, Tommy hears tracks and engine noises, and risks a look. Coming down the hill towards his platoon are over 25 BMPs, the lead ones about 200 metres away, and closing the distance fast. Tommy shouts *"Stand to!"* to his fire team and reaches for a LAW. In the 10 seconds it takes to aim the lead BMP is now only 100 metres away. Tommy fires, there is a deafening roar and when he looks he sees that he has hit the target. A few other trenches have fired and hit, but there are now 20 BMPs

50 metres away. One of his privates has fired the other LAW, but it's time to get ready for infantry.

Day 3, 11:25

500 metres behind Tommy, Rupert can see the problem. Of the 10 trenches that comprised 5 Platoon's position, only six remain. Thankfully these include the antitank platoon missile launchers, who are engaging the battalion assaulting A Company on Hill 218, and the SF Trench. The platoon headquarters no longer exists, and the other two sections are down to one trench each. His troop starts to engage BMPs again, with lethal effect. Then the anti-tank missiles from 4 and 6 Platoon start to arrive, and Rupert instructs his troop to engage tanks again. His loader has put his other radio onto the B Company net, and Rupert realises that B Company commander may not know what has happened. He tells Smitty to get on with it and speaks to B Company Commander.

"Hello 0A this is T30, to your right and rear. Your front right platoon has lost is commander, is at half strength and being assaulted by at least one company. Enemy are dismounting now, am engaging"

Rupert is not the only person to have seen the enemy getting out of their vehicles. The 6 Platoon MFC is calling mortar fire down on it, which starts to arrive. The defenders have a huge advantage with their indirect fire, which is that they have all their targets registered and are therefore accurate first time. The mortar platoon is excellent, and each tube is firing at over ten rounds per minute; a wall of 81mm mortar bombs lands 75 m north of Tommy's trench.

Tommy doesn't notice that, as he and his fire team are now in a fire-fight with a platoon that dismounted from four BMPs about 15m to his front. The BMPs are now struggling to fire onto his trench as they're a bit close and Tommy's trench is inside the limit of their gun depression, but it's only a matter of time. The 24 infantrymen who got out are having no such problems, and are winning the fire-fight. To his right, one man is hit and falls to the bottom of the trench.

Rupert sees the problem and orders Smitty to switch to the chain gun and engage the infantry. Smitty, never one to be troubled by restraint, pours burst after burst into them, each burst of 20 rounds or more. Although his is not well sited to use the beaten zone, every little bit helps. Rupert glances left, and sees that 4 Platoon is in a similarly desperate state. Further west, A Company are faring better, as the firepower of the four Warriors behind Rupert take their toll, and C Company seem to be providing better support. The FOOs and MFCs are working well, and indirect fire is landing all over the dismount area.

The situation is summarised below:

Figure 11.7– Situation Day 3, 11:30 hours

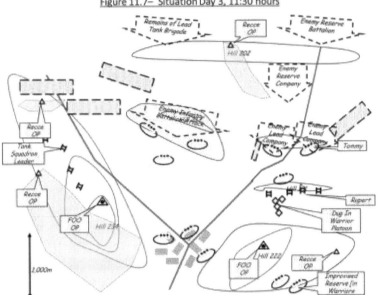

On Hill 192 Tommy and about a third of his platoon are in close combat with the remains of the lead company. To his west, 4 Platoon is in a worse state, with the enemy company almost through their position. Looking towards Hill 202, Rupert can see what must be the reserve company of the enemy battalion starting to move. If that can overwhelm 4 Platoon and hit 6 Platoon then the way is open for the next battalion to assault the village, and the battlegroup's position will have been destroyed.

"Hey boss" pipes up Jonah, *"Isn't about time for us to move, or do you like getting hit by artillery?"*

Rupert takes one more look at Hill 192. There seem to be about 7 BMPs not on fire, and 3 T72s. Time to earn his pay;

"*Good point Jonah, prepare to advance. Load Fin!*" Onto the squadron net "*T31, T32, this is T30, prepare to advance.*"

A stunned silence.

"*T30 this is 0A*" The squadron leader is still alive then; "*Go for it! Move now! Out.*" He's seen the risk.

As the tanks reverse back from the ridge Rupert briefs the crew. "*Right, there are four T72s on that position, and about eight BMPs. There is another company coming to attack and we have to get up there to stop it. Smitty, we'll be firing on the move, short range so just aim on. Jonah, don't hang about but keep it as smooth as you can.*" He looks left and right through his episcopes, "*Let's go!*"

Jonah floors the throttle, black smoke belches from the exhaust as 1,200 horsepower kick in and T30 starts accelerating to the ridge. He sees the first T72 "*Fin tank on*"

"*Can't see it Boss, still too low.*" Fortunately Rupert has gunnery controls too. "*I'll do it myself*"

"*Loaded!*"

"*Lasing...Firing now... Target!*" Fortune favours the brave and the sabot round obviously cleared the ridge.

"*You Jammy sod, Boss.*" Banger the loader is struggling to load the gun and keep his feet as the tank lurches about as it accelerates down the hill.

"*No sticks!*" shouts Rupert – as he makes another friend in 6 Platoon. "*OK come right and we'll go 30 metres right of where we were before*"

"*Got it Boss*"

"*Loaded!*"

"*Fin, tank on! Aim on.*"

Day 3, 11:35

Things are getting desperate for Tommy. Although the BMPs and tanks that were worrying him seem to have been destroyed, his trench is the only one at the front of the position still fighting, and it's become a bullet magnet. Every surviving enemy soldier of the company that assaulted seems to be shooting at him. He is also under enemy mortar fire, which is now falling alarmingly close. As far as he can make out, the only thing keeping the enemy from grenade range are the SF machineguns from 6 Platoon, who are firing about 10 metres in front of and behind his trench.

Tommy himself is firing to his front and, increasingly, to his rear as the surviving 3 Section trench has similar problems to his own. The wounded man in the bottom of the trench is reloading magazines from bandoliers, groaning every time he is trodden on. Although the enemy isn't in hand grenade range, he has taken to firing RPGs at the overhead cover. This is not doing much for Tommy's quality of life, but little of the blast gets into the trench – and it has sorted out his target priorities.

B Company commander has seen over half his company destroyed in just 10 minutes. He knows that one of the rules of attack is to reinforce success, and a glance over at A Company tells him that it is B Company that will be hit again, even if it survives the arrival of the reserve company. His FOO and surviving MFCs are working well, but he needs men on the ground. Even as he thinks this artillery starts to fall again, this time on 6 Platoon and Hill 181. The enemy FOOs clearly know their job.

The Battlegroup commander also knows how desperate things are for B Company. If they are overrun, as it seems they must be, he is entirely reliant upon C Company being able to hold off the enemy reserve battalion, which his recce section on Hill 202 – amazingly, still alive – tells him is starting to move. He also knows that the battlegroup to his west is under similar pressure, and is starting to worry about a thrust from their area down the other road, through the minefields. While C Company might hold one battalion, it won't defeat two.

The key decision a commander makes in a battle is when and where to deploy his reserve. The options are either to counter-attack and reoccupy the B Company position, or to boost the defence of the minefields, from Hill 234. While he is pondering this choice he hears of Rupert's advance. Opportunity created, decision made. He orders his reserve to counter attack the enemy on B Company's position. The RSM asks for, and receives permission to join the attack, taking with him two more Warriors filled with ammunition resupply. The Colonel calls the Brigade commander to request some Apache support.

Day 3, 11:40

Tommy's fire team is now killing people at 10 metres range. Their overhead cover has partially collapsed and their immediate prospects are not great. The 3 Section trench seems to be in a similar state. The stark fact is that Tommy has no chance of escape and little of surrender. The choice was fight or not fight; he chose to fight.

Rupert's troop arrives. Having knocked out all the T72s they are now very, very worried about RPG men. They advance slowly, using their chain guns to obliterate anyone who looks like they might have an RPG. Of the ten RPG men who dismounted, nine are now dead and the tenth has thrown his away. Rupert and his troop advance again to the ridge. They can see nothing, which Rupert realises is because the enemy reserve company is already advancing – they crawl forward, keeping a wary eye on Hill 202. Suddenly, at 700 metres they see the four tanks and 12 BMPs of the reserve charging at them. Three shots, three hits, three kills. The troop starts to reverse, three more shots, one of which kills the enemy company commander. The range is down to 500 metres, but the Challengers front armour is immune to the BMP, which can't fire on the move. Three more shots, three more kills. Rupert's troop is now passing Tommy again, and is safe from Hill 202. Nine BMPs cross the ridge. Rupert's troop hit and kills another three, and the squadron leader's four tanks hit another two. The last four BMPs really have no options – surrender is nigh on impossible and stopping just makes them an easier target. The last four are dispatched at point bank range, just as the RSM and the reserve arrive. The enemy attack has been fought to a standstill.

Rupert and Tommy have been fighting for 70 minutes. In that time they, and their colleagues, have destroyed over 130 armoured vehicles, and killed or wounded over 700 men. They have lost four of their own tanks, plus 100 killed and wounded. The day is still young, the enemy hasn't given up and they're about to do it all over again.

Now you know why it is called high intensity warfare.

Chapter 12 Tommy Gets Fed; Logistics

As we saw in the last chapter, Tommy and his pals consume huge volumes (and weights) of materiel in the course of implementing their country's policies. It should be obvious that a rifle without ammunition, a radio without a charged battery and a tank without fuel are about as much use to Tommy (or the country) as a chocolate fire guard. In this chapter we'll look at how Tommy and his colleagues are supplied with what they need to perform their task. This is a skill known as logistics, and is fundamental to successful soldiering. Logistics occupies a substantial portion of the manpower of any armed force. Voltaire may be right about God being on the side of big battalions, but on the battlefield a battalion with no bullets is a mobile cemetery looking for a graveyard.

ECHELONS

There is a little bit more organisation that we need to cover. In Chapter 10 we looked at how the combat power is organised. Logistic support is similar, but different. In the logistic world the army is organised into three (sometimes four) echelons.

> Firstly the F echelon contains the fighting troops, plus all the spare combat supplies that they can carry on their person or in their vehicle.

> The A Echelon (which is sometimes split into A1 and A2) contains a resupply of compact supplies and spare parts for the F Echelon.

> The B Echelon deals with replacement soldiers and non-combat supplies, such as clothing.

So if Tommy needs more combat supplies it's an A echelon problem. Everything else is B echelon. Whatever the case, the onus is on the A and B Echelons to take the supplies to Tommy, who is busy enough in combat. As Tommy can't fight for long without logistic support all planning includes both the tactical (what Tommy will do) and the logistical (how he'll be sustained while doing it). There is an unfortunate tendency for the uninformed to consider firepower more important than logistics[199]. It is very much the reverse.

COMBAT SUPPLIES

These comprise the military equivalent of the fast-moving consumer goods – with the one bonus that they don't deteriorate like fresh food. The primary difference is that whereas a supermarket's customers drive to the supermarket, Tommy can't do that as he is busy manoeuvring to defeat the enemy – so the logisticians have to deliver to him wherever he is.

Tommy has to eat, and food is therefore a combat supply. There are various arrangements for this. Typically Tommy will receive one-man day ration packs. He may carry three or four day's food, although of course this puts up the weight on his back. He needs something like 4,500 calories per day (around twice the usual male intake) because of the arduous nature of his job and the length of his working day (24 hours). Tank crews are more likely to get crew rations, i.e. boxes to feed four men for 24 hours, rather than one-man packs. British Army rations are superb, and if Tommy is on operations with allies he'll find that they are a strong bartering currency, particularly with Americans.[200]

Tommy also has to drink, and Rupert's tanks need water when they overheat. Water is heavy, and Tommy needs lots of it to brew tea and avoid dehydration[201]. At most he'll carry one or two litres in a combination of camel packs[202] and water bottles, and he will always want to drink (but not carry) more. It is essential that the water is clean and pure. Although Tommy is issued with purification tablets, the consequences of bad water are so severe (in terms of military capability, odour, sanitation and hygiene), that they are only used in

---

[199] Politicians prefer photo shoots involving F echelon machinery to rows of (say) fuel bowsers.

[200] The American field ration is known as an MRE. Whether this stands for "Meal Ready to Eat" or "Meal Rejected by Ethiopians" is a matter of debate.

[201] In Iraq and Afghanistan the requirement was for 6 litres of water per man per day.

[202] A camel pack is a slim, soft container of water worn on the back, usually under clothing. It contains water and has a pipe to deliver it to Tommy.

extremis. Vehicles usually carry a 20 litre "jerry can" or two of water. Armoured fighting vehicles also have internally stored water to feed the BV. The challenges of providing clean water increase enormously in a war involving nuclear, chemical and biological weapons.

Ammunition is obviously a combat supply. Studies are regularly conducted on how much and what sort of ammunition will be consumed in various war scenarios. The requirement is, by definition, highest in high intensity wars. This ammunition is sent forward, automatically. Ammunition is heavy, as is its packaging. Moving ammunition, artillery ammunition in particular, consumes significant amounts of transport.

For a dismounted infantry unit Petrol, Oil and Lubricants (POL) are not a large burden. For a tank regiment, or armoured infantry regiment it is huge. Not only do tanks consume prodigious quantities of diesel, (which is the British Army standard fuel)[203], they also require a range of specialist oils and greases. It is not uncommon for a tank to require carry five to ten different lubricants, to grease everything from battery terminals, gun systems, engine and transmissions through to the commander's pistol.

The final combat supply is Nuclear Biological and Chemical (NBC) warfare stores. NBC war is covered in detail in Appendix Three. However NBC protection is largely based on filters, and these need replacing frequently and regularly.

We'll ignore the manufacture and storage of combat supplies, and assume that they have arrived in theatre, i.e. in the geographic area that Tommy is fighting in. But do note that ammunition may have been sitting in a bunker for a decade or more. Obviously the supplies need to move towards Tommy, and generally they do this on a truck along a road know as a Main Supply Route.

---

[203] The author recalls being the umpire of the first all diesel battlegroup during the latter days of The Cold War. Unfortunately my vehicle (a ferret scout car) was petrol fuelled. While the battlegroup were mortified that they could not look after their umpire, there was nothing they could do. I eventually filled up at my personal expense at a local petrol station. Claiming that expenditure back proved impossible.

Tommy is a fearsome warrior but he is impotent without combat supplies[204]. The enemy knows this too, and this makes supply dumps and the main supply routes (MSRs) targets for artillery, ambush and mines. All this means that delivering combat supplies is more complex and more dangerous than restocking a supermarket. The trucks may well have to go on unpaved roads. Multi-wheel drive and high ground clearances are at a premium, (even sappers can't mend roads instantly), but the supplies must get through.

Eventually the convoys will arrive in the Brigade Administration Area, or BAA, which is run by a staff officer of the brigade headquarters. This is a series of hides, full of loaded logistic vehicles, which holds one or two day's combat supplies for the brigade's battle groups. It also contains the logistic headquarters of the battle groups, and is therefore where the fighting units meet the logistic ones. In the British Army this is called the A2 Echelon, and is run by the Headquarters' Company Commander. While Tommy and Rupert are converting ammunition to empty cases and dead enemy, The A2 collects the battle group's next load of combat supplies from within the BAA, which may be up to 20Km from the battle, and brings it forward when required.

Tommy's company commander will include logistics in his planning. The CQMS[205] will then drive to the A2 echelon, collect the vehicles with drivers, and lead them to the company's replenishment location. When he arrives, each platoon sergeant will bring a working party to collect his platoon's allocation. This will then be carried to the platoon location, split between the sections and thence to the individual riflemen. The working party will then return empty containers to the CQMS, who will set off for A2 again. This is a bit of a palaver, and the company is vulnerable while it happens.

If the company is mechanised, or if it's an armoured squadron, the replenishment will be set up as a "rolling replen" if at all possible. The SQMS will find a suitable location, usually en route to the

---

[204] Arguably, with bromide additives to tea, he is impotent with them too – but in a different sense.

[205] CQMS=Company Quartermaster Sergeant, in case you had forgotten. In an armoured regiment he would be an SQMS (S for squadron).

squadron's next hide, and line up his trucks. The tanks pass down the line of trucks, pausing at each one to full up with diesel or take on ammunition. The diesel bowsers also carry some lubricants – if tanks need them they ask for them, sotto voce[206]. They'll also pick up rations, drinking water and mail. If the SQMS is any good he'll also have a vehicle dispensing[207] soft drinks, hot pies, chocolate bars and the like.

Bear in mind that rolling replens are usually performed in the dark, with no lights and no talking. It is an operation that requires practice, and the cardinal rule is that no one gets off a vehicle lest they get crunched. Even then things can go wrong; some of the truck drivers may not have worked with an armoured unit before. At the end of the replen the tanks will halt and stow their ammunition – which requires time and the turret to be traversed all over the place. For this reason rolling replens take a while, perhaps 30 minutes for a tank to pass through and complete re-stowing.

Rolling replens can be done at battlegroup and brigade level. However the latter is avoided as such a concentration of logistic and combat vehicles is too big a target. It can also get horribly complicated, as the variety of ammunition types generally causes confusion. Fuel only rolling replens are sometimes necessary for long road moves.

When everyone is replenished the fighting troops will be off to wherever the war takes them, and the SQMS will return to the A2 Echelon – which may well have moved while he was replenishing his squadron.

Now, tanks and artillery pieces can't always hold one day's ammunition inside them, and sometimes fuel consumption rises. The solution is to create an A1 echelon. This lives in the battlegroup area, rather than the BAA and is therefore closer to the fighting troops. As and when they need more combat supplies they can replenish from A1, usually by a rolling replen being established just

---

[206] The reader may not believe it, but a well conducted replen can be inaudible from as little as 500m away. While it is hard for a human ear to put an accurate direction on the direction of a tank engine at tick over, it is very good at getting a direction for a human voice.
[207] Selling on credit

behind the combat elements, with troops pulling back to replenish as the opportunity arises. This takes time, and places the logistic vehicles in danger. In the first Gulf War the British had to acquire armoured, tracked logistic vehicles to provide a "hard A1." Depending on what is going on, replenishing from the A1 will be coordinated by the SQMS or the SSM.

Although rolling replens are efficient, in as much as they get the combat supplies to the troops as quickly as possible, they are not always tactically appropriate. The alternative is a hide replenishment, where the SQMS will bring the logistic vehicles to the troops in their hide, and replenish them there. This inevitably takes longer, and creates noise in the hide.

In counter-insurgency operations squadrons and companies are likely to operate from fixed locations, as will the A echelon. The norm is for the logistic vehicles to come to the fixed locations. The challenge is that this inevitably produces a predictable series of road movements; they're predictable therefore vulnerable to ambush and IEDs. The only solution to this is to replenish by air, using cargo-lifting helicopters to deliver combat supplies. Of course, this is more expensive (helicopters cost more than trucks) and the helicopters themselves are vulnerable to anti-aircraft fire. However, moving by air increases the speed and number of routes possible. As we shall see in Chapter 13, clearing and securing a route for logistics convoys takes a significant effort and, as Afghanistan has shown, carries substantial risks.

SPARE PARTS

Soldiering involves complicated machinery – which can break. The more complicated the machine, the more things to break and the more different sorts of spare parts are required. While spares have been a problem for armoured troops since the tank was invented, the expansion of electronics is increasingly affecting even dismounted infantry.

A few spare parts are carried by the fighting troops. These are almost invariably vital, simple and easy to change. Obvious examples are return springs for machine guns or bits of track for tanks. However, the overwhelming majority of spare parts are simply too bulky, complicated, or rare to burden Tommy with.

Some will be carried by the company fitter section, but the vast bulk of them are held by the Quartermaster Technical, who lives in the A2 Echelon. He has trucks full of spares, and some clever chaps who know where to find them. For an armoured battlegroup he may well have a total of over 10,000 items on his trucks for maybe 4,000 different pieces of equipment. Everything from a tank road wheel (easy to find), to a tiny pea bulb to illuminate the aiming mark in a tank gun sight (not so easy to find).

For example if the return spring in Tommy's rifle breaks he requests another one from his platoon sergeant, who in turn contacts the company armourer (who is actually part of the Light Aid Detachment). The armourer issues it, and demands another to replace it from the QM Tech. The QM Tech issues the one he has, and demands another from further up the chain. There is a strict priority system, which ensures that scarce resources go to where they are needed most. It can be seen that this takes time and is bureaucratic. However, it is necessary as the only alternative would be to hold more stores forward, which in turn would mean yet more stores forward in the BAA and beyond. The system works, not least because it is exactly the same system as is used in peacetime.

There are some weaknesses. If Rupert's squadron is attached to an Infantry Battlegroup his spares will have to come from his own Tech, and his own A2. This in turn means that although his combat supplies will come via the (infantry) battlegroup A2, his SQMS will also have to visit his "parent" A2 for spares. This creates delay and increases SQMS fatigue.

The next weakness is financial. The entire system relies on holding adequate numbers of spares in the right place. This is expensive and the spares budget is often cut. Some items, like a thermal sight, have very long lead times and therefore building the spares back up to acceptable levels in the event of conflict may not be as fast as is required[208].

---

[208] Politicians adore having rapid reaction forces – and regularly announce them. They fail to realise that any idiot can get into a fight; the clever bit is to win the fight and that needs logistics. The French Army, encumbered with similarly delusional political leaders, has the same problem. Their FAR

The final one is structural, in as much as the system assumes that an entire brigade is deploying. If smaller forces are deployed it is all too easy to neglect to send all of the spares required and the organisation to deliver them. If they are sent, the proportion of fighting troops to support troops diminishes, and the cost for a small amount of deployed combat power rises inexorably.

CASUALTIES

As we have seen throughout this book, one of the certainties of going to war is that soldiers and civilians are going to be killed and wounded. Historically, the dead were buried where they fell and an emergency burial report filed. At the end of hostilities they were then exhumed and moved to war graves[209]. More recently the bodies are repatriated in much the same way as the wounded. What the practice would be if casualty rates increased is beyond the scope of this book. The point to note is that at some deep level, Tommy needs to know that, if at all possible, what's left of his corpse will end up in a marked grave. Huge efforts are made to collect bodies and body parts, generally successfully.

If Tommy needs to know that his grave will be marked, he also needs to know that the most strenuous efforts will be made to keep him from needing it if he has been wounded. As we saw in Chapter 4, at the moment Tommy is hit the best his mates can do for him is win the battle. The fundamental principle is that medics come forward to the casualty, and not the other way round. As operations in Afghanistan have shown, there is no limit to how far forward a medic will go. Modern medical technology means that it is possible to start treatment at the place where the casualty is (subject to his mates making it safe and secure for the medics to work).

The combat medic's job is simply to stabilise the casualty. This usually requires a combination of stopping bleeding, repairing sucking chest wounds, topping up vital fluids and dealing with pain. A well trained medic can achieve a huge amount with relatively little

---

("*Force Action Rapide*" i.e. rapid action force) is known as "*Faire Avec Rien*," do with nothing,
[209] This is what happened in the Falklands War of 1982.

equipment. Having stabilised the casualty, the next step is to get him into the medical evacuation chain.

In general war the chain starts with the combat medic in the company ambulance. He takes casualties to the battalion aid post. There they will be seen by a doctor, sorted in order of priority, treated if possible or necessary, and then collected by ambulances from the dressing station. Thereafter they are in the medical system; next stop, a field hospital and a surgeon.

In less intense wars the probability is that the casualty will be evacuated straight to a hospital. In Northern Ireland this was almost always performed by road[210]. If Afghanistan it's usually by helicopter, and indeed the helicopters are becoming increasingly a mobile trauma unit – once the casualty is on board he will be getting medical attention from a doctor within the "golden hour[211]". In this respect Tommy is probably better off than many of the British rural community for whom getting to A&E and in front of a doctor within 60 minutes of being injured is unlikely.[212]

Evacuation and treatment is on the basis of medical need, so wounded enemy and civilians will also enter the system on an equal basis. Triage is performed at the Battalion Aid Post.

In times of peace there is a tendency for military medical services to be run down and there is a general level of under provision. This is then boosted, belatedly, when the next war starts. Military medicine is not cheap – as the onward march of medical science and body armour has progressed, more horrendous wounds become survivable. This increases demand for well-equipped and trained combat medics and sufficient helicopters to evacuate the casualty to first rate medical facilities expeditiously. Military medical services

---

[210] It was not uncommon for non-combatant republican sympathisers to block roads with women and children to delay ambulances getting to and from the incident.

[211] Trauma surgeons agree that any casualty has a significantly greater chance of survival if he (or she) arrives at hospital within an hour of injury. Scandalously, in Afghanistan the British target is 2 hours.

[212] While this is not a book about the NHS, I think it is quite sobering that a first world country can't provide A&E infrastructure as good as the service it supplies for its troops in a third world country.

probably illustrate more starkly than any other part of soldiering how cuts to the defence budget are paid for in Tommy's blood.

BATTLEFIELD CASUALTY REPLACEMENTS (BCRs)

These are the soldiers required to replace Tommy's fallen or wounded casualties. They are not reinforcements, which are additional soldiers (almost always in formed units) to achieve an increase in tactical strength.

In general warfare reserves will be called up and some allocated as BCRs. They are assembled, equipped, retrained if necessary and sent forward. They are collected by the battle-groups in their B Echelon (which lives in the divisional administration area, some way behind the BAA), and then transported forward. Similarly, some units will have taken such heavy casualties that they can no longer function as a fighting unit. They are broken up, and their main go into the reserve pool. Again, they are collected by the B Echelon and sent forward.

In counter-insurgency operations it is generally assumed that casualty rates will not be as spectacularly high as in general war[213]. Replacements usually come from the natural flow of people into and out of units.

SUMMARY

While a bold tactical action can snatch victory from defeat, you can't argue with logistics. The system has to be robust and centred round military capability where the rubber hits the road with Tommy and capable of surviving reversals. When you hear politicians and pundits talk about "front-line capability" in a military context, remember that Tommy, in that front line, needs the support service to keep him supplied with bullets to fight the enemies of Her Majesty's government. If he gets his leg blown off, he also needs them to keep him alive. Most of an army's manpower does not

---

[213] There was national outcry when one of the British Brigade commanders in the First Gulf War revealed that he expected to take 30% casualties, which was the anticipated rate in The Cold War (assuming Western victory). As it transpired, Saddam's ability to conduct high Intensity warfare was inadequate, so the casualty level was a fraction of this.

work in what a politician would call the "front line", but that does not mean that they are not a vital part of "front line capability."

Logistic operations hinge on keeping supply routes open and secure. This is a particular problem in counter insurgency operations, where the supply routes become vulnerable along their entire length. The rise of the improvised explosive device with modern electronics, which provide a variety of means of detonation, makes ground travel dangerous and time consuming. We'll look at this in more detail in the next chapter.

Chapter 13 Tommy Plays Piggy In The Middle; Counter Insurgency Warfare

One of the unanticipated effects of the British withdrawal from empire after the Second World War was that its armed forces, primarily the Army, got plenty of experience of counter–insurgency warfare, all over the globe. In addition, the Northern Ireland "Troubles[214]" ensured that, if nothing else, politicians obtained substantial first-hand experience of dealing with armed insurrection.

We first need to appreciate the differences between general war, at whatever intensity, and counter-insurgency. This will require some fairly broad simplifications and glib statements, but they're necessary to understand the context of Tommy's role. The first simplification is to sort out the jargon: for this book counter-insurgency warfare, asymmetric warfare, counter-revolutionary warfare and counter-terrorism operations are all the same thing. It involves Tommy, in mortal peril and equipped to kill, operating in an area populated by civilians, in which his use of force is constrained and where the opposition is not a national army, in the sense of one operating under the control of an established government[215]. I shall use the word "insurgent" to represent Tommy's opposition.

Now, we know that warfare is all about ground, and we have seen that capturing it and exploiting it to destroy enemy forces is Tommy's basic trade. Counter-Insurgency, or "COIN", is about ground, but it is also about people. The indigenous population is key to both sides for winning a COIN war. In a COIN operation ground is rarely something to be captured by force of arms, but is always something to be dominated by armed presence.

---

[214] The "Troubles" could not have been a war otherwise the captured terrorists would have been Prisoners of War, rather than the dangerous criminals that they were.

[215] I make no apology to current and former members of the Irish National Liberation Army for not treating them as the army of a nation state. Any idiot can call themselves a national movement – very few can actually be one.

The next difference is that in general war the outcome will be decided by a clash of arms, which in turn will resolve who owns the disputed ground and whose armed force is dominant. This may or may not lead to a change of government of the ground, and that is not a military objective or factor. If Tommy and Rupert capture the enemy's ground or destroy the enemy forces, or both, then the war is won.

In COIN operations the insurgents wish to change the government within the same ground. The entire process is political and Tommy and Rupert must appreciate that. As any officer cadet knows, but few politicians and fewer editors seem to recognise, COIN wars do not have a purely military solution. They will continue until an accommodation or solution is found for whatever the underlying political or economic problem is. The von Clausewitz maxim that "war is the continuation of politics by other means" holds true, although it would perhaps be more accurate to state that insurgency is the replacement of politics with violence and intimidation.

We also need to ask why Tommy is there at all. Military aid to civil powers is constitutionally fraught in all democracies. Ignoring the legal complexities, which are huge, the reason for Tommy's deployment is usually that the police are about to collapse under insurgent pressure, or indeed have already. Anyway, most police are neither trained nor equipped for close combat. A collapsing police force implies that local government is dysfunctional and that the local population is therefore disconcerted, unsupported and frightened. There may well be more than one insurgent organisation, who may have diametrically opposed aspirations.[216]

So what does all this mean for Tommy? The familiar bit is that he can still get killed and wounded, so the requirement for his medical skills and body armour will be pretty much the same as in general war. As for the rest, although the ground per se is not at dispute, Tommy must dominate it. This will require intensive patrolling, which we'll come to. The overall military aim will be to return the responsibility for dealing with the insurgency to the local civil

---

[216] Through most of the Northern Ireland Troubles there were at least four terrorist groups including republicans and unionists

powers. However those civil powers will not be able to resume their work without local consent. This means that Tommy has to win the hearts and minds of the locals not just for himself, but for the local civil power that he is there to support. As winning hearts and minds is a high priority, Tommy is going to have to be very careful about using weaponry – collateral damage can set the hearts and minds campaign back years, or decades. This also means that the media are going to be important.

In terms of using his weapon, Tommy will learn that there is no easy way of identifying insurgents until they start shooting[217]. Intelligence and reconnaissance operations are likely to be common and key. When he does open fire, Tommy must shoot straight, and lawfully. The consequences of a lawfully fired bullet missing the lawful target, (an insurgent) and hitting a child are immediately strategic as the adverse publicity will have international repercussions rather than tactical. Tommy is aware of this, and the stress is significant as the decision to fire his weapon could result in criminal charges being brought against him personally – even if the decision was correct.

So, how does Tommy go about COIN warfare? One of the first things that must be established is a network of secure bases from which Tommy can operate. Usually these will be capable of accommodating at least a reinforced company. They will be close to a road and town, have (as a minimum) anti-visibility screens all round them and may be fortified. The base must not be overlooked (to prevent insurgent snipers making Tommy's life short and unbearable), and so is likely to be on a hill. There will be sentry posts, gates, and ideally a helipad within the perimeter. The patrol base will also need accommodation for the soldiers, plus kitchens, showers, power and a good radio connection. Buildings should be blast proof. Clearly the sappers are going to be busy. Expedience means that initial deployments will be into locations that are less than ideal, and that the sappers will be forever upgrading them. One final point is nomenclature; although this complex is effectively

---

[217] And not always then. In some countries, unfortunately including Iraq and Afghanistan, local celebration culture often involves firing weapons (which are widely owned and often AK-47s) into the air. The consequences can all too often be tragic.

a fort, it should not be called that as the aim is to integrate with the local population, not subjugate them. "Patrol Base" or "Camp" are better terms.[218]

So, let's imagine that Tommy and his company have occupied Patrol Base Baldrick,[219] which has been converted from part of an industrial estate on the edge of a town called Blackville with a population of 10,000 or so. The other two companies of the battlegroup are in similar bases, perhaps 10 to 20 Km distant. As well as the patrol base, the company has been allocated an area of around 10km by 10km to control and dominate.

Blackville has a police station, although the police are utterly demoralised through attacks on them and their families. Absenteeism is rife and their ability to prevent crime is minimal. Blackville is becoming increasingly lawless, with insurgents roaming the streets, collecting "taxes" through intimidation[220] and posing as an alternative government. The police have yet to arrest any insurgents. The whole town has been brought to a halt. Commerce is dying, and there are regular protests and demonstrations about a wide range of issues. Shootings, bombings and general thuggery, not all inspired by insurgents, are daily occurrences. Those residents who can are leaving the area, which creates an increasing number of derelict houses.

PB Baldrick itself is part way to being complete. It is not overlooked, has anti-vision fencing and its own generator. Troops' accommodation is in modified containers, sanitation is basic but the quality of life is better than that in the back of a Warrior or the bottom of a trench. The company is organised into its headquarters plus patrols platoon, base platoon and operations platoon, with the company's three platoons rotating between roles every four days.

---

[218] It is unfortunate that the US Army routinely refers to its peacetime locations in the United States as "Fort".

[219] Names from Blackadder seem to have become a part of British Military life.

[220] Insurgents need money to purchase weaponry, training and fund propaganda. Obvious sources are bank robberies, extortion and taking over the drug trade.

Base platoon provides sentries and gate guards. This requires four men in daylight and eight in the dark. The platoon also provides the fatigues men to do tasks like unloading logistics, providing runners and cleaning communal areas. The platoon sergeant has worked out a routine, which ensures that stags are 2 hours, with a fresh man coming on every hour in the night. It also ensures that everyone gets a decent amount of sleep. The platoon also provides one section as a quick reaction force, known as a QRF. This section has all its kit on and is usually close to the operations room, although as the size of PB Baldrick is about 50 metres by 50 metres, nowhere is that far from anywhere else. Being the base platoon is dull, but at least people get sleep.

Patrols platoon is the one tasked with dominating the local area, thereby providing local security, primarily to the patrol base but also to the town. A patrol programme is designed and adhered to; significant effort is expended in finding ways to avoid routines. Patrols platoon is busy, but Tommy enjoys it as it gets him out of PB Baldrick, which is already feeling claustrophobic.

Operations platoon carries out planned operations against insurgents. These range from supporting the police by patrolling with them, establishing Observation Posts (Ops) overlooking likely targets or known areas of insurgent activity, searches and ambushes. The company headquarters mans an operations room, which is in radio contact with any patrol in their area, as well as battalion headquarters. The company commander, second in command and CSM all join patrols as often as they can, with the proviso that only one is out of camp at any one time.

PATROLLING

The insurgency will not be defeated if Tommy and his colleagues merely sit inside their perimeter defending PB Baldrick. They have to get out and dominate the area. In this context, domination means going where they like, when they like in the hope of meeting insurgents and the local population. While the insurgents have been easily able to terrify a policeman's family, they are not keen to encounter Tommy, and so avoid areas in which Tommy is active.

Generally a patrol will consist of one or more multiples, a multiple being two or more fire teams, commanded by a corporal (if it's just two teams) or more normally the platoon sergeant or platoon commander. Teams will stay within line of sight of at least one other team, and will be 100 metres to 200 metres apart, so they are able to mutually support each other with accurate rifle fire. They will pick routes to confuse any insurgent, doubling back, making quick turns and switching formation. At times they will halt and observe. Sometimes they will run. Sometimes they will walk.

At all times all team members will be looking for anything suspicious, trying to recognise faces and trying to get a sense of the level of tension. If they see the number of people on the street thinning out they will suspect that they are about to be attacked, if they see children playing they will be more relaxed. The must also look confident, professional, tough and yet approachable. They must be seen to act impartiality and within the rule of law.

So what does Tommy do on patrol? Well, any number of tasks. Typical patrols might include route checks, making sure that the insurgents have not planted bombs in manholes or under culverts. As the patrol moves about it will perform vehicle and personal checks, setting up vehicle check points to stop cars and lorries, identifying the occupants and checking the load for weapons or bombs. The patrol might provide police support, providing close security to a police patrol investigating a crime. It could also include searching buildings, taking photographs of people and places and removing pro-insurgency posters and graffiti.

The list of possible tasks is endless, and a good, imaginative company commander will find plenty to do. The activity yields information, which can be developed into intelligence. More importantly, every time a multiple steps onto the street, the actions of any insurgent there are constrained. It is impossible to measure how many insurgent actions are interfered with, but the overall insurgent activity should start to fall. It is also good for Tommy's morale to be doing something specific, rather than just promenading about waiting to be shot at.

One of the key skills is being able to chat to people. In Northern Ireland the British Army was able to chat with the populace, which yielded much intelligence.[221]   In places where Tommy does not speak the language then the whole task becomes harder, and there is reliance upon interpreters.   Even then, Tommy will be encouraging his men to say hello in the local tongue. Part of the pre-deployment training package will include local phrases and customs – perhaps it is not seemly for young males to speak directly to women, for example. Tommy and his team have to get this right first time or risk alienating the local populace.

There are three ways to patrol. Tommy can go on foot, in a vehicle or in a helicopter. Patrolling on foot is cheap and easy to arrange and gets Tommy close to the people whom he is trying to reassure. He is also moving slowly, which means he sees more, and information is everything.   The disadvantages are that he is vulnerable, limited in what he can carry and slow to cover the ground. Remember, Tommy's company has an area of 100 square kilometres to dominate. Even if he can see and be seen for 1,000 metres in all directions, at 4 km/h his multiple is only covering 4% of the area an hour. If an insurgent sees Tommy's multiple heading for the market he knows that he can get up to mischief at the bus station, and he knows how long it will take Tommy to get there to prevent him.

Patrolling in vehicles increases the speed and coverage, and the range of equipment that Tommy can have to hand. Even a lightly armoured Land Rover, such as the now infamous "Snatch", offers better protection than being on foot. There are some downsides: vehicles are hard to hide and noisy, so Tommy is less likely to surprise anyone. They need a driver (using up at least one man per team), maintenance spares and fuel, all of which increases the logistic burden.   If we're in a scenario where using armoured vehicles is appropriate then we have the benefit of more sensors and much more firepower – if we dare deploy it. On the downside, heavy tracked vehicles make an awful noise, which will upset the population at night and they break roads, kerbstones and the like. They are also not very approachable, and the men in the back are doing nothing useful until they get out.

---

[221] Although it sometimes took a while to get used to the accents and idioms.

Riding in helicopters gives Tommy great mobility – should the insurgents start something he can be there in minutes. It is also relatively safe; unless the insurgents have shoulder launched anti-aircraft missiles. This makes it a perfect place to mount a quick reaction force, or QRF. One benefit of using an airborne QRF at least occasionally is that it means that insurgents will tend to view any helicopter as a potential QRF, whether it has Tommy in it or not. The downside is that it is expensive and noisy. The sound of a helicopter overhead is oppressive and the rotor wash of low flying does not win the hearts and minds.

The best solution is usually to combine foot and vehicle patrols, using the vehicle's speed to move the foot patrol quickly from one part of town to another. This puts quite a load on the multiple commander, but that is what he's trained for. More importantly, it means that the local population will see lots of the soldiers and the insurgents will find it harder to operate. Every time that Tommy appears in public he is undermining the insurgents' claims that they control or influence a neighbourhood. Provided he is polite and sensitive, he will also undermine the insurgent's portrayal of Tommy as the jackboot of authority. Eventually the insurgents will have to come out and take Tommy on, or risk their influence waning. Before that happens we had better consider Tommy's rules of engagement.

RULES OF ENGAGEMENT

Most of the local population are not active insurgents. Tommy needs to convince them to throw in their lot with him. They must be open to this persuasion; if they had wanted to throw in with the insurgents they would already have done so. However nothing loses support like killing the locals' children or blowing their homes up. Tommy has to be very careful if and when he fires. Rupert, Biggles, Gary and Katie must be even more punctilious, as their weapons are more powerful.

However Tommy is there to stop the insurgency, not to turn his other cheek. If people start shooting at him he must be allowed shoot back, immediately. At the basic level rules are generally straightforward, and will be something like "*You may engage anyone who has a clearly visible weapon and, is about to fire it or has fired it at you or anyone under your protection (i.e. everyone other than an insurgent) and there is no other way of stopping them."* Of course, this leads to the question of warnings. The rules of engagement might also say *"You must shout a warning before you fire, unless to do so would jeopardise your life or the lives of those whom you are protecting"*. More complicated and powerful weapons (particularly those using explosive such as M203 grenades, artillery and FGA) will have additional rules requiring positive confirmation of the target and the lack of civilians in the danger area.

Now, while this gives plenty of opportunity for budding lawyers to kick up a fuss, it also gives Tommy a clear mandate to be able to use his weapon. Assuming that he shoots straight, he is going to start killing and wounding insurgents. Generally it is better to capture insurgents alive, as they can be interrogated, so in principle Tommy is keener to capture than kill.

While we're on the subject, one particularly idiotic yet common and emotive phrase is "Shoot to kill." Hopefully you now understand that shooting to wound only is nigh on impossible. And Tommy is hardly likely to "Shoot to improve the target's health and happiness." If people are too squeamish to see insurgents killed then either don't send Tommy, or equip him with non-lethal weaponry. But don't expect him to use a less than lethal option if he's facing an insurgent with an AK-47 or similarly deadly weapons.

Each weapon needs its own, clear and unambiguous rules of engagement. When may Tommy throw a hand grenade, or a smoke grenade? Can that smoke grenade be white phosphorous? When can Rupert fire his main armament, or call in an airstrike. These questions cannot be ducked and should be worked out well in advance, because Tommy and Rupert need to know the rules when they are training before deployment, so that they can practise them. As the military and political become intertwined in COIN warfare, it is also important that politicians understand and accept the rules, and the reasoning behind them. It is important that the authority to use the weaponry is delegated to the men on the ground, and to as low a level as possible. There were occasions during United Nations operations in the former republic of Yugoslavia where a UN functionary had to be found in New York to give authorisation to drop a bomb. By the time he had been found, briefed and had made his decision the moment had passed.

Of course, as the weapons become more complex and destructive, the rules and their implementation become more complex. For an air-launched weapon both the pilot and the forward air controller have to be satisfied that the rules are being complied with. Inevitably, and rightly, this delays weapons release. Of course this in turn increases the chances of the insurgent escaping, possibly by mingling with a crowd, or firing his weapon. This translates as increased risk to Tommy and the population that he is trying to protect.

TERRAIN

One of the areas of debate amongst revolutionaries is whether it is best to start insurgency in urban areas, where the people and the wealth are, but so are the police, or in rural areas, where there is more space. Lenin subscribed to the former theory, Mao, Che Guevara and Fidel Castro to the latter. By the time Tommy and Rupert get involved this decision will have been made by the insurgents, but there are significant differences in how they conduct COIN operations. This should not be a surprise, as we're talking about differences in ground and we know that this is fundamental to soldiering.

Urban

Urban areas are densely populated. This makes it easier for the insurgent to hide, and indeed easier for him to find targets. It also limits the firepower that Tommy can use, as the potential for collateral damage is close to 100%. There are some advantages. Within the population there will be at least some who have information on insurgent identities and activities to pass to Tommy. Distances are short, so Tommy can see more people per hour on patrol, and can get to incidents quickly – increasing the probability of capturing an insurgent. There is also more potential for the use of surveillance cameras and other technical devices.

The urban environment also presents the insurgent with opportunities and challenges. The main opportunities arise from the high density of targets, government buildings, commerce and infrastructure, police forces, Tommy and of course the local population. The challenges to the insurgent include the likely presence of informers within the population, that Tommy passes him more frequently and that the insurgent has no open areas in which to train or test weapons. If movement control is well established the insurgent also has a logistic problem, in as much as getting explosives, weapons and personnel into the town requires him to run the gauntlet of check points and surveillance cameras. Storing them is also more complex and risky.

Rural

The low population density means that if Tommy can find an insurgent the potential for collateral damage is low so he can bring more firepower to bear. It also means that there is a far better opportunity to establish who lives where and therefore to identify strangers. The flip side is that whereas in town identifying an insurgent is like trying to find a needle in a haystack, in the countryside it's akin to finding the needle in the hay meadow. Distances are longer, so reaction times to incidents are slower and proportionately more movement will be by road. The population are more vulnerable to intimidation – Tommy can't be everywhere at once –so it is much harder for them to assist Tommy even if they want to.

For the insurgent, remote areas give him the opportunity to zero weapons and train new recruits. There are ample opportunities to cache arms, explosives and food. The long roads afford him plenty of opportunity to set up mines and bombs. The one thing he must do is avoid direct fire contact with Tommy, who is better armed and trained. Note that this does not preclude sniping, but the wise terrorist will adopt a shoot and scoot technique; if he stands and fights he will die or be captured.

If the insurgent is lucky, there will be an international border which he can slip across to completely evade Tommy. This will work well until the governments on either side of the border cooperate closely. If the insurgency is being opposed by a coalition of nations, rather than just one country the insurgent can reasonably assume that this will take some years for the coalition to operate seamlessly together. For example, even the closest of allies are reluctant to share details of intelligence gathering capabilities which in turn means that the intelligence itself is unlikely to be fully revealed.

It can be seen that if ground were the only consideration Tommy's best plan would be to contain the insurgency in the towns and fight it in the countryside. The insurgent is better of acting in the towns, and recovering and preparing in the country. Of course, the ground is not the only factor, but this simple truth explains in part why it is so very hard for Tommy to bring the insurgents into anything like a decisive battle.

COIN Operations

We have discussed patrolling, which is the bread and butter of COIN. There are some more active operations that can be mounted if time, resources, intelligence and rules of engagement permit. The first one that we'll look at is the ambush.

An ambush is a simple concept – find out where the insurgents are going to be preparing some attack, get there first and kill them when they turn up. By achieving surprise, which is paramount, and a violent use of firepower, an ambushing force can easily kill two or three times its own number in a few seconds. But like almost everything in Tommy's world, the fact that it is simple does not make it easy. The diagram below shows the basic layout for a linear ambush.

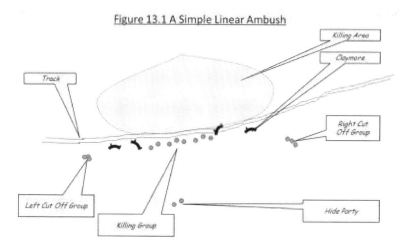

Figure 13.1 A Simple Linear Ambush

Tommy's forces are deployed into four main groups. The cut-offs have a dual role; to provide warning of the insurgent's approach and to prevent any of them escaping the ambush. In a linear ambush there are usually two cut-offs, one at each end. They will include an NCO if possible, and have communications to the commander. To keep noise to a minimum this will probably be a piece of cord. When they see the enemy coming they tug the cord – and various code systems exist to provide a more sophisticated system. They may well have radios too, but the noise of speaking may preclude their use.

The Killing Group's job is straightforward. On command they kill everyone in the killing area. Some of them will then go forward to search bodies for information.

The hide part is really for long-term ambushes, where it may be necessary to take extra men and rotate them through the other groups. It is the only place where it is possible to sleep, eat or talk. It also provides depth to the position, and a protection against being flanked by better trained insurgents.

Assuming that the target is insurgents on feet, Tommy is almost certain to use Claymore mines, rigged to detonate on command and therefore legal under the various conventions. A Claymore comprises about 1Kg of explosive and 700 or so ball bearings. It is directional[222], and when fired will produce an arc of destruction around 50 metres deep and 50 metres wide at the deepest point.

Everyone is in cover and well concealed, as an ambush relies upon complete surprise for its success. Ideally there is no easy access to cover from the killing area. Every individual in the killer group should be able to reach out and touch the man to the left and right, and should have a clear and unobstructed view into the killing area. Ranges are dictated by terrain, as ever. As a rule of thumb, closer than 20 metres increases the chance of being seen and reduces the field of fire. Over 50 metres increases the chances of some of the enemy being able to escape.

---

[222] Setting claymores up facing the wrong way is alarmingly easy to do – even though they helpfully have "This side to the enemy" embossed on the appropriate side.

The theory is simple. Tommy sneaks in and sets the ambush well before the enemy arrives. When the cut-off sees the insurgents he pulls the cord to alert the killer group, who in turn alert the other cut-off. The insurgents continue along the track until the ambush commander (at the centre of the killing group) decides that it is time to "spring" the ambush. He opens fire, as does the rest of the killer group. The claymores are detonated and all the insurgents killed – any who try to escape are killed by the cut-offs. Bodies are searched and possibly collected, and the ambush party heads for home. What could possibly go wrong?

The most common problem is that the insurgents don't show up at the anticipated time. Tommy can cope with them being late: ambushes are lying in wait, with the emphasis on wait. If necessary the ambush can stay there as long as it takes, provided that it has enough men and can be resupplied safely and securely. Of course this makes it a large undertaking as there will have to be a duplicate ambush party in the hide, but beyond that anything is possible. The British Army has had successful ambushes that have spent over 100 days in position. However if Tommy didn't come equipped for a protracted stay, he'll just disarm the claymores, lift them and extract himself from the position.

The most dangerous problem is that the insurgents either see or are informed of the ambush, and attack it from another direction. Planning, security and excellent field craft and camouflage are the only solutions. However it the insurgents are well trained and diligent, they may well have flanking patrols out to either side of the track and these may see the cut-offs or the hide party. If this happens the first Tommy will know about it is that he is in a fire fight. The commander should have a plan for this, but don't forget that they could well be outnumbered and, as Burns said, "the best laid schemes o' mice an' men gang aft agley[223]".

Misidentification is always a problem. If light is poor and people are unlucky, a group of civilians may be mistaken for a group of insurgents. The unfortunate consequences are unlikely to make helpful headlines. A worse problem (for Tommy) is if the

---

[223] It is another of Murphy's Laws of Combat that "No plan survives contact with the enemy". Less poetic than Burns but more succinct.

intelligence is wrong, and where they expected say ten insurgents, there turned out to be fifty or more. While killing everyone in the killing area is simple, getting the rest is not and they outnumber Tommy.

The last problem occurs if the initial burst of fire is not well executed and the insurgents are well trained and motivated. The standard anti-ambush drill is to turn towards the fire and charge. If the insurgents get to the killer group it's in big trouble.

Two final points on ambushes; firstly ambushes take place in day or night. Instant illumination is needed at the moment of opening fire. This comes from flares and sometimes "ambush lights" which are a car headlight connected to a battery. Secondly, although I have described a rural track, the ambush site could equally well be a building or house.

SEARCH

An insurgent needs weapons, plans, money, photographs and indeed everything else that anyone (including Tommy) going to war needs. He has to store it somewhere and eventually intelligence may identify a weapons dump location.

Before the location can be searched and the weapons found, it has to be secured. This involves inserting one cordon facing out (to stop people and insurgents coming into the search area) and one facing in to prevent people and/or insurgents leaving. Each cordon is simply a ring of observation posts with interlocking arcs of observation.

The actual searching can be delicate, particularly if the objective is a derelict house, as booby traps are a major risk. Specially trained soldiers (probably sappers, again) will perform the search, quite possibly with sophisticated jamming and detection equipment. It will involve sniffer dogs and photographers, as well as police and legal staff to note anything damaged during the search and pay compensation (Tommy is still trying to win hearts and minds, don't forget). The operation can be protracted, which in turn makes the cordon troops vulnerable as they can't move without compromising the integrity of the cordon and thus of the operation. Protecting them requires more patrols, using up more troops and leaving other parts of the area unpatrolled, which will give insurgents there a free rein.

This is worth it if the search yields a significant haul. Anything recovered will provide more intelligence and evidence to convict. And of course removing weapons and explosives increases the logistic pressure on the insurgents.

BOMBS & MORTARS

The insurgent's best weapon is a bomb. They are straightforward to make, are spectacular and can kill Tommy and terrorise locals without the insurgent actually having to engage Tommy in a direct fire battle, which the insurgent may well lose. Bombs can defeat armour, particularly if they utilise explosive formed fragments, demolish commercial and government buildings and, of course kill, people. There are several types.

Firstly, suicide bombs, which are all too familiar. The only defence against them is to kill the suicide bomber before he detonates himself,[224] assuming of course that the suicide bomber has sole control of detonation. This is a challenge, and is likely to need many bullets hitting the bomber in the head. Even more alarming is the vehicle born suicide bomber as the amount of explosive that he can deliver rises from under 50kg to over 5 tons. The only practical defence is movement control, using explosive detectors to prevent bombs access to city centres. However, it is important to accept that some bombers will get through – one insurgent with a grenade will cause mayhem. A better prevention method is to develop and exploit intelligence to stop the bomber and the arms, but this is not a quick solution.

In those cultures and belief systems that do not reward martyrdom, the proxy bomb is an effective insurgent weapon. The insurgents kidnap the family of a (say) taxi driver and compel him to drive a car containing a bomb to Tommy's camp gate, threatening to kill or violate his family if he does not. A sensible insurgent will have made the car a replica of the one that the driver normally uses, so no suspicions will arise at the gate until the car arrives. The only

---

[224] After, of course, making sure that he is not a Brazilian plumber.

protection against a proxy bomb is blast protection within the camp, and slick drills.

If the insurgent knows where a target will be and when, he may be able to plant a time delayed bomb. The most famous use of one was the attempt to kill the British Prime Minister, Margaret Thatcher, at the Grand Hotel in Brighton. The bomb was planted several weeks before the conference and detonated by an electric timer, which started counting down when the bomb was armed. While safe for the insurgent, these bombs do rely upon schedules not being changed. They also leave a forensic trail; the Brighton Bomber was caught and convicted, albeit two years later.

A simpler option is the under-car booby trap. These have a tilt switch and detonate when the vehicle starts moving. They are cheap, safe (for the bomber) and quick and easy to place – typically less than five seconds. They are held in place by magnets[225] and contain around 1 kg of explosive – easily enough to destroy the car and driver. They are an excellent terror weapon.

Command wire bombs work well for attempts to, say, demolish a culvert while Tommy is walking or driving over it. The command wire, which can be hundreds of metres long, is connected from the detonator in the bomb to a battery, carried by the Insurgent, at the other end of the wire. Advantages include immunity to batteries running down; the ability to detonate the bomb at the precise moment and immunity to jamming. The downsides (for the insurgent) are that the command wire must be hidden, and when the clean-up team finds and follows the command wire they'll find the firing point, which might yield forensic clues like a couple of hairs. The other disadvantage is that technically it is quite simple to detect an underground wire.

---

[225] The Hollywood portrayal of car bombs as being wired through ignition circuits, (which requires the bomber to defeat the car alarm system, pick the door lock, connect the terminals correctly, hide the device, arm it and then exit the car leaving no trace and resetting the alarm) are plain wrong. Planting a tilt switch operated car bomb just requires the bomber to pretend to tie a shoelace as he passes the car, reach under it and place the device, pull the arming button and walk on – less than 5 second's work.

A development of the command wire bomb is for the insurgent to use a laser to trigger the bomb. When the insurgent sees Tommy step onto the culvert, he shines a laser at the bomb, which incorporates a laser detector. The laser detector completes the circuit between the detonator and the batteries. While this saves the insurgent from having to conceal a command wire, it does mean that the bomb has to include batteries. The disadvantage of including the batteries is that they have a high metal content, and are thus easier to detect. They also may go flat, and thus not detonate the bomb as Tommy passes.

Replacing the command wire (or laser) with a radio makes bombs still easier for the insurgent, and technology has come to help him as he can now use a mobile phone in place of a radio. The two weaknesses are keeping life in the batteries of the receiver and detonator, and the vulnerability to jamming. Again, battery technology is improving all the time, reducing bulk and increasing life. Jamming radio signals is all well in theory but means that Tommy will be festooned with yet more radio equipment and carrying still more (heavy) batteries. He also has to become adept at remaining in the jammed, and therefore safe, area. This increases the training load, as well as constraining tactical options. Jamming mobile phone signals is possible, but does not do much for commerce or hearts and minds.

Finally the insurgent can make a pressure plate, which detonates the bomb when Tommy steps on it. This could be mechanical or electronic. Again, the challenge for the insurgent is to keep the metal content as low as possible, without compromising the battery power and life. Most of the IEDs in Afghanistan are pressure plate triggered.

There are some places that an insurgent would like to bomb, but can't get to. The obvious place is the inside of Patrol Base Baldrick, and indeed any others. Depending upon the sophistication and equipment available to the insurgent, he can use artillery, military mortars or make his own. The IRA became adept at making their own from gas cylinders. Some contained as much as 50kg of explosive, and had multiple barrels. Using military equipment is better, but as many Taliban and Fedayeen have found the hard way, operating a mortar close to a patrol base invites heavy return fire.

And, as Gary could tell them, hitting the target with the first round is hard, even with sophisticated fire control equipment, which they probably don't have.

The simple but stark truth is that in any counter- insurgency operation Tommy has an unpleasantly high chance of being blown up. While cash is being thrown at explosive detecting technologies, it is hard to provide one that will give Tommy sufficient warning. His best defence lies in being observant, getting close to the locals, interdicting on the insurgents' supply chain, building intelligence on the bomb makers and, above all, moving quickly and at short notice. Slow, predictable road movements, such as the logistic resupply of PB Baldrick, should be replaced with helicopter movement if at all possible. If road moves are unavoidable then they will become major operations, consuming Tommy's time with keeping himself alive and equipped, rather than taking the fight to the insurgent. This was clearly illustrated in Afghanistan when the US Marines (who have lots of helicopters) were taking over operations in Helmand. The majority of USMC casualties were gunshot wounds, where they had been in fire fights with the Taliban. The (overwhelming) majority of British casualties were blast injuries caused by stepping or driving on IEDs.

Bomb Disposal

The likelihood is that Tommy will find some bombs before they detonate, and others will malfunction (a "fizzle"). Making them safe and obtaining information from them is the role of very specialist, very brave individuals known as Ammunition Technical Officers. These remarkable people often become the specific target of the bomber, with multiple devices being set in related locations. In set up the operation is broadly similar to a search. Tommy cordons off an area and removes the local population. Then the bomb disposal team arrives, disarms the bomb and returns to base. He will of course gather intelligence from his work, and this is fed into the (highly classified) battle of measure and countermeasure.

While Tommy has increasingly sophisticated equipment to find IEDs, the best source of information about their location comes from the local population. One battlegroup in Helmand, which found and cleared a huge number of IEDs in their six month tour, calculated that for every one device that they found themselves the locals tipped them off about five more. Winning the trust and respect of the local population is fundamental to success in COIN.

SHOOTING

Much of the insurgent's interaction with Tommy will be through shooting. The level of the insurgency, the insurgent's capabilities and training and, of course, the ground will shape what Tommy faces. In general in most urban areas it is likely to be a single shot sniper, RPG or bursts of machine gun fire. In all these cases the insurgent needs to be careful, he is in line of sight with and in range of Tommy, who is probably a better shot.

If there are no-go areas, like Sadr City was for much of the 2nd Iraq War, then if and when the political will is found to reassert control, Tommy will find himself fighting something quite close to a high intensity operation, but with civilians in the way. Rules of Engagement based limitations on his weaponry and tactics and (usually) having to give the insurgent the opportunity to fire first which is never ideal. Tommy is unlikely to enjoy this experience, particularly if there has been delay and the insurgents have been able to plant IEDs on the approaches. Political vacillation is paid for, as ever, in Tommy's blood.

In open country there will be battles, but the odds are more in Tommy's favour as he can bring more firepower to bear –up to and including airstrikes. However, as the level of firepower deployed increases the adverse effects of a miss and the possibility of inadvertently killing civilians (or at least unarmed insurgents) escalates too. There are rules of engagement for each weapons system, so the entire operation can become very complicated. These complications cause delay, which usually works in favour of the insurgent.

The exception is if there is an international border close, over which the insurgents can shoot, or flee having shot – with or without the connivance of the government. Shooting over international borders, or mounting spontaneous invasions gives Tommy the ability to elevate a minor firefight to a full blown international incident. Sealing and policing borders is hugely expensive in terms of both cash and manpower. Failing to do so can prolong insurgencies almost indefinitely, which can be even more expensive, depending of course on the value ascribed to a pint of Tommy's blood.

RIOTS

The insurgency will generate rallies, marches and demonstrations as part of the political process. It is almost inevitable that at least some of these will degenerate into riots, with concomitant looting, thuggery, damage to property and assaults on the forces of law and order. Tommy may well find himself in riot gear, supporting or replacing the police efforts to maintain the rule of law.

Riot control is relatively straightforward but, as "Bloody Sunday" showed, it is one of those things that do not go a little bit wrong. The security forces' aim is to contain the rioters geographically, which is done by forming baselines of men in riot gear blocking the street, ideally with vehicles there to provide structure. In Ulster in the 1970s the British Army had a wheeled APC, universally known as a "Pig." A number of these were fitted with fold out extensions to widen the vehicle when it was acting as part of a baseline. The extensions were called wings, and about five seconds later the "Flying Pig" entered service with the British Army.

The only problem with being on a baseline in riot gear for Tommy is that the rioters tend to hurl bricks, stones and paving slabs at him. The less civilised ones throw petrol, nail and blast bombs as well. Nowadays, the combination of helmet, visor, body armour, shield and training will keep Tommy pretty safe, but it is prudent to cool the rioter's ardour. There are three ways to do this; rubber bullets (which are nowadays made of plastic and called baton rounds), water cannon and CS Gas. All are theoretically non-lethal, although accidents happen.

Forming a baseline is generally a platoon task. Usually three fire teams will actually man the shield wall, one team will provide baton gunners and two teams will become snatch squads. The process is straightforward; ringleaders are identified, a volley of baton rounds fired, snatch squads dash out, grab the fallen ringleader and bring them back[226], where they are identified, processed and arrested. It is hard, physical work and the processing side can consume manpower quickly if rioters have to be arrested, instead of interned.

The big fear is a sniper, to whom the baseline is hugely vulnerable. Some of the platoon will be on anti-sniper cover, with rifles up scanning for targets. That said, the most they are likely to see is the muzzle flash of the sniper's first (and probably only) shot.

One area of debate in the rules of engagement is whether or not a petrol bomb is a lethal weapon, and therefore whether a petrol bomber can be shot. Clarity on this is essential, but rarely forthcoming in time. Similar clarity is required about nail and blast bombs. The clarity is essential not only for Tommy, but also for the young thugs who get involved on the other side of the baseline, who may find that a piece of bravado has been interpreted as action with lethal intent.

INTELLIGENCE

The key to containing an insurgency is intelligence. In the military sense, intelligence means information on the insurgents and public that has been collected, collated and considered. This is then used to deduce what operations might be useful in either damaging the insurgents, collecting more intelligence or (ideally) both. It should be obvious that language is fundamental; if Tommy can't speak to the locals he can only gather a fraction of the data that he otherwise could. In these cases the entire campaign's success rests upon the quality, quantity and reliability of interpreters.

Intelligence comes from a huge range of sources. At the lowest end are patrol reports, completed by every patrol, on what they saw and heard. Above that are the notes and logs of those sent out to observe specific locations, often the houses or businesses of suspected insurgents or sympathisers. We then move into the realm of interrogation reports, bugging, telephone intercepts and, at the top end, the murky world of informers.

---

[226] The snatch squads need speed and strength. The encouragement of the ringleader to cooperate requires some robust handling.

Ideally Tommy will have access to vehicle data and personal data, and the legal power to require people to identify themselves. If he stops a suspicious car he can call in the registration number and verify that it is the right car in the right place. At the same time, of course, the fact that the car has been stopped is recorded. Over time a picture of movements will develop, and abnormalities and patterns searched for by computer. The emergence of facial recognition software has also generated many more opportunities for computer analysis of events to identify patterns of behaviour. CCTV feeds from main public areas will help the intelligence effort enormously (or at least they will for as long as the CCTV camera remains operational).

The world of recruiting informers is slightly above Tommy's pay grade, but also in the shadows. It is a specialist area, highly sensitive and not very pleasant. Similarly, bugging and phone interceptions are performed by other agencies. Tommy may get involved in interrogation, at least in the early stages, when he captures an insurgent or suspected insurgent. It is important that Tommy is completely aware of what he may and may not do in the course of restraining the insurgent and bringing him to a secure location. Generally a susceptible insurgent will be more impressed by firm but correct handling at the moment of capture. Once the captive has been handed over to specialist agencies he is no longer Tommy's concern. At some level, if the captive has knowledge that is likely to speed the ending of the insurrection, it is in the public interest that the information should be revealed. This is unlikely to be an entirely pretty process, and may involve sleep deprivation, robust questioning and severe mental pressure. If the chattering and political classes cannot accept that necessary unpleasantness they should not have chosen to counter the insurgency in the first place[227].

Of course the intelligence effort works both ways – the insurgents need to know what Tommy and his pals are up to. One way to do this is to watch them closely. Operational security is a priority, but it also allows Tommy to have some fun. For instance, one day in a

---

[227] Where reasonably robust interrogation ends and torture begins is a very grey area.

vehicle checkpoint he may decide to stop all blue cars[228]. To the insurgent watching Tommy, this might mean that they have information from an informer that an operation involving a blue car is being planned. To an insurgent in a blue car in the queue, it may be sufficiently alarming to make him pull out of the queue and try a different route. If Tommy gets the vehicle's registration number it is information, and if he also has a spare team waiting in the right place he may yet nab an insurgent.

Intelligence causes tensions within headquarters. At any command level the job of an intelligence officer is to collate information and generate intelligence. The operations officer's job is to exploit that intelligence to damage the insurgency. The problem comes when using the intelligence risks making the insurgents aware of a source and not using it increases the risk to Tommy's life. For example if a source has revealed the location of a bomb, immediately clearing it may compromise the source. Continuing to send Tommy on patrol past it protects the source, but of course creates the possibility of Tommy being killed. Neither outcome is desirable, but there are no easy answers to establishing the priority. In the absence of firm, united leadership the competing points of view can damage the campaign's efficiency.

United leadership does not just refer to the army. At some point the police forces are going to have to take over much of the work. Certainly, in the initial stages of the conflict, the police are likely to be institutionally mistrusted by soldiers. It will take time (measured in years, if not decades) for the mistrust to be focussed away from the entire police force onto individuals. Only at that will there be some trusted policemen (or other government authority) the possibility of a return to normality.

HEARTS AND MINDS

This phrase occurs again and again in COIN warfare, to the extent that it has become a cliché. It is worth considering what it means where the rubber hits the road, i.e. with Tommy.

---

[228] The author has observed that it is important to have some basis for selection of cars to stop. "Random" systems always seem to intercept a disproportionately high number of cars driven by pretty young women.

In any insurgency the local population will be divided into those who sympathise in part (or more) with the insurgents aims, and those who don't. The latter group will also include many who oppose the government, on the grounds that it allowed the insurgency to happen. Tommy's job is to persuade them all that life is better working with him to defeat the insurgents, rather than against him.

As we have alluded to before, the first step is to minimise, and ideally eliminate, collateral damage and to pay compensation generously and promptly when it occurs. Of course the insurgent knows this, and will do his utmost to induce Tommy into creating the damage and, if possible, extort some of the compensation. It is axiomatic that Tommy must only engage within the rules of engagement, and must hit the target. A bullet has to stop somewhere and a round that misses an entirely legitimate insurgent target and continues on its trajectory to hit a civilian (or his house, car or donkey) is a disastrous outcome. To avoid such events Tommy needs additional range training, and lots of it.

Another step is for Tommy to be identifiable as a human being, rather than an alien warrior. This means that when Tommy is on patrol the population needs to be able to see his face and eyes. This is best achieved if Tommy eschews his helmet and dark glasses. There are downsides to this. The lack of dark glasses will tire Tommy's eyes more quickly and foregoing his helmet increases the chances of death and injury. This again is an area which politicians need to understand. Rightly, everyone is concerned to reduce and avoid casualties to Tommy and his pals. However, ordering them all to wear helmets all of the time does actually run the risk of reducing Tommy's effectiveness and prolonging the battle to win hearts and minds. The British Army is particularly fortunate in having a wide range of headgear as a legacy of the long history of its Regiments[229]. If nothing else, they promote curiosity with the public. The simple fact is that in a beret (or equivalent) Tommy looks like a human and is approachable, in a helmet he's closer to Robocop or an Imperial

---

[229]As are the French with their Kepis and the Italian Bersaglieri, whose hats seem to have chickens roosting in them!

Storm Trooper[230]. As a helmet is heavy and hot, Tommy generally prefers to wear something else.

Having established his humanity and competence, Tommy has to demonstrate his value. The most obvious way is to provide security, and thus a return to normal life. The problem is, of course, the insurgents who are determined to prevent normality. Tommy's arrival in PB Baldrick is likely to produce an increase in insurgent operations, at least in the short term. The probable response is for Tommy to control movement, which may mean shutting some commercial and social access routes. Again, in the short term this will have a negative effect on the general population, but if security increases through reduced insurgent activity Tommy will reap the rewards.

Two of Tommy's colleagues are of huge value, particularly in less-developed nations. Sappers can build roads, schools, hospitals and the like, and medics can save lives and increase health. It is important to coordinate the provision of aid with the establishment of security[231]. Firstly there is no point inoculating a child against typhoid if it gets killed by an insurgent bombing the next week. Secondly, it is a great bargaining tool with local leaders ("Tell me where the insurgents live and we'll build you a school"). Obviously the information needs checking. It is vital that any such agreements are kept to: if Tommy loses his reputation for being honourable the whole campaign is jeopardised. Again, there is no point in building a school if the insurgents can blow it up the next week, which means continuing security is a prerequisite.

The best route to a population's acceptance is by becoming part of their economy, and increasing their wealth. Few people wish to bite the hand that feeds. Of course, this option is fraught with danger; corruption is often endemic and if the money doesn't flow to the locals it will cause resentment and alienation. There are also

---

[230] Interestingly, some British police forces are finding this out the hard way. Having exchanged their smart white shirts for "more practical" black ones, they are being accused of looking sinister and threatening.

[231] Which implies that the Army needs to deliver the aid as it's also delivering the security. The profusion of organisations all seeking to help in Afghanistan is inefficient, flawed and it undermines the military's ability to offer carrots and sticks.

significant security implications, and cultural ones. Less-developed countries may not be able to cope with the bureaucracy imposed on Tommy; there may be straightforward legal differences that make it exceptionally hard to create a satisfactory contract.

SUMMARY

COIN operations are long, slow, dangerous and frustrating. The military and political worlds are intertwined, and running through it all is the shadowy world of intelligence gathering. There are no quick fixes and the ultimate solution will not be a military one. However the challenge is more interesting than straightforward soldiering, and Tommy may (just) have an opportunity to make a great advance, be it through finding an arms cache or arresting an insurgent. More likely perhaps, (and Tommy has no way of knowing), his professionalism, personal charm and determination might prevent a teenager from joining the insurgency. Without fresh recruits the insurgency will wither. Eventually.

For Tommy a COIN campaign will involve endless hours of patrolling and being on sentry. He is also likely to be living in a hovel. For almost all of the time nothing will happen. When it does it will be sudden, violent and brief. Unlike the battlefield, casualties may well include civilians and children. Some of the things that he sees and does are likely to scar him for life.

For Tommy to be effective he needs to be well trained, motivated and disciplined. We'll look how this is achieved in the next chapter.

Chapter 14 Tommy Learns his Trade; Training

Throughout the preceding chapters one of the recurring themes is that Tommy is part of a team, and that to survive on the battlefield this team must be cohesive, well-motivated and able to co-operate with other teams, sometimes at short notice, in order to achieve the mission. The most brilliant plan will fail if the soldiers carrying it out are not prepared to fight. In practical terms opting out of combat doesn't mean Tommy surrendering; he could just lie down in cover and hope that the battle goes away. Every time that Tommy gets up from the ground he is making a conscious act of will – knowingly risking his life – to continue implementing the plan.

The purpose of battle procedure is to ensure that Tommy is delivered into battle at the right time, in the right place and with the right kit. Leadership is how Tommy is inspired routinely to demonstrate the bravery that is a fundamental requirement of soldiering. However, it all starts with training, which is what we will consider here.

BASIC TRAINING

As ever, well start from the bottom. Let's therefore imagine Tommy's younger brother, Timmy, as he enters basic training to follow in Tommy's noble footsteps. Most first-rate armies no longer have universal conscription and the British certainly don't, so Timmy is a volunteer. This is fundamentally important; Timmy has chosen to be a soldier, and indeed has passed a series of tests and interviews to get to the training depot. While he can easily leave at pretty much any stage in his training and can be ejected from it if he cannot achieve required standards, he wants to be there and he wants to succeed. Of course, his aspiration is made partly in ignorance:[232] one of the purposes of basic training is to identify and remove those who are not suited. However, the simple fact is that most people can soldier if they want to enough.[233] As he arrives at

---

[232] Which is one of the reasons for this book.

[233] The mass conscriptions of the two world wars actually produced people who wanted to soldier - at the very least; they wanted to be soldiers more

the depot, Timmy's overwhelming emotion is likely to be trepidation – not so much as to what the training involves but as to whether he is indeed going to be able to endure and achieve his ambition of becoming a soldier.

The aim of basic training is straightforward; to turn a collection of individual civilians into a group of soldiers, ready to progress to more advanced training and become full members of the team. The process takes three to six months and starts with a very short haircut, usually within an hour of arrival. The reason for this is simple; the recruits have to work together and the quickest way to start a team forming is to give them a shared unpleasant but survivable experience. A 60 second short back and sides is just that![234] Timmy's next stop is the stores, where he will be issued a bewildering array of clothing and equipment. He'll then head back to his barrack block, where he will be shown everything from how to wash, through making beds to how to wear, clean, iron and polish his uniform.

The next couple of months will consist of long hard days as Timmy gets fit and learns the basics of weapon handling, map reading and foot drill. He'll spend his nights cleaning everything that he has been issued, touched or slept in. His day will start unimaginably early with inspections and finish very late, possibly with an exhausted Timmy sleeping under the bed that will be inspected the next morning to avoid crinkling the sheets. On the upside, he'll be introduced to sport, fed vast quantities of good food and need never worry about being bored.

Getting fit is likely to be quite unpleasant. Timmy will find himself pushed well out of his comfort zone and into areas of pain and exhaustion. Of course Timmy he could stop running and opt out but then he would be out of the group. If he takes the next step he is still in the group, and one more step isn't that hard. Timmy is learning that being a soldier costs pain, but at the same time he is

---

that they wanted to be conscientious objectors, draft dodgers or prisoners. The same is probably not true of US draftees in Vietnam (there being no direct threat to the US or any of its close allies), which accounts for some of the problems that arose in that conflict.

[234] There is no equivalent for female recruits. A missed opportunity for Vidal Sassoon, perhaps?

investing that pain into the shared benefit of the group. The longer he keeps going the more he has invested and the more he has to lose by stopping, a thought process familiar to anyone who has run a marathon. Timmy's mates and instructors will encourage him, robustly if necessary, to take the next step. And the one after that. Getting fit also risks injuries – and these are a major concern of both staff and Timmy. Rushing physical training injures recruits, (sometimes irreparably – for example broken legs rarely recover well enough to permit a trainee to return to training) and wastes money.

Timmy will also spend plenty of time learning and practicing foot[235] drill. The uninformed often question the need to learn drill in a "modern age."[236] While foot drill originated in the 17th Century as a way of manoeuvring formed bodies of men on a battlefield, and as such has been supplanted by fire and manoeuvre and using ground, it still has an important place in soldiering, particularly in training. Soldiering requires discipline and instant response to orders. This is a mental process, and drill develops it. It also develops self-discipline. For example, one of the hardest things to do is remain absolutely still, which is as necessary in an OP or ambush as it is in standing to attention on a drill square. Soldiering requires team work; on the drill square Timmy learns to do exactly what his peers are doing at exactly the same time. Drill invariably involves highly polished boots, burnished badges, pressed trousers and starched shirts. Tommy has tens of thousands of pounds worth of kit (or more) issued to him by the taxpayer, which he is responsible for maintaining. Timmy starts to learn maintenance by polishing his boots to his instructor's elusive satisfaction.

But most of all drill is about pride. Marching in his squad, Timmy is demonstrating to the outside world that he is not a civilian, strolling

---

[235] It's called "foot" drill to distinguish it from "mounted" drill (on horses), "cycle" drill (on bicycles – sadly now passed in UK), "battle" drills and "gun" drills.

[236] The author was as guilty of this as any other, particularly when he started as an instructor at Sandhurst and saw how much time was devoted to drill. However his view soon changed – you can tell a lot about an individual's character while watching them drilling for hours. Those who get a thrill from being part of the team are obvious, as are the shirkers.

along as part of a loose crowd but a soldier, part of a noble profession, proudly marching along at 120 30-inch paces to the minute with his comrades in arms. Pride is fundamental to soldiering; whenever any soldier is interviewed about why he (or she) did something brave or dangerous, the answer is always the same: *"I didn't want to let my mates down."* For Timmy, Tommy and Rupert, letting one's mates down is an awful prospect, because it constitutes betrayal of the ethos they themselves have created. Once Timmy is through basic training he knows that he has the ability to be a good soldier and that this includes an unlimited liability to not let his mates down. Lying safe on the ground while his mates are up and fighting is the most fundamental betrayal of his mates and himself.

Rupert's brother Robin is having an equally sharp introduction to military life in Officer training. As well as learning basic soldiering like Timmy, Robin will also discover that his prime obligation is to his soldiers.[237] On this basis it has been argued, with some merit, that the lowest form of military life is therefore an officer cadet. However, Robin is always called "Sir" by his non-commissioned instructors, although their long years of service have given them an ability to make this salutation profoundly ironic. After his first term or basic training Robin will then spend another two terms learning and practicing the process of command and the art of leadership, as well as acquiring the technical skills required.

Timmy will learn military procedure, although he might not realise it at the time. At any moment throughout his training he knows where he has to be, when and with what equipment. Someone will always be in charge, and if there is a problem it is up to the person in charge to fix it. He knows that he is taught by a Corporal, and that the path to peace and happiness lies in fulfilling his Corporal's orders expeditiously. He becomes aware of Sergeants and Officers, who he knows are higher in the chain of command that the Corporal. He knows that on all routine matters he deals with his Corporal. If it is above the Corporal's pay grade then the Corporal will arrange to go up the "chain of command."

---

[237] The motto of Sandhurst, the British Officer training academy, is "Serve to Lead" – which says it all.

At the end of basic training Timmy will be fitter than he thought possible, smarter than his most demanding grandmother could imagine and probably at least half a stone lighter. He is capable of being in the right place at the right time with the right kit. He'll have learnt how to use a rifle, and will be at least an adequate shot. He'll have met his chemical warfare kit, and worn it in a building full of tear gas. He will have carried telegraph poles to the tops of distant hills and brought them back. His hair will still be short, but his self-confidence and pride in himself will be palpable. On his last day he'll put on his smartest uniform, highly polished of course, and perform a passing out parade with his friends and family in the audience. After the parade they will, rightly, fawn over him. Timmy is now a soldier.

Robin will still have a long time to go; his training can take up to a year as he has more to learn. Much of the additional learning burden is to do with the orders process and battle procedure. The essential difference between Robin and Timmy is that while Timmy slots into the military team at the bottom and is responsible only for himself and his kit, when Robin is commissioned he will become responsible for the lives, actions and welfare of ten to thirty soldiers.[238] This daunting responsibility usually tempers the ecstasy of being commissioned.

FURTHER TRAINING

From time to time all soldiers receive further individual training, perhaps learning to be a mortar man or reconnaissance platoon commander as well as in less obviously military skills such as HGV driving and accounting. They will also go, as individuals, on promotion courses, learning the skills that they need for the next level of command. These vary enormously by branch of service – the point is that there is a well-established, formally structured progression. Where possible, say in vehicle maintenance, the

---

[238] Having taught at Sandhurst, the author has seen few young men more anxious about their immediate future than new young officers the morning after their commissioning party.

military qualifications match civilian equivalents – Tommy is being prepared for life after soldiering.[239]

Robin and Timmy (and indeed Tommy and Rupert) are still learning when they are with their Regiment or Battalion; this is particularly true of Robin. Aged 23, he has people old enough to be his father calling him "Sir" and relying upon his recommendation and prowess to gain promotion. While it is by no means only Robin's word that counts, his performance as a platoon commander or troop leader has a significant impact. If he does well, his sergeant and corporals rightly share in the glory. If he does not they will share in the blame and others will obtain advancement. As you can imagine, this puts pressure on Robin and he has to develop the character to be able to deal with it. As a young officer there are innumerable mistakes that could be made; Robin needs to work out how to avoid the worst of them and mitigate the impact of the more minor ones. Although he has substantial theoretical powers a wise young officer is a humble one.

We have seen that relatively simple tasks like shooting straight are actually quite complicated. The answer is practice, practice and practice. While rifle ammunition is relatively cheap, anti-tank missiles are not. A whole range of simulators exists to enable soldiers to keep their skills current. Much as the accountants hate it and simulator salesmen deny it, there is no substitute for live fire training; as while no-one ever got killed on a computer simulation, accidents do happen on ranges. Tommy has to be utterly confident handling weapons that if abused will kill him or his mates.

Command processes are practised in mock-up headquarter complexes on broadly paper based exercises. Tactics and the use of ground are practices on TEWTs (Tactical Exercises Without

---

[239] This can cause problems as men with military experience are sought after by civilian employers, who can entice Tommy to leave with higher pay and a more stable life (with less prospect of being killed or maimed). In extreme cases, for example helicopter pilot training, Tommy (or Rupert) will be required to serve for a minimum amount of time post qualification. Five years is the norm.

Troops[240]). But the whole battlegroup must practise together with everyone there. This is done in two ways. There are now huge simulators, which link together 50 tank simulators, plus infantry and FOO simulators, which all fight in the same battle, either against the simulator administrators and computer controlled forces or against another battlegroup in another simulator. These are spectacularly expensive and highly realistic.

But nothing beats getting into the field, and becoming tired, wet and muddy. Blank ammunition and laser sensors enable realistic engagements and logistic demands. There are also now fully instrumented training areas where entire battles can be played back in detail, errors identified and lessons learned. The British Army, which has a healthy obsession with live fire training, also has an extensive range in Canada where up to a battlegroup can exercise performing live fire exercises[241] for weeks at a time.

All of that keeps everyone proficient. When real operations arise, like the ones in Iraq and Afghanistan, specialist training centres are established and complete battlegroups go through them together.[242] These training centres get operational feedback all the time, and so the training is literally as up to date as it can be.

If all this sounds like a lot of effort and cost, it is. However, a fundamental tenet of soldiering is "Train hard, fight easy."

PROMOTION (AND YET MORE TRAINING)

One of Rupert's tasks is writing annual reports on each of his soldiers – which are moderated by the Company Commander. These reports are the basis of the entire system, and are fundamental to identifying those soldiers with the capability to progress. With tight competition for places, it is very hard for a private soldier to stand out from his peers. Sportsmen naturally

---

[240] There are a range of acronyms for other exercises with components missing. The most anti-climactic is NEWD, Night Exercise Without Darkness.

[241] Bear in mind than tank projectiles can travel 10km and artillery shells 40+km and you can understand what a wonderful facility this is.

[242] Of course, training on Salisbury Plain in February for operations in Iraq during the summer doesn't stimulate heat exhaustion casualties.

catch the eye. One of the skills that Rupert and Robin have to develop is ensuring that all their private soldiers have a chance to shine. Tommy and Timmy can help themselves enormously by their general demeanour, always being punctual and properly turned out, smiling and speaking up. While this is relatively easy in barracks, it is more of a challenge on a field exercise in the middle of a British winter. Any army requires excellent NCOs and is always on the lookout for talent to nurture and develop. Napoleon famously alleged "Every French soldier carries a marshal's baton in his knapsack." While rising from private soldier to Field Marshal is a serious challenge,[243] being commissioned from the ranks is common[244]. The enforced objectivity of the reporting system actually makes soldiering one of the most meritocratic employment environments.

TRAINING FOR THE INSURGENT

First rate armies invest heavily in training. Lesser armies spend their money on decent kit but forget to budget for maintenance and training, and are often too proud to learn the culture of promotion by merit. Impoverished armies barely have kit, spending most of their time on the cusp of banditry to provide food. Broadly for conventional warfare the more you spend the better you are. If the army is relatively new a wise government secures training support from a more experienced Army of a friendly state. The British Army has trained the armies of many friendly powers, although of course the vagaries of geopolitics sometimes mean that friends sometimes become enemies.

Training for an insurgent is more complex and dangerous (as is every aspect of being an insurgent, but this book is not about him). However it is worth considering further as insurgents are Tommy's

---

[243] Achieved by Field Marshall Sir William "Wully" Robertson, Bart. He enlisted as a trooper in the 16th Lancers in 1877, became a Troop Sergeant Major in 1885 and (with the support of the Officers of his Regiment) was commissioned into the 3rd Dragoon Guards as a 2nd Lieutenant in 1888. He became Chief of the Imperial General Staff in 1915 and was made a Baronet in 1919. The British Army is a great instrument of social change.

[244] When the author taught at Sandhurst (the British Army Officer training academy) 20% of his students had served in the ranks as private soldiers.

most common recent enemy. Any insurgency that is successful enough for Tommy to become involved in fighting will have some form of state sponsorship, which may well be hotly denied in public.[245] This will, at the least, yield a supply of weaponry and some of those weapons may be advanced (for example, during the Soviet occupation of Afghanistan the Americans happily supplied the Mujahedeen with Stinger missiles, which at the time were state of the art).

The insurgency has committed members, at least some of whom will have received military training from the sponsor state. The insurgency will also have logistic, intelligence and operations functions. What it will not have is the time, budget and facilities to conduct intensive collective training in the way that first rate armies do. This is not to say insurgents do not train. Many insurgents are supremely fit and superb shots. As their training is unconstrained by health and safety, and their discipline not reliant upon Acts of Parliament the individual insurgent can be a formidable fighting man, and an implacable foe. But for an insurgent to become a fully trained and effective fighter, he (or she) has to overcome some formidable challenges.

The first is saying alive and free. Wherever he is, the insurgent is hunted. For example, to practice with his rifle he needs a range. At all stages of the journey to the range, the actual shooting, and the return journey he is in deep trouble if Tommy finds him. If the insurgents establish a training camp, the logistic effort starts to take over and impede both training and insurgent operations. Training camps need materials to construct them; trainees and instructors need food and accommodation. All of this creates more movement, which intelligence agencies might spot. Training camps themselves are worthwhile target, and Tommy actively seeks them out.

Having built a camp, the insurgency needs to find instructors. Anyone teaching new recruits is not attacking Tommy. This has a strategic impact upon the insurgency; if Tommy is not being struck

---

[245] It is entirely possible that there are some insurgencies which accord with the aims of a British government, at which point they become freedom fighters and may receive training from the likes of the SAS. This is beyond the scope of this book.

hard he will be winning hearts and minds. The net result is that much of the insurgent's training, particularly in anything more advanced than individual skills, may well be conducted on the job. This is a very Darwinian way to go about it, as making mistakes when fighting Tommy is usually fatal. Moreover, a high insurgent death rate is bad for recruiting, which means Tommy is winning (although he might not know it at the time, and the victory parade may be years away).

The insurgent's best solution is to train in the safety of a supportive country. Unfortunately this involves risky international travel[246] and, probably, some compromise on the objectives of the insurgency to accommodate the aspirations of the supporter. If insurgents were minded to compromise they would probably not be insurgents in the first place and shifting ideology can do irreparable damage to an insurgency.[247]

While Tommy and Rupert train together in a system that has evolved to build trust and interdependence, the insurgent rarely has the chance to train as a formed unit in an established system. While the insurgent is possibly the equal of Tommy as an individual fighting man, unlike Tommy he does not have a large and sophisticated team to support him. The insurgent therefore has to keep one eye out for himself – particularly if Tommy's intelligence effort has penetrated the insurgency. How does the insurgent know whom to trust? The answer is that he doesn't, and he is therefore suspicious of all new faces and many old ones. Of course, personal relationships do exist between insurgent rank and file and their

---

[246] The risks of international travel are reduced to almost zero if there is a supportive state next door and the border is not well defended. This was the case in Ulster for much of the Troubles, and is the case in Afghanistan.

[247] Consider the Irish Troubles. Republicans started with the IRA, which split into the Provisional IRA and the Official IRA. PIRA split and the Irish National Liberation Army emerged. To the delight of the British, INLA and PIRA went to war with each other, which provided fertile ground for intelligence, plus a lot of terrorist casualties for zero effort. INLA folded, the peace talks started and PIRA spawned the Real IRA and Continuity IRA. It makes the tribulations of the Judean Peoples Liberation Front in Monty Python's *Life of Brian* seem trivial.

leaders, but they may be complicated by family or tribal relationships.

The challenges of training an insurgent to fight Tommy head on can be reduced by the insurgents avoiding face to face confrontation and by specialising. Many insurgent activities such as bomb making, research, publishing, electronics development, chemical synthesis and the like can actually be conducted by one person in a garden shed, attic or basement. Provided there is a secure courier network (a big caveat) there is less need for concurrent teamwork. Under-car booby traps, one of the best attack weapons used by the Provisional Irish Republican Army (or PIRA), are a case in point. Seamus can make the bomb at home from household items. His designs include arming systems so that the bombs are relatively safe to transport and store. The couriers, Oona and Murphy, can collect the bomb and deliver it to Liam. When Liam has identified a target, he can have Frankie, one of his up and coming young thugs, walk to the target car and plant and arm the bomb in a matter of seconds. The only skilled person is Seamus, who is three steps removed from Frankie. More importantly this five person team has conducted a joint attack without ever having to all be in the same place at the same time. The flip side is that Seamus is only a bomb maker, and possibly the only bomb maker. When the intelligence identifies him he is unlikely to present a militarily formidable target.

LEGALITY

Although the insurgent is less well trained, has a far more dangerous and lonely life and has to avoid head on conflicts with Tommy he does have one major advantage. He absolutely believes in the cause that he is fighting for. For Tommy it's a bit more complicated; quite possibly he joined the army before the Westminster wonders decided that this war was going to involve him. Before we look at the mechanics of delivering Tommy into battle, we should consider who decides to send him to war in the first place. In Britain Rupert and Tommy's oath of allegiance is to the Monarch, not to Parliament and certainly not to the Government. The oath does include an unambiguous undertaking to obey all lawful orders given by the Monarch or her Generals and Officers.

The key word is lawful: for example, it is not possible to order Tommy to shoot a prisoner (as that would be against the Geneva Conventions, and therefore unlawful and not binding).   Generals therefore have to satisfy themselves that the instructions that they have received from politicians to make war are themselves lawful. As recent events have shown, this is not always as straightforward as it seems. A significant amount of officer training is in the concept of just war and lawful war, and what does and does not constitute a lawful order.

Note also that the oath is not limited to warfare; it is to the protection of the Monarch in "person, crown and dignity" which permits the use of the British Army in, say, disaster relief. It also allows for use of the Army to provide emergency services — conceivably including breaking strikes, as happened in the Fireman's Strike in the 1970s. But again, the Generals must be satisfied that they are protecting the Monarch's "crown and dignity" rather the immediate future of a politician. Rash statements by politicians can lead to constitutional crisis.   The media, free from the responsibilities of direct power, often cause problems. "Something must be done to stop the killing in Syria" is not a policy; if it is developed into a proposal, defining who should do what to whom (and where) it may well be discovered that the proposal cannot lead to lawful intervention. This is not just a lucrative academic debate for lawyers; Tommy and Rupert feel it keenly. Rupert is particularly concerned as he will be giving the orders that may get Tommy killed and, if they do, it will be he who writes to Mrs Tommy and his parents.

By the time Tommy gets ordered to war he can be confident that the orders have been rigorously scrutinised and are lawful — he does have the right to contest the legality of the order, although this rarely happens.[248] It's now time to look at the mechanics of getting Tommy into action.

---

[248] It did in 2005 when an RAF Officer refused to go to Iraq. He was court martialled and lost, as it was not his job to determine whether a war was lawful. That is the job of the Heads of the Armed Services and the Attorney General.

Chapter 15 Tommy Get His Orders; Battle Procedure

So, we now have an armed force, trained to be loyal to itself and sworn to serve the monarch. The next step is to deploy it into battle at the right time and place, properly prepared and willing to fight. The mechanics of this process are known as battle procedure, which incorporates the giving and receiving of orders. Let's imagine that Tommy has deployed to another war and that the battlegroup is in a series of company hides[249]. It's just after dawn, 6.00 am. Battlegroup headquarters receives a warning order from Brigade:

"The Brigade is to capture an insurgents training camp in the area of High Mountain. Orders Group at Brigade Headquarters at 09:00. No move before 18:00."

The Orders Group is where the Commanding Officer and his Operations Officer will receive their orders for this attack. The no move before time is the earliest time at which the brigade will move; every part of the brigade needs to be ready to move then. Receipt of the warning order immediately triggers a whole series of activities within the Battlegroup. The Operations Officer (a keen, experienced Captain) finds High Mountain on the map, sends for the Commanding Officer and, crucially, at 6.15 issues the battlegroup's warning order to its companies.

"The battlegroup will be conducting offensive operations against an insurgents training camp in the area of High Mountain. O Group at Battlegroup Headquarters 12:00. Building entry stores to be collected by companies from the A2 Echelon at 07:00. No move before 18:00."

Two tests of how effective a headquarters is are the speed with which it issues warning orders and the accuracy of its "no move before" times. Getting warning orders quickly down the chain of command means Tommy has more time to prepare (or sleep). Changing a no move before time is unhelpful; bringing it forward

---

[249] A hide is a concealed and secure position out of contact with the enemy. It is not established as a defensive position – if the company is attacked in its hide by a serious force it will move rather than stand and fight.

induces administrative mayhem and Tommy may not have everything that he needs. If it is set too early, effort is wasted and Tommy loses sleep.

Notice that the Operations Officer has anticipated having to break into buildings, and ordered the ladders, grappling hooks and other equipment to be brought forward early. This means that Tommy can practise with them before the Commanding Officers even sits down to get his orders. This anticipation and concurrent activity is one of the hallmarks of a well-trained battlegroup (and army).

When the warning order gets to the Company Commander he sends for the Company Sergeant Major, his three platoon commanders and the Company Quartermaster Sergeant. The latter gets sent to collect the ladders from the A echelon. The CSM and platoon commanders come up with a programme for training with hooks and ladders, which will be with them in a couple of hours. Tommy and the majority of the company are left sleeping, cleaning weapons, washing and eating breakfast. It is going to be a long night for them, although they don't yet know that.

So, within half an hour of the warning order being issued, the entire brigade is starting to prepare for the action. Although none of them yet has detail on the mission, they are getting on with key preparation. They are also able to allocate time, as they know when they have to be ready and when their commanders will be receiving orders. This allows Tommy to plan when he can eat and sleep. Fatigue management is a key military skill; seasoned soldiers are expert at catching sleep whenever they can wherever they are.

Remember, warning orders initiate the next battle. In a fast moving campaign, and particularly in high intensity warfare, it is by no means guaranteed that the current battle will be completed before warning orders arrive for the next one. While at company level and down commanders are generally only involved in one battle at a time, at battlegroup and above they are generally involved in two – the current battle and the next one.

ORDERS

The warning orders may be supplemented as the day goes on, but the next major step is the issuing and receiving of full orders. There are broadly three ways in which this can be done. The least attractive is in writing, delivered by computer or fax. While this is secure, efficient and fast and has the minimum scope for error, it removes the opportunity for human contact and deprives the commander of the opportunity to impose his personality, charisma and leadership on his subordinates. It's the difference between reading the book and seeing the play.

By far the preferred method is for all the subordinates to meet the commander face to face in a secure location. While this involves a lot of movement, which consumes time, it brings everyone together. If face to face is not possible, orders can be given by radio (ideally with some documentation sent through by fax or dispatch rider). We'll return to this later; for now, let's advance the clock to 12 noon.

The Commanding Officer has had a busy morning. He got his orders from the brigade commander at 9am, and from 10am worked out a plan for his battlegroup's part in the brigade operation. The process of developing a plan is known as an appreciation[250]. The commander considers the aim (or mission – i.e. what he has to do and why), relevant factors such as ground, the enemy, time and space, and comes up with a plan. It is important that the commander remembers that the appreciation is a dynamic process. Many factors will change during the interval from receiving his orders and completing the operation, and a good commander continually reviews his plan in the light of events. Plans evolve during the course of the battle - not least because the enemy will be doing his utmost to make the plan fail. The Commanding Officer has to tread a thin line between producing too simple a plan, risking that his subordinates failing to grasp all the important points, and too much detail, which will be hard to change if it is rendered irrelevant by events. As with much in military life, keeping it simple is generally best.

Having developed his plan, he prepares to give his orders. Much of the work will be done by his staff, primarily the Operations Officer,

---

[250] Jargon alert! The British Army changed "combat appreciation" to "combat estimate" when it belatedly switched to "mission command" in the 1990s. Appreciation better describes the process.

supported by the Intelligence Officer and the Signals Officer. The content of orders changes, but the sequence never does, at any level of command.

Typically the RSM will have arranged a building or tent, seats for the commanders and a map and model. The company commanders will have arrived early and collected map updates, air-photos, signals instructions and myriad other pieces of information before they sit down. Also present will be the specialist platoon commanders (mortars, anti-tank and recce, as well as any attached troops, such as Gary the gunner, the sapper and (in this case) Katie. At 12.00 precisely the RSM will order *"Sit up!"* and salute the Commanding Officer as he arrives. The Commanding Officer will then start[251]:

"Relax, ladies and gentlemen. These are orders for a battlegroup night attack on an enemy position near High Mountain. Orders. Ground."

If there is a sapper attached he will describe the ground relevant to the operation. This is likely to include maps, models and photographs. In a perfect world the Commanding Officer will have seen the ground and shown it to his company commanders from a viewing point or helicopter. If there is no sapper then the Operations Officer will do the description.

---

[251] The style with which a commander delivers his orders is largely a matter of (his) personal taste, which has of course been shaped by his time in the battalion. Generally an amount of formality and saluting is involved subconsciously reminding everyone who is boss (i.e. an officer whom they have sworn to obey). The audience is usually seated, the commander standing.

Figure 15.1 The Ground Near High Mountain

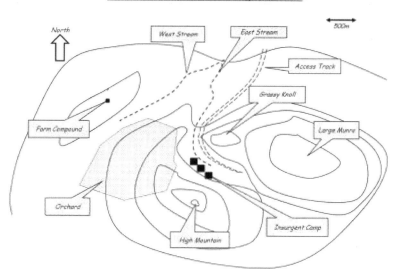

"The insurgent camp, which is our objective, is located in a fold in the land between Large Munro and High Mountain, the slopes of which are generally short grass on a stone base. Note the grassy knoll 500 metres to the north of the buildings. Note also the outlying farm compound (which we think is abandoned – certainly there has been no human activity there for a week or more), the orchard (which has workers in it most days), the two streams (which, although fast flowing, are only knee to waist deep and are fordable) and the track (which is really passable only to donkeys, mules or well driven 4x4s). The camp itself comprises three separate building complexes, each surrounded by a masonry wall five to ten feet high. The buildings are masonry build, roofing is corrugated iron and window shutters are metal. Some of the buildings are three stories high. You have photographs."

Next comes "Situation – Enemy Forces", given by the Intelligence Officer. *"From surveillance we know that around 75 insurgents are currently in this camp, split evenly between the compounds. They appear to be preparing for an operation; they have been seen zeroing weapons and the like. About 25 of the insurgents are permanent inhabitants, the other 50 arrived three days ago. It is thought that their operations will be launched next week, to coincide with local elections. As always, they're armed with AK47s and RPG7s. No heavy machine guns or anti-aircraft missiles have been* seen in or around the buildings, and there is no evidence of minefields. We suspect that this group is well-led, it certainly seems disciplined, but we have no name for the commander. It is reasonable to assume that they are experienced and capable."

Then "Situation – Friendly Forces" from the Operations Officer. "We know that the forthcoming elections are likely to spark insurgent activity, and therefore operations are being launched across the province tonight. Our brigade's mission is to prevent insurgent activity in the area of High Mountain, in order to enable peaceful elections. One other battlegroup is attacking a similar camp a few kilometres to the east. The plan is that the attacks will launch simultaneously, and the intention is to have this camp secured by 9am tomorrow to allow follow up operations in the mountains by the other battlegroups in the brigade for the next few days, thereby limiting the insurgents' ability to interfere with the elections. Tonight we have support from half the brigade's Apaches, led by Katie, plus fast jets on standby. Various UAV's are already on task, providing pictures and target designation if required. They are controlled by Gary. Colonel?"

The Commanding Officer gets to his feet and starts to speak. "Mission. The mission is to capture the encampment in order to prevent insurgent interference with the local elections. The mission is to capture the encampment in order to prevent insurgent interference with the local elections.[252]

"Execution, general outline. Right, this is a deliberate night attack. Phase One is the approach march, which will be done as a battlegroup. Phase Two is A Company securing High Mountain, C Company securing Large Munro and Grassy Knoll and B Company moving to the Eastern edge of the Orchard. Phase Three is B Company capturing the buildings and Phase Four will be the reorganisation. Now, the crucial bit is Phase Two, as once we occupy this ground the insurgents are unable to move."

---

[252] It is axiomatic that the mission is ALWAYS repeated in full. It is the single most important part of the process – if the battlegroup knows what the mission is and the overall purpose in the absence of any further information they will use their best endeavours to achieve it.

The Commanding Officer will then continue with giving detailed instructions to each of the Company Commanders, plus Katie, Gary and any other attached unit commanders. For example:

"B Company, Simon. In Phase 1 you will act as battlegroup reserve, travelling at the rear. On Phase Two I want you to let A and C Companies get ahead of you. Make sure that you have a well-established link with A Company and do not come out of the orchard. Phase Three – well it's up to you how you do it, but work from north to south. C Company will have a platoon plus the Anti-Tank Platoon on the grassy knoll, so you'll have plenty of fire support. Again, ensure that you have good communications as the Anti-Tank Platoon comes under your command once we launch into Phase 3. Phase 4, once you have cleared all the buildings fire three green flares. Then get a helicopter landing site established and marked as close to the compounds as possible."

And so it goes on. Once every commander has his orders the focus turns to coordinating instructions which comprise timings, orders of march, routes, and a whole bunch of vital but technical stuff which is beyond the scope of this book.

The next heading is Command and Signal, given by the Signals Officer. This runs through who is in command, code words, passwords, radio frequencies, emissions control and the succession of command (i.e. who takes over if the Commanding Officer is killed).

The final part is Service Support, which deals with logistics, and is usually given by the A Echelon commander. Everything from food and special equipment to when Tommy's backpack will be collected and returned will be detailed and explained.

At the end of all this, and while commanders prepare questions, Gary the gunner gives a time check to synchronise watches.[253] It is an hour since the "O Group" began, so it is now 10am.

If anyone has questions they ask them. Once there are no more, the commander will ask questions of the subordinates to ensure that they have taken the information on board. The company

---

[253] Remember, the whole army works to gunner time - they may miss the target but they are never late!

commanders then start their own process of appreciation prior to issuing their own orders to their platoon commanders at noon. They have to move back to their company locations and may have the opportunity for a look at some of the relevant ground (in this case they have ample air photographs). He'll also check with his CQMS on the logistic side (the CQMS may be at A2) and receive an update from his second in command (a junior captain) upon the state of the company and progress in ladder handling.

The orders format is the same, although there are fewer people and they know each other better. As the Company Commander has no staff he will give all the orders. The CSM will have arranged for a model to be carved out of the ground and labelled, and placed everyone where the Company Commander wants them to sit. The Company Commander then starts speaking.

"Gentlemen, orders. Ground." The company commander will take describe all the ground, although he will pay more attention to the buildings that are his objective.

"Situation, enemy forces." This will be almost identical, passing on as much information as he has.

"Friendly forces." He describes the battlegroup plan and will mention the other simultaneous attack by another battlegroup in the brigade. He'll then turn to the battlegroup plan.

Figure 15.2 The Planned Attack on High Mountain

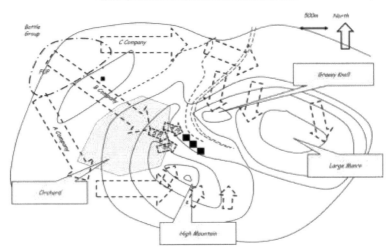

"We'll move as a battlegroup into the FUP.[254] We'll be at the rear and the FUP will have been secured and marked by recce platoon. When we leave the FUP C Company, to our left, is flanking round to positions on Grassy Knoll and Large Munro. A Company, to our right, is skirting the orchard to positions on High Mountain. We go through the orchard, and take up positions on the eastern edge. At H Hour we assault the buildings, with covering fire from C Company and the Anti-Tank Platoon, who will be on Grassy Knoll. A Company's snipers will provide covering fire onto the buildings as we assault, as well as preventing any reinforcements from coming in. Apaches will be overhead; the two supporting us will be call signs A11 and A13. They will be on our radio net,[255] and available for fire support. All clear so far?" He looks each platoon commander in the eye and continues*

"Mission; to capture the buildings in order to prevent insurgent interference with the local elections. Mission; to capture the buildings in order to prevent insurgent interference with the local elections."

Note that every platoon commander in the battlegroup now knows that the reason for their mission is to prevent insurgent interference with local elections. If the Commanding Officer and all the Company Commanders die, they all know what the Brigade Commander wants to achieve, and can therefore get on and use their best endeavours to that effect.

"Execution – general outline. This is a straightforward deliberate night attack. Phase One is the move to the FUP, Phase Two is the advance through the orchard, Phase Three is the Assault, with fire support from C company and the anti-tank platoon on the grassy knoll. Phase Four is the reorganisation.

"Four Platoon – Johnny. You will lead in phase one; we'll be following battlegroup headquarters. Make sure that you find the Recce Platoon guide and then follow the FUP markings in the usual way. Phase Two, you'll be left forward. Stay in the orchard, and

---

[254] FUP=Forming Up Place – where soldiers shake out into assault formation prior to an attack.

[255] This means that all the platoon commanders will be able to talk to the Apache pilots directly.

keep going until you're close to the edge. Then shake out into assault formation and wait my order. Phase Three, you will assault the northern building. It will just have had two hits from the anti-tank, but you'll probably have to blow your own entries. Once you are inside, clear the building. Be careful with the eastern windows; although C Company and the Anti-Tank Platoon know you are there, it is going to be dark and noisy. When you have cleared a room with an eastern view, put a blue Cylume[256] in the window. Stay in the building until I order you to move in Phase Four.

Five Platoon, Keith. Phase One, you follow me; I'll be following Four Platoon. Phase Two, you're the reserve – so follow me up through the orchard. Phase Three, once Four Platoon's assault on the north building is under way you will launch into the centre one, but on my order only. Same details as Four Platoon and watch the eastern windows. Phase Four, once you have captured it, stay in the buildings.

Six Platoon, Liam. Phase One, bring up the rear, following Five Platoon. The CSM will be your last man. Phase Two, you're right assault as we go through the orchard. Stay in the orchard and keep an eye out for A Company to your right – they should not be in the orchard but stranger things have happened. When you get to the eastern edge go to ground and wait. Phase Three, reserve. I intend you to provide additional fire support, so all of your platoon will carry a LAW. Half of them will fire a salvo on my order just before Four Platoon launch their assault. Once I have ordered Four Platoon to move, DO NOT fire again. Once the first two houses are secured you will assault the southern one, again, on my order only. Phase Four – stay in the building and await orders."

A pause, and then a summary.

"Right, this should be straightforward but it'll be dark and there will be insurgents about. You must keep your wits about you and you must exert strong fire control and make sure that the Toms[257]

---

[256] A fluorescent chemical light.

[257] It's an English regiment, so the soldiers are generally referred to as "Toms" – in a Scottish regiment they would be "Jocks" and in a Welsh one "Boys"

understand – particularly yours Liam. I do not want a surprise second salvo of LAW up my chuff as I move forward!"

Again, he runs through Coordinating Instructions. This will include a large section covering actions on mines, actions on meeting insurgents en route, or in the FUP or between the FUP and the houses. He'll question the Platoon commanders thoroughly, and then cover Command and Signal and Service Support. You can see that the Company commander has included far more detail on how the company will act, while retaining the outline of the battlegroup plan. He also decides that he wants to practise occupying an FUP at night, and sets the rehearsal time for 17:00 and confirms to the CQMS that he wants a hot meal delivered for 17:30 (armies march on their stomachs).

It's now 13:00, still five hours before the no move before time and the platoon commanders go through the appreciation and order writing process. The platoon commanders head back to their platoons (most of whom are sleeping)[258]. After a quick chat with his sergeant, Keith, (who commands Five Platoon – which includes Tommy as one of the fire team commanders), decides to brief the whole platoon at once, rather than just the section commanders. Keith's Platoon Sergeant wakes the section commanders, tells them that there is an O group for all not on sentry in half an hour and orders Tommy to report to the platoon commander to make his model.

"Here is a map Corporal[259] Atkins. I need one model of the area and a detailed one from this photo of the houses. Make sure you keep north the same way in them both. Here's my model kit.[260]"

"Got my own, thanks Boss."

---

[258] Hollywood movies may have soldiers playing the harmonica at rest. In the real world were anyone to try it the instrument would be removed by their audience, who would be trying to sleep.

[259] Although Tommy is actually a Lance Corporal, normal practice is to abbreviate this to Corporal in speech.

[260] All infantry commanders have a tin full of coloured ribbons, Lego bricks, white cards and the like to enable them to quickly make clear models of the battlefield.

As Tommy gets to work, Keith checks his map, works out bearings and prepares his plan, suiting the best man for the job where possible. He reckons that his main challenge will be to get into the building. As he works the Sergeant has a look at Tommy's models. *"Not bad lad, at this rate we'll be sending you to Brecon soon.*[261]*"* The Sergeant then organises the seating; section and fire team commanders in front, their soldiers behind. He reaches out to a tree and snaps off a thin branch, trimming it with his bayonet to make a pointer.

At 13:45 Keith looks at his entire platoon (less three men on sentry duty), smiles and starts:

"Right chaps, helmets off and listen up. These are orders for our part in a battlegroup night attack tonight. We've got the time, so I thought I would brief you all as it is important that you all get the picture. We'll be rehearsing our bit later. Orders! Ground. Take a look at Corporal Atkins's excellent handiwork." As Keith describes the ground his Sergeant points out the features on the model. Tommy watches the pair of them working in harmony and is impressed by their teamwork. Keith continues with the "situation" and then gets to mission.

"Our Mission is to capture the Centre House, in order to prevent insurgent interference with the elections. Our Mission is to capture the Centre House, in order to prevent insurgent interference with the elections."

"Execution General Outline – Phase One, we move as part of the company from here, through the battlegroup FUP – where we'll wait for a bit – and up to the orchard. We'll move in platoon column to the FUP, Corporal Adams and Four Section in front, then me, then Corporal Brown's Five Section then Corporal Clovis with Six Section. Sergeant Rees will bring up the rear. When we get to the FUP we'll shake out Four Section left, Five right and Six rear, following me. Now, the bearing from the FUP to the objective is 2245 mils

---

[261] Brecon is the school of the British Infantry – the next step in Tommy's career is to attend the Section Commander's Battle Course which will earn him promotion to Corporal. The Platoon Sergeant is well aware that a word of praise is a strong motivator.

magnetic[262] *– make sure you have that set on your compasses. Visibility should be OK, but don't spread too far. Once we're in the orchard, we stay in the orchard. There should be nothing to our left within 500 metres. Six Platoon is to our right, so Corporal Brown, whoever your right hand bloke is needs to keep alert and calm. We don't want a blue on blue in the orchard. Once we get to the eastern edge of the woods, lie down in cover and wait for H hour.*

Phase Three, the assault. At H Hour a salvo of missiles from the Anti-Tank Platoon will hit the houses from our left. At the same time, 6 Platoon will put around 10 LAWs into it from our right. That's our cue to go, but watch me. When I get up, Corporal Adams you head to the left side, Corporal Brown go right. We'll probably need to blow mouse holes.[263] *The charges are on the way and you all know Sergeant Rees was once an assault pioneer*[264] *and we'll get some practice in later. Lay the charges and blow them quick. Now, we don't know the inside layout, so when you go in don't shoot at each other. Clear the first room, get everyone in and go firm. Depending on what we find, I'll nominate which section goes forward first. All this time, Corporal Clovis and Sergeant Rees will be in the wood edge, providing overwatch onto the top windows. I'll call you in once we're underway and when you come in you should be prepared to go straight into room clearing. Now Corporal Atkins, if you clear a room on the eastern side remember that C Company and the Anti-Tank Platoon will be watching – although they should be engaging the next building. Put a Blue Cylum in eastern windows so that they know where we are.*

We'll fight our way through, bottom to top. Remember Four Platoon will be doing the same next door, so it will be bloody loud –not every bang will be us or the enemy as Four Platoon will be house clearing next door. Once we've secured the area we're into Phase Four – the reorg. STAY IN THE BUILDING. Get any casualties down to the entry

---

[262] Remember that magnetic north is not the same as the north on the map. Keith has done the work of converting the bearing for them, removing one potential source of error (provided he got his maths right!)

[263] A hole created by a one or two pound explosive charge detonating on the outside of the building.

[264] An assault pioneer is an infantryman trained in mines, explosives, barbed wire construction and similar matters.

point. Any prisoners of war to Sergeant Rees (also at the entry point) and adopt all round defence. Get loading magazines from your bandoleers as we may have to support the other platoons.

Questions?"

Having answered them, Keith then goes through the rest of the orders, again in detail and he questions key men. When he gets to the end it is 14:15. Across the brigade all 7,000 soldiers now know what they have to do, why they are doing it and how they are going to achieve it. As they rehearse entry drills, make up charges and pack their kit the entire formation is working to a single purpose; "to prevent insurgent interference with the elections."

We'll leave Tommy there, and move on. What we have seen is the process by which Tommy and his mates receive their orders and prepare for an operation. It is a systematic process that works because everyone at every level has been trained to do it and has practised it repeatedly until it is not second but first nature.

You now know that getting even one company into the field ready to fight and able to win takes time and process. Remember this when you are next watching one of Hollywood's productions, or indeed listening to one of Westminster's finest talking about "rapid reaction forces." Skimping on battle procedure substantially increases the risk of something going wrong, and thus the mission failing and Tommy getting killed.

Chapter 16 Tommy and Rupert Talk; Communication, Command and Leadership

Warfare is a team game and therefore communication between team members is fundamentally important. This is particularly the case for commanders – if they can't communicate they can't command. Every commander needs accurate, timely information on where his subordinates are, what they're doing, what condition they're in, where the enemy is, what the enemy is doing and what is being done to him. Tommy needs to know where the enemy is, where his pals are and when fire support is coming in.

Tommy can communicate with his fire team by voice, hand signals and, if necessary, man handling them as they are usually within 10 metres of him. To talk to anyone else he needs radios (although hand signals will still work). Above company level a commander will not be able to see all his command and so is reliant upon radios and runners[265].

The company commander also needs to keep track of what is going on largely achieved by maps and china graph pencils. Radio operators listen to what is said, note the contents in a radio log and plot it on the map using standard symbology. Increasingly map displays are becoming computerised and position reporting automated. Although this technology works reasonably well for armoured vehicles, it is harder for individual soldiers and, of course, the enemy does not broadcast his locations in a compatible format.

The battlegroup commander also wants to know the situation, and he expects to hear this from his company commanders. Every headquarters maintains a rear link, usually operated by the second in command, which has the role of passing the same information in a collated format to the next higher level. The result is a number of radio networks or "nets;" each net has a control station (invariably

---

[265] A runner is a man who carries a message from commander A to commander B. It is a job given to experienced privates – as they have to be able to find commander B. They also have to be very fit (commander B will send a reply) and lucky – battlefields are dangerous places to run about!

the commander's headquarters) plus the radios of all that commander's subordinates. Have a look at the diagram below.

Figure 16.1 Radio Nets

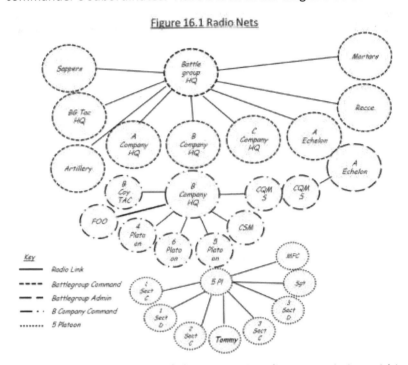

The diagram shows some of the 20 or 30 radio nets existing within the battlegroup, and who is on them. Working from the top, the battlegroup command net has all the companies on it, plus supporting arms such as artillery and sappers. All of these also have their own different nets (each on a different frequency) through which they command their troops. I have only shown B Company, which has its three platoons, FOO, CSM, and CQMS. At both company and battlegroup there is also a "TAC" which is the tactical headquarters i.e. the commander himself – who will typically be moving with his men. Headquarters are always on two command nets – one as a subordinate station and one as a commander. They will also be on the administration net and may well be listening in on one of their key subordinate nets and, possibly, a flanking battlegroups command net. The Artillery battery commander is also on the artillery net (not shown) talking to the guns, as is the FOO. Similarly the MFC is on both the 5 Platoon net and the Mortar

Platoon net. I have shown the CQMS on two nets, the company command and the Admin net, where he can speak to the A Echelon.

Understand too that people can join other nets; for example in defence a company may listen to the recce platoon's net to get early information on the enemy advance. It is also fairly common for a company on one flank to join the net of the next door company from an entirely different battlegroup. Learning the structure of the army with particular attention to all the radio nets is fundamental to the training of any commander, from section up.

At platoon level there is one net, which all the fire team commanders are on, plus the MFC. Increasingly, every soldier has a radio either on a platoon net or a section net. You can see that there is a huge amount of complexity, and strict discipline is required to prevent chaos as only one person can speak at a time. This is known as voice procedure, effectively a language that everyone with a radio has to learn.

There are four basic transmissions. Firstly, "sighting reports", which are sent when the enemy is first seen, and is not being engaged. They have the same format as contact reports. The next are "contact reports," sent when the enemy is engaged. The format is simple; when the contact started, where the enemy is, what the enemy consists of, what the enemy is doing and what the sender is doing about it. If the sender is actually engaged in the direct fire battle himself, he will probably send an earlier report, simply saying his call sign and "Contact! Wait out." If he gets killed, and therefore can't be spoken to on the radio at least the Company Commander knows that the enemy have arrived.

Once a platoon is in contact he will update company headquarters on progress of the battle using situation reports. It will include his location, what the enemy is doing, what he is doing and administrative considerations – usually confined to ammunition and casualties. Generally a sitrep will be sent every 15 minutes or so, until the contact ends. Finally there are "fire missions", which we have seen before. In most cases the FOO / MFC will be able to see the target, and therefore the command net will be spared the whole rigmarole of adjusting fire over the command net.

In addition to these standardised statements, commanders will issue orders. If the radio is not encrypted, and is therefore insecure, this will involve encoding the sensitive parts of his orders manually. This can take time, and errors occur. The British Bowman system is encrypted (and has embedded GPS so the system knows where all the radios are).

Armoured Squadrons usually operate on "all-informed" nets, in other words every vehicle in the squadron is on the same net. This speeds information flow, but can generate lots of traffic. This in turn requires precise and concise transmissions, as there could well be twenty to thirty stations on the net – all of whom have something to say.

One common confusion arises when two different stations see the same enemy at the same time. Unless they get their grid references spot on (a challenge, particularly in mobile warfare) there will be a time when their commander might think he is facing twice as much enemy as he is. A key command skill is to restore clarity, and once in contact many commanders will produce broadcast sitreps down to their own troops, thus ensuring that everyone has a common battle picture.

While the Company Commander fights the battle, the 2IC takes the information, collates it and transmits it up the chain to the battlegroup headquarters, on the battlegroup command net. Spare a thought for the armoured squadron 2IC, who as well as fighting his tank using the intercom (right ear), is listening and operating on the squadron net (also right ear) and on the battlegroup command net (left ear) simultaneously[266].

---

[266] The only person who might have it worse is the Armoured Operations Officer. Some Commanding Officers have their Ops Officer in their tank as loader. He then gets to load the guns, work the radios, mark the maps, devise the plans, prepare the orders, talk to the brigadier and make the tea. Katie also has to multi-task - in extreme circumstances she could be working four radio nets while trying not to fly her Apache into a mountain!

THE DIGITAL BATTLEFIELD

In the digital age, this may seem an archaic method, and indeed it is. Every Bowman[267] radio has a GPS in it, so the system knows where every commander (or at least his radio) is. If the radio were also connected to a range finding sight then it could automatically send a location and classification of the target. If the target is being viewed electro-optically it could take a picture and send that too. Having fired its gun it can then update the logistics, and while it's at it, take a reading of the fuel on board and send that. Data that would take perhaps twenty seconds to transmit as voice could be passed in milliseconds, and of course be processed immediately at the receivers end. In the armoured world, this extends to the vehicle's engine management system and fire control system, so details of how much fuel and ammunition the vehicle has can be passed automatically via the data system.

All this information could then be distributed to everyone who needed it, automatically and in near real time. This would simultaneously reduce the workload on commanders, speed the flow of information and therefore get us inside the enemy decision cycle[268]. It would also confer tactical advantages. If Rupert knew where every friendly tank was, which this system should tell him, then if he detects a tank the system can tell him whether it is friendly or not. Rupert therefore gains the ability to engage the enemy at recognition range rather than waiting to identify. Blue on blues should also become a thing of the past. Best of all, if much of what used to be passed by voice is now a data transmission there is more time available to command. Systems such as this are now being fielded by advanced armies, though a process known in the British Army as "digitisation".

---

[267] BOWMAN is the current British Army radio system.

[268] Jargon alert! "Decision Cycle" means how long it takes the enemy to react to events. If Tommy attacks, how long before the enemy commander delivers a counter-attack on the ground? Quick thinking commanders and well trained troops should react faster – say by anticipating the counter-attack and having a machine gun and fire mission waiting for it. Fast decision making is more discussed than achieved.

It is not yet perfect though. One of the key roles of the system is to filter and distribute information. This means that defence contractors have to design and write filters into the software to determine what is displayed to whom, when. The challenge is of course that in various parts of the battle, differing pieces of information have different values and someone has to programme the command system to sort this out. The situation is further complicated by the emergence of drones and UAVs, which are now able to provide real time images (Optical TV or thermal). There is a real danger of information overload on commanders and, worse, commanders not getting the relevant information on time. Bear in mind that as the amount of information to be carried by a signal increases there are challenges on having sufficient bandwidth to transport it all, and never forget that VHF and UHF radio signals are line of sight. Mountains, hills and even woods play merry hell with the quality of communication, as do buildings. In Afghanistan Tommy and Rupert's pals have frequently found themselves in combat in an urban area without usable radio communications[269].

Another problem at the sharp end is that Tommy and Rupert's eyes are busy fighting the enemy. Having to look at screens reduces the time he has available to look for the enemy. If you can't see it you can't kill it.

The system also has to cope with people losing radio contact. This happens to Tommy frequently, particularly in built-up areas. When he emerges from the sewers (or wherever else he has been) his position will not have been updated for (say) 15 minutes as he crawled along underground. How is Rupert, now accustomed to firing on detection, to know that Tommy is not the enemy when he sees him emerge in front of him? Conversely, what happens if an enterprising enemy sergeant kills Tommy, keeps his radio and then continues to move. Rupert's screen will tell him it's Tommy, which he'll believe right up until the enemy sergeant puts an RPG round into his tank's engine.

---

[269] Which is why they claim that BOWMAN stands for "Better Off With a Map and A Nokia." To be fair, BOWMAN was specified for high intensity armoured warfare, which is unfortunately not the war being fought in Afghanistan.

There is also of course the usual concern about the durability of equipment - Tommy has to be able to operate if the digitization infrastructure fails, which means he still needs to master the old system anyway. While digitisation is able to massively increase the efficient distribution of information, it is not a panacea and indeed, may open a Pandora's Box of questions. It is certainly not cheap, but then again neither is training commanders and nor is losing wars.

Finally there is the human aspect. The sound of a competent and calm commander issuing instructions by voice is more charismatic than some text appearing on a screen. The point of digitisation is not to supplant voice radio, merely to free up more time on a busy net for combat related conversations, taking out ambiguity and unnecessary traffic. It's fair to say that Bowman is getting there, but has some way to go.

COMMAND AND LEADERSHIP

We have now seen how Tommy, with his consent, is trained to fit into the military environment and to obey orders. We have also seen how Rupert has been trained to put his men first, to formulate plans and to promulgate them through the orders process. It is time to consider command and leadership in a little more depth. Rupert has to be both leader and commander.

The command part requires him to assess events, decide what to do and communicate that to his subordinates. This is fundamentally a cerebral process. It is taught at various stages in a soldier's career and is refined through practice. Commanders also have to learn to balance the extra time required to produce a near-perfect plan against the benefit of having a workable plan earlier. In practice the commander's job is to make viable decisions based on imperfect information. People will die whatever the commander decides, and the commander will (rightly) feel responsible. This makes for stress on levels that are almost unimaginable to the civilian. Occasionally commanders are unable to operate at this level of pressure – in which case they have to be replaced. One of the many things that commanders have to monitor is whether their subordinates are coping. One of the first signs of overload is commanders neglecting to sleep. It is not uncommon for them to be ordered to bed by their superiors, or even their sergeant major. A good headquarters protects its commander from fatigue and makes sure that he is rested and fed. This applies at all levels, although fatigue studies have shown that the most vulnerable are section and company commanders.

Commanders have to assimilate information speedily and process it quickly and objectively. Rupert has to learn to filter the information that bombards his eyes and ears, distinguishing between the important and the urgent, the relevant and the irrelevant. Information overload is a real risk, particularly when Rupert is tired. Platoon commanders are particularly vulnerable to getting too involved in the battle; once they start concentrating on firing their own rifle they are cutting out other information sources. This does not mean that commanders don't fight, just that they have to pick their moment[270] and always remember that there are other things that they have to do.

At all levels, commanders act as the filter between what is happening the level above them and what is happening within their commands. If they get it right, they anticipate problems and solve them before they become serious. When they get it wrong their soldiers die.

The other part of command is the ability to communicate plans succinctly, clearly and convincingly. While the sacrosanct format of the orders process helps, it cannot solve the problems of the inarticulate or the unconvincing. A significant part of officer selection tests the ability to speak in public and there are minimum educational standards that have to be obtained. As Tommy progresses up the ranks, he will receive academic training in addition to military training.

If the command process produces good plans and clear orders, and battle procedure delivers the force to the right place it is leadership that delivers mission accomplishment. Leadership is a full time task,

---

[270] For example, in the Battle for Mount Tumbledown during the 1982 Falklands War one of the Company Commanders of the Scots Guards ended up using his bayonet at a desperate moment during the final assault – a graphic an example of leading from the front. He received the Military Cross.

not something that is switched on for combat. From the moment Rupert arrives at his battalion for the first time he is being assessed by everyone on the simple premise of "Do I trust him with my life?[271]"Everything Rupert does has an impact on the answer to that fundamental question. It is asked not just by soldiers; his brother officers are equally critical as one weak or bad officer reflects poorly upon all the other officers. Mismatches do happen and are unpleasant; the usual solution is to transfer the unfortunate officer to another unit.

Leadership is required at all levels of command and the requirement for it drives much of the syllabus of officer training. While it is debateable as to whether leaders are born or made, leadership can certainly be developed. It is useful to consider leadership in two ways: the attributes of a leader and what the leader actually does. Most armies produce strikingly similar lists of the characteristics of leaders. All of them include integrity. A leader must be demonstrably honest, which is not the same as not being demonstrably dishonest. No one trusts a dishonest man, and in the military context leaders are asking followers to trust them with their lives. Integrity requires courage, as the right path is not always the easy path.

Leaders need professional competence, both technical knowledge and the ability to conduct appreciations and make robust plans. Of course they can usually obtain detailed technical advice, often from one of their soldiers, but they do need to know enough to understand the advice and its implications at one.

They also need to be decisive and able to communicate. Communication is, of course, a two-way street and leaders must able to listen. Within the military, where leadership is combined with rank and the rank has draconian power attached, it is not always easy for the senior to get the junior to speak openly. The senior needs to be aware of this and become an astute observer of human behaviour. Leaders also need to be frank with themselves, work to improve their skills and above all have the humility to ask for advice.

---

[271] Of course, being British this is never made explicit and may be disguised by a range of euphemisms like *"Does he fit in?"*

Now this is all well and good on paper – it is somewhat harder to put into practice. How Rupert actually leads is a matter of personal style. Clearly he will have to study diligently and practise his military skills – all of which the training system arranges for him. More importantly he must get to know the soldiers whom he commands, which means spending time with them. As a new platoon commander he'll spend most of his day with his soldiers, whether fitness training, rifle shooting or maintaining vehicles. If he is lucky he will get an opportunity to demonstrate professional ability early – whether it is successfully map reading during a filthy dark night or giving an impressive set of orders. First impressions count; as we have seen, his soldiers all benefit from Rupert's success and none of them want a weak platoon commander. A wise sergeant will do his utmost to ensure that Rupert's early actions go well – without being seen to do so. Rupert must understand that he is not in a popularity contest (being "one of the blokes" is easy, but irrelevant). He needs to earn his soldiers' respect, and that involves diligence hard work.

Some officers find it easier to talk with soldiers than others – unsurprising given the wide disparity in background, education and aspiration (but not pay: a corporal earns about the same as a second lieutenant). However provided the communication is there, the actual style matters less. Rupert will know he is doing well when they stop calling him "Sir" and start calling him "Boss." Nicknames are one area that affords opportunities for Rupert to slip up – generally he will call soldiers by their surnames and NCOs Corporal X or Sergeant Y. In Welsh Regiments, which abound with soldiers called Williams, Davies, Jones and Evans, Rupert may well end up calling them by their (often inventive) nicknames[272] – but should insist on them calling him "Sir", "Boss" or "Mr Smythe.[273]" Ranks exist for a reason, and the structure needs continual reinforcement. This is particularly challenging within the close confines of a trench or armoured vehicle.

---

[272] The Welsh tend to identify soldiers with the same surname by the last digits of their military number – Williams 54 or Williams 68. Nicknames can develop from these, Jones 430 may be known as "tea time" or Evans 125 as intercity. This can produce some bizarre conversations...

[273] Assuming that "Smythe" is Rupert's surname.

Establishing a new officer's authority is a sensitive process, and Rupert is not alone. While the company commander and second in command will keep a sharp but distant eye on him, Rupert's main ally is his sergeant. If at all possible, Rupert will have an experienced platoon sergeant who knows his job well and is deemed suitable for working with a new officer. The relationship between them is fundamental, and Rupert will be acutely aware that while he has a year's training and no experience his sergeant has at least as much training and about ten years' experience. However, Rupert's job is to command and the sergeant's to support. Establishing mutual respect is not always an easy smooth process – and it may well test Rupert's courage.

COURAGE

It is generally accepted that there are two sorts of courage, which are closely related. The first is physical courage – the willingness to confront danger such as height, fire, punches and bullets. The second is moral courage; the will to do the right thing rather than the easy thing.

Physical courage is about confronting the risk of pain, death or both. In most circumstances the risk arises as a requirement of doing the right thing. Physical courage can be developed, as any child learning to play rugby can attest. Armed forces generally encourage risk and contact sports. Boxing is important, as is "milling."[274] Assault courses and confidence courses require soldiers to move fast at heights that will cause serious injury if they fall.

Displaying courage requires the conquest of fear, and is important that Tommy and Rupert know what fear feels like, and that they can conquer it. *"Knowledge dispels fear"* is the motto of the British Army's Parachute School. The more soldiers can know about combat the less it should frighten them when it happens. Extensive, realistic live fire training helps as, of course, does actual combat experience.

---

[274] Milling involves two people, matched for side, in a frenetic bout of boxing – usually for a minute of two. The object is to demonstrate aggression by landing as many punches on your opponent as possible. The miller will simultaneously be developing courage as his opponent will be doing the same to him.

In some ways, the combat environment aids bravery. For a start, Tommy will be (at the least) apprehensive, and therefore their bodies will be releasing adrenaline. As well as pumping up his blood glucose and oxygen levels, it has the effect of slowing things down and narrowing the field of concentration – and the more Tommy focuses on achieving his task the less he is aware of the risks.

One of the causes of wonderment to many modern commentators is why soldiers went "over the top" in the First World War, or indeed why they are so routinely heroic in more recent conflicts. The fact is that very few British soldiers opt out of combat. Having volunteered in the first place and then worked hard to become part of a mutually loyal organisation, Tommy is intensely proud of being and accepted member of an elite[275]. Not letting one's mates down as a fundamental core of the belief system. So when the shooting starts, what else is Tommy going to do but fight alongside his mates?

There are, of course, some soldiers who find the actuality of combat overwhelming – generally they are removed (usually without shame – they were brave enough to enter the combat zone). It is generally accepted that people have a finite amount of courage. It can be replenished, but if the "tank of courage" ever runs dry it is unlikely that the unfortunate person will recover. Management of battle shock and providing soldiers with support and opportunities for a respite is an important part of Rupert's job.

Rupert will find that his moral courage is tested frequently – then classic (but not trivial) example is the soldier who fails to salute, one that is faced by many young officers in their first couple of months.

Soldiers are required to salute any officers any time that they see them;[276] in practical terms whenever they pass within a few metres. Imagine Rupert passing two soldiers from a different company[277] as he walks about the camp. They should start saluting when they get

---

[275] The brilliance of the British regimental system is that any regiment is an elite to its members.

[276] Soldiers will tell you that they salute the rank, not necessarily the individual. That is the point.

[277] It is rare for soldiers from Rupert's own platoon to cause a problem as they have nothing to gain from undermining their platoon commander.

within a few metres of Rupert, but they don't. Rupert now has some choices to make, and fast. He could choose to ignore them, thereby avoiding a petty confrontation. But Rupert will know that they know that he "bottled out." He could immediately confront them; "*Why aren't you saluting?*" or he could give them one chance of redemption by saying "*Good morning gentlemen.*" Being a wise chap he opts for this, in effect pointing out to the miscreants that he can see them, and they should be saluting. Most often that is the end of it; the soldiers salute and say "*Good morning, sir.*" If they don't Rupert has to act, as both he and the soldiers know that his authority has been deliberately challenged.

What Rupert does next is his choice, but it will be something like "*Hey you two, come here.*" The soldiers stop and one of them says "Sir". The least Rupert can do is say "*I'm sure it's the custom in this Regiment for soldiers to salute officers.*" To which the soldiers will reply, if they're wise. "*Yes sir. Sorry Sir.*" Then salute. Rupert will return the salute and say "*Carry on*". Incident over, authority re-established, moral courage demonstrated. At the other extreme, Rupert could demand their names and have them charged for conduct to the prejudice of good order and discipline,[278] which would result in them being fined or even imprisoned – in practice this would be a gross over reaction. The point is that Rupert saw something wrong and, at the risk of appearing a martinet, did something about it and enforced the law.

While the example is almost trivial, even backed by rank and the full weight of military law confrontation is neither easy nor pleasant and choosing to confront requires moral courage. If Rupert is unable to confront a surly soldier, in 25 years' time he will never be able to confront a politician to establish the legality of a proposed war.

To summarise; passing accurate and timely information is fundamental to modern warfare, and the process, requirements and technology are complex. However ultimately the question of

---

[278] "Conduct to the prejudice of good order and military discipline" is an offence under Section 19 of the Armed Forces Act 2006. For the nostalgic, it used to be an offence under Section 69 of the Army Act 1955. The maximum punishment for an offence under s19 is two years imprisonment, although there are many lesser punishments available.

whether Tommy risks his life in pursuit of his government's aims is down to how well he is led. The requirements of a military leader are many and complex, and place the leader under terrible stress.

The relationship between leader and follower is best developed by training, practice and experience. Even then, it can all go horribly wrong when the bullets start to fly. In spite of all the technology that we have considered, soldiering is fundamentally a human activity, not a technical one.

Chapter 17 Tommy's Destiny; A Glimpse of the Future

In spite of the fervent wishes of every Miss World for "world peace" and Ringo Starr's "peace and love," the newspapers show that these noble aspirations remain unfulfilled and there is no evidence of an imminent, sustained outbreak of global harmony. A pessimist[279] would point to the growing world population and finite resources such as a likely source of *causus belli* for the foreseeable future. The actions and pronouncements of some countries are hardly comforting either. It is a safe bet that warfare is here to stay for some time, and so Tommy will be busy.

As Nils Bohr said, "Prediction is difficult, particularly if it involves the future." However, nothing worthwhile is ever easy and there is no downside to this book's forecasts being wrong. So let's take a deep breath and have a glimpse into how Tommy's world might develop.

TYPES OF WAR

The nature of warfare will change, largely as a result of technology and experience. One incontrovertible lesson of the First Gulf War was that it is the utmost folly for a less capable army to take on first rate armies, particularly the Americans, in conventional, high intensity warfare. Saddam Hussein was unfortunate (or fatally miscalculated) in as much as NATO members had been training and equipping for that sort of war for over 40 years. The simple battlefield truth is that the Iraqi Armed Forces were completely overwhelmed and utterly destroyed. In many ways the Iraqis learnt the lesson better than the US and UK, switching to Feyadin and irregular attacks from populous areas rather than conventional warfare for the Second Iraq War. Saddam still lost, but the cost to the allies was far higher, and whether they "won" or not remains a debate. The seeds of the 9/11 attacks may have been sown in the devastation of the Mutallah Ridge. The rational response to being overwhelmed by the superb armed forces of a regime you despise is to attack the regime at its weakest point rather than at its strongest.

---

[279] A pessimist is often defined as an optimist with the facts.

There is therefore a basis for presuming that the days of high intensity warfare are over. While that may be so, there are plenty of armies in less stable regions that are developing the capability and there are over 100,000 tanks in service in the world. (For comparison, British tank fleet is about 300, the American about 5,000 and the Chinese 8,500 – although many of these are archaic). The point is that most states have armour, and thus if there is a state on state war, the armour will be used. Armour concentrations are highest where there are disputed or emotional boundaries –like between the two Koreas or India and Pakistan. While there is no immediately obvious scenario for Tommy's involvement at the moment, if any British soldier had suggested in 1985 that within two decades there would be a brigade fighting in Afghanistan he would have been laughed out of court and given immediate military history lessons. Unfortunately training and equipping for high intensity warfare is expensive, and governments on the brink of insolvency are unlikely to invest sufficiently.

While the future of high intensity warfare may be an open question, lower intensity and counter insurgency wars look set to stay, and indeed expand. As we have seen, these are protracted operations of increasing technological sophistication. If failed or rogue states that are acting as havens for terrorists and insurgents continue to be deemed a threat to the security of the UK Tommy is in business for the foreseeable future and beyond.

While nuclear proliferation continues it is important to remember that the only nuclear weapons ever used were dropped on a country that had no means of retaliation – it is unlikely that any of the current nuclear powers will initiate a course of action that leads to atomic war. Chemical war is more likely – once the politicians get passed the "weapons of mass destruction" label, are they really going to use atomic weapons because someone tried to poison Tommy (who, thanks to his training and NBC suit, survived) when they won't use them against an enemy who actually killed Tommy with a bullet or bayonet?

Of course, NBC weaponry is terrifying to the (uninformed) public, so we are likely to see some form of attack by some terrorist group or another. Whether it is a dirty bomb or a nerve agent release, Tommy will have a role in cleaning up, at the least. There is more information on nuclear, chemical and biological warfare in Appendix 3.

INFORMATION SYSTEMS

The continuing computer revolution allied to GPS and increasingly sophisticated communications means that the links between sensors, weapons and commanders are likely to multiply. This should generate quicker, more accurate, more lethal engagements with fewer own forces casualties and less collateral damage. So far, so good. The challenge is in avoiding both overloading commanders with non-essential information or, in seeking to avoid information overload, neglecting to provide key information. While the old, manual systems were labour intensive they had well-trained soldiers filtering information at every level. Writing software to replace this human analysis is challenging, and an evolutionary approach is likely to be more successful that starting from a blank sheet of paper. While the mechanics of logistics and tracking where everyone is can (and indeed is) be done fairly simply, more complicated command related functions will take far more time – and indeed may not worth the effort. Add to this the long history of failed government IT projects and it becomes hard to believe that battle procedure will change much.[280]

One of the effects of the ever increasing information technology is that gun sight and helmet camera footage is now available to the media, and through them to the public. While this is fine and dandy if the war is going well, the public never likes to see people being killed in its name – deliberately or by mistake. The information technology is therefore going to make it harder to obtain public support for the war, or maintain it when things go wrong – as they inevitably will.

SMART, BRILLIANT AND AUTONOMOUS WEAPONS AND ROBOTS

"Smart Weapons" was a phrase that arose in the 1970s to describe laser guided munitions, and has since been used to describe the increasingly clever guidance systems that we have discussed.

---

[280] Another of Murphy's Laws of Combat is "Always remember that your weapon system was made by the lowest bidder."

"Brilliant Weapons" describes the incorporation of increasing decision making within the weapon fusing and guidance systems, for instance giving sub-munitions the ability to select targets themselves, and to communicate with each other to ensure maximum coverage and minimum overkill - avoiding the circumstances where two sub-munitions attack the same vehicle while neglecting the vehicle alongside.

Autonomous weapons are those which make the decision to engage themselves. The technology has existed for some time. For example, the Predator Unmanned Aerial Vehicle (UAV) is currently a very efficient airborne sensor system. It is flown by a pilot sitting on the ground, thousands of miles away. He receives data from the UAV via a satellite link, which also sends his commands to the UAV flight system. Effectively the pilot has been replaced by a satellite link. The Predator also has an autopilot, and is perfectly capable of flying itself to and from the battlefield, which means that pilots can concentrate solely on flying Predators in the battle area. This reduces the "aircrew"[281] requirement by over 50%. The latest versions of the Predator are armed with at least the Hellfire missile. At the moment missiles cannot be launched without manual authority, but there is no technological reason for that. The real question is a philosophical one, are we content to make machines that are allowed to decide to kill humans (even if they are the enemy)?

There is another interesting corollary. Without doubt the Predator is a battle changing weapon and is nigh on impossible to shoot down. Any rational enemy who can't play the ball will, like a third rate soccer defender, play the man instead. Predators are operated from bases in the continental United States and elsewhere. If the effect of Predators is such that the insurgents look like losing the obvious solution is to destroy the Predator base. If that looks too challenging, (and targets don't come much harder than a USAF

---

[281] Aircrew used to mean people who flew. Predators and the like are currently operated by pilots. An increasingly hot debate exists in Biggles' world about whether it is necessary for a UAV to be operated by someone trained to fly fast jets [who is a very high price guy] or actually anyone with basic piloting skills [a much lower price guy] or indeed, given the increasing autonomy UAVs, whether the operator needs to be a pilot at all.

base), kill the pilots or their families as they drive to work from their (off-base) house – as we know, car bombs are cheap and easy to make. Being too capable on a battlefield almost forces the opposition into terrorism.

Advancing technology also raises the prospect of a robotic Tommy – Tombot. While Tombot can probably now keep up with Tommy's movement, his cognitive software is weak. As we have seen, Tommy has to take in large amounts of visual and audio data, process it and act in an instant. We have also seen that Tommy's actions change depending upon the circumstances– the upshot of which is that writing the control laws for Tombot is a challenge. Most likely the first Tombot will be used in bomb disposal – with a human making the decisions for them and Tombot ignorantly stepping into danger in place of Tommy.

So what would the enemy make of Tombot? The insurgent cannot win a conventional war. His best hope is to sap the national will to win by sending a steady stream of body bags home. When he sees Tombot performing a task that Tommy used to do the insurgent has a choice – destroy Tombot in place of Tommy, or let Tombot pass and kill Tommy later. If the insurgency is being won by a stream of body bags, what happens if that is switched to a box of Tombot parts, plus an invoice for another one? And what happens if and when the insurgent has destroyed all the available Tombots? Does Tommy stop the operation, in which case the insurgent wins? Or does Tommy hold in position, awaiting more robots, in which case the insurgent has secured a substantial tactical advantage as Tommy is tied in position for longer than planned, meaning he can't be somewhere else winning hearts and minds. (As a supplementary question, can Tombot win hearts and minds?) Or does Tommy continue without Tombot and take his chances? In which case we're back to where we started, albeit with higher expenditure (Tombot will not be cheap).

Although Tombot may be used for some dangerous tasks, the current reality is that Tommy is faster, better, more flexible and cheaper that Tombot – and will be for some time to come.

LETHALITY AND SURVIVABILITY

It is a reasonable assumption that weapons will continue to develop, and if they do so will the counter weapons. The challenge of blade versus armour has continued since Ug the caveman first sharpened a stick or tanned a hide sometime before the Bronze Age. The target, *Homo Sapiens*, will continue to evolve, but more slowly. Tommy is already operating close the physical limits of what a human can carry, so anything new has to weigh less that the equipment that it replaces, rather than more. The strength of Tommy's knees and back are becoming a real design limit.

There is research work being conducted of providing Tommy, or at least his American counterpart (Hank the Yank) with a powered exoskeleton. Halfway between a suit of armour and a robot, these might enable Hank to carry more equipment and protection. Of course, he'll also have to carry a motor and fuel, so logistic burdens will increase.

In the meantime, increasingly effective blast weapons will lead to increasingly effective body armour. Three versions of body armour have been introduced by the British Army in almost as few years, reflecting the struggle to balance enhanced survivability with the ability to fight. The harsh fact is that dismounted combat is inherently dangerous and will remain so.

The continuing advances in medical technology mean that Tommy is more likely to survive. The unpalatable corollary is that by protecting their vital organs, Tommy's mates are surviving events that would have been fatal just a decade ago. The number of limbless ex-soldiers is increasing inexorably, and with it the strain on medical services. The increasing demand on medical staff and prompt casualty evacuation is showing the deficiencies in an army that was structured to win The Cold War. Military medical care is superb;[282] the challenge is getting the injured Tommy to it quickly but without killing anyone else. Helicopters are likely to continue as

---

[282] In the 1992 Falklands War of the 503 British casualties who got to the field hospital at Ajax Bay only 3 died of their wounds. There are hospitals in that can't achieve that in spite of having a bespoke building rather than a bunch of tents, almost in the Antarctic, with two unexploded bombs in it.

the ambulance of choice, but their expense and vulnerability remain a limit. Clever stretchers (containing computerised IV drips, blood pressure monitors etc.) may be a partial solution if a way can be found to deploy them far enough forward to get them to Tommy before he dies.

If Tommy's chance of physical survival is improving, his mental survival is not. More veterans of the Falklands War have committed suicide than were killed in the conflict itself. Most people connected with servicemen are well aware that they have been disturbed and that some are coping less well than others.

AFFORDABILITY

State of the art weaponry is expensive – it generally exists at the cutting edge of science and has to be usable anywhere on earth. Production runs are short, and therefore costs are awfully high[283]. Much of the impetus behind British (and NATO) weapons development until the 1990s was the simple need to be able to win a conventional, high intensity war in Europe. This involved destroying a huge number of armoured vehicles before they could advance from the inner German border to the Rhine. As the consequence of being unable to achieve this was thought to be nuclear war, cost was less of a concern – the rapid destruction of multiple detected targets was everything. The result was that it made political and economic sense to throw technology at the military, buying them newer, better equipment reasonably frequently.

The Cold War ended in the 1990s but much of Tommy's current equipment either dates from then, or from weapons that were planned then. While they are expensive, at the moment there are few incentives for governments to spend heavily on developing new military technologies. Those new weapons that are produced are likely to be American – Tommy's masters will have to decide

---

[283] In the 1980s someone extrapolated the rate of defence inflation and predicted that by 2010 the royal Navy would not be able to afford a frigate. The theory was much derided as simplistic at the time, but as we look forward to aircraft carriers with no aircraft it is time to address procurement costs head on.

whether they are prepared to pay a premium price to be fully integrated with Hank the Yank.

However, as we have seen, the secret of winning battles is training. Provided Tommy can have enough cash and time to train he will remain formidable – even if his rifle is older than he is. Although the British Army has a deeply embedded culture of whether its generals manage to secure adequate training funds from the politicians is yet to be seen – but the omens are not good.

There is no doubt that the defence budget will remain under pressure. Anticipate many defence "reviews", promising smaller, better and lighter forces, just as every other cut has. But, as you now know:

> God is on the side of the big battalions, and so is Allah. Or has the government found a new religion?
>
> Protection is heavy – does the government really want less protected forces, with the concomitant increase in casualties?
>
> Better forces require more training, which means spending proportionately more on that, unless of course the government is relying upon divine intervention.

There are no easy answers. But destroying a capability, either incrementally or wholesale, without a clear theory of how armed forces are to meet the requirements demanded from them in the voter's name is reckless and morally and intellectually bankrupt.

ORGANISATION

There has been a general trend for the number of military personnel per front line soldier to increase. In part this is due to the ever increasing maintenance burden of ever more sophisticated weaponry and secondly to the expansion of communications and headquarters. While the first is reduced by the slowing pace of new weapon procurement, the latter will continue. The search for efficiency (i.e. lowering the ratio of payroll strength to bayonet strength) may further weaken the British Regimental system. It is unlikely to change the size of a company or battalion by much; their size has evolved over centuries and most armies have similar sizes. Within companies there may be some switching of the number of men in a platoon and section, but given the dearth of new equipment whatever is done will have to fit into existing vehicles.

Within the wider organisation of the army (and indeed all armed forces) there is an opportunity to wield an axe and restructure completely. Whether any politician arrives with sufficient authority guts and disregard for his career is an open question – but there hasn't been one since Cardwell reforms, which started in 1868.

The Certainty

In 2025, somewhere hot, cold or temperate[284] Tommy is still fighting Her Majesty's enemies. Approaching 40, a proud father and now a Company Sergeant Major, Tommy has now seen, defied and survived most of the dangers in his world.

As his company advances into yet another attack, Tommy's knees are telling him that he is too old for this; neither the passage of time nor the emergence of new technologies has lightened the load on his back. He can feel the adrenaline starting to kick in as the company closes with the enemy – combat is still dangerous and he's still frightened.

The younger soldiers, (with whom Tommy still keeps up on company runs – but only just), take great comfort from the fact that although the battlefield is patently dangerous, Tommy has lived in it for almost two decades and is its master. Like Tommy, they are afraid of many things.

Most of all they fear letting their mates down.

---

[284] It its temperate it is bound to be raining – particularly if it's supposed to be summer.

Chapter 18 Appendix One; More about Direct Fire Weapons

This appendix contains additional information about how direct fire weapons work, and why. The information is here to prevent it interfering with the general flow of the text in Chapter Three. While there is more technical detail here, please never forget that it is Tommy who fires the weapons and he is human.

BALLISTIC TRAJECTORIES

As you know, everything on the planet is subject to gravity and bullets are no exception. When they leave the gun barrel they start to accelerate downwards towards the earth's surface. Tommy has to aim high enough to make sure that they get to the target before they hit the ground. This aim off is complicated by the fact that the bullet is also a victim of air friction, which slows it down. Thus the further away a target is, the slower the bullet will travel towards the target. The bullet will also have been under the influence of gravity for longer and thus the slower it is travelling towards the target, the faster it will be heading for the ground. The chart below illustrates the effects of gravity on projectiles travelling at various speeds. Note that their initial velocity is parallel to the ground and that the vertical axis has been exaggerated.

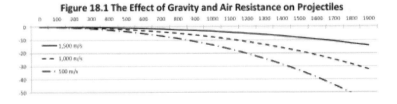

Figure 18.1 The Effect of Gravity and Air Resistance on Projectiles

As you can see, even a tank firing a projectile at five times the speed of sound needs to aim 15 metres above the target! This requirement is incorporated into the sight design or, if computerised fire control is being used, is included in the computer's calculation. Note that the effects get worse at longer ranges – Tommy firing his rifle at less than 300 metres does not have to worry about it until he becomes a sniper and starts to shoot at targets at 800 metres.

THE FORCES ACTING ON A GUN BARREL

While the bullet is travelling down the barrel it's a bit like a champagne cork leaving a bottle of Moet with a bunch of pressure behind it. The diagram below shows the forces on a barrel. As you can see, they are more complex than immediately obvious. The implication is that this is a barrel is an expensive piece of metal – particularly when you start thinking about tank gun barrels which may be 5 metres long or more.

Figure 18.2 - The Forces Acting on a Rifled Barrel

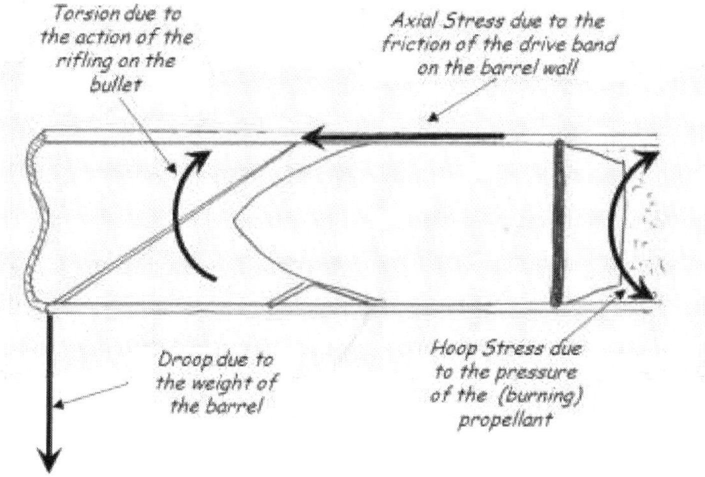

Torsion due to the action of the rifling on the bullet

Axial Stress due to the friction of the drive band on the barrel wall

Droop due to the weight of the barrel

Hoop Stress due to the pressure of the (burning) propellant

These forces are further complicated when the barrel starts to heat up, as it will when several rounds have been fired. Hot metal is not as strong as cooler metal, so the barrel may droop more (not visibly to the human eye) and expand, reducing the effects of obturation and accuracy. The result of this is that barrels are made from expensive steels, and treated with great care by Tommy (unless he has fixed his bayonet to it and is in the process of disembowelling one of Her Majesty's enemies).

JUMP

As the propellant in the cartridge burns it generates expanding gas which forces the bullet accelerate up the barrel. There is an equal and opposite force at the breech, which tries to push the entire rifle through Tommy's shoulder. While Tommy prevents this, the force is important because it makes the weapon move while the bullet is still in the barrel, sending it to some place other than the one Tommy aimed at. This is known as "jump" and it acts only as long as the bullet is in the barrel. Once the bullet leaves the pressure in the barrel is released and thus the force on Tommy's shoulder is reduced to zero.

Figure 18.3 - Jump

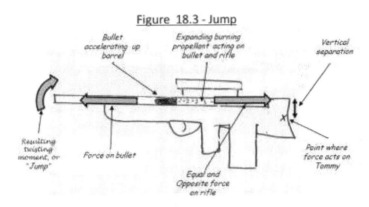

The diagram illustrates several points about jump. Firstly, assuming that Tommy holds the weapon the same every time, the jump will be the same every time. We can therefore adjust the sights to cancel out the effect. This process is known as zeroing, and it is fundamental to hitting targets, thereby killing the enemy and staying alive. Of course, Tommy's shoulder and build is unique to him so a weapon zeroed by Tommy will not be accurate for Dick or Harry.

Soldiers fire guns from all sorts of positions, standing, sitting, lying etc. Note that jump changes for every position. Generally soldiers zero "prone", as they are safest on their belly and that is the most stable position. They then have to learn and apply corrections for shooting from (say) sitting, kneeling or standing positions. If they get the correction wrong they will miss. They learn through constant practice on the ranges – only live firing produces jump.

Rifle designers seek to reduce jump by keeping the line of force into Tommy's shoulder as close as possible to the axis of the barrel. Unfortunately this requires mounting sights higher, which makes them more vulnerable to being knocked out of alignment when Tommy is crawling about the undergrowth.

Finally, we can see that firing from the hip is unlikely to be accurate, as Tommy is then relying upon his strength to contain jump – even if he managed to line the barrel up with the target in the first place. It is also one of the reasons why accuracy with a pistol is rare – significant strength and practice are required. For most soldiers in most roles it simply isn't worth the effort.

AUTOMATIC LOADING

Up until the 1960's the British Army used a bolt action rifle, [285]and this is still the design for many sniper and sporting rifles. However, as we have seen above, Tommy is likely to miss with his first round, so he needs to take another shot as quickly as possible without changing his position (so that the jump remains the same). This is only possible if the weapon loads itself. There are two approaches to this.

The first and simplest is known as blowback. The breech is not locked when the gun fires, so the pressure of the gas also forces the breech block backwards, ejecting the cartridge case. A return spring then pushes the breech block forward again, collecting another round from the magazine on the way and thus loading the gun. Blowback is simple, compact, cheap and rugged. However there are a couple of serious disadvantages. Firstly moving the breech block before the bullet has left the barrel alters the centre of gravity of the weapon, and thus amplifies the effects of jump. This is why revolvers are more accurate pistols than automatics. The second is that the reloading process starts while the bullet is in the barrel. Once the cartridge moves obturation is ended, and some of the propellant gas will escape round the cartridge. This amount is likely to be variable from gun to gun and cartridge to cartridge. It therefore cannot be predicted and thus reduces accuracy further. Blowback is therefore most suited to weapons that are likely to be used at short range and where small size is desirable. It is used in most automatic pistols, such as the Browning 9mm or the Glock, and sub-machine guns like the Uzi.

For longer range weapons a different approach is required, which is known as gas operation. Figure 18.4 shows the usual method for

---

[285] The Lee Enfield, which had been in service since the First World War.

achieving this. Note that this adds a substantial number of moving parts to the weapon thereby significantly increasing cost, training and maintenance requirements. It also reduces reliability.

Figure 18.4 – Gas Operated Automatic Reloading

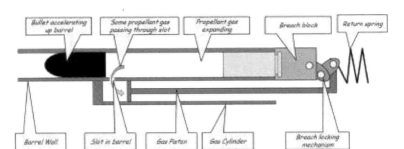

Once the bullet is past the exhaust port, propellant gas starts pushing on the gas piston. This pushes the breech block back, starting the process of extracting the cartridge case from the breech and then ejecting it from the weapon. There is a bit of clever design here which means that the cartridge case is not removed until after the bullet has left the barrel. Once the cartridge is extracted ejectors flip it out of the way. The breech continues back, compressing the return spring. Once the return spring is fully compressed and the bullet has gone, it expands, sending the breech block back forwards collecting a fresh round on the way. The round feeds into the chamber, the breech closes and locks and the gun is ready to fire again. The process takes about 1/10th of a second, so by the time Tommy has dealt with the recoil and is back on target he can fire immediately.

From this design to being able to fire fully automatically is a small step. If the design of the catch that holds the hammer back is modified then rather than having to press the trigger again the gun can be made to fire the moment that the breech is locked – provided of course the trigger is still pressed. While this has the advantage of putting more rounds in the general direction of the enemy, given the effects of recoil it is likely that the second and third rounds in a burst will not hit the target. The less stable Tommy's firing position the more likely this is to be the case. The benefit of firing more than one bullet is that there is a greater chance of achieving suppression. But firing accurately on automatic requires a more stable platform. This is generally achieved through using a bipod, tripod or rigidly mounting the weapon in a vehicle. The weapon has now become a machine gun.

Machine Guns

The gas operated automatic loading process described above is used for the overwhelming majority of machine guns, although there is some variation on the mechanics of feeding in the rounds depending upon whether they come in link, belts, drums or magazines. The machine gun is likely to have a heavier barrel (to deal with the high temperatures) and either a bipod or tripod. Most machineguns have the fixings for either, and the same fixings serve to mount them in vehicles, where they will also have an electrically operated trigger.

There is a relationship between the barrel length, the bullets velocity and the rate of fire. Generally a machine gun has a cyclic rate of fire of 600 to 1,000 rounds per minute. It can't fire any faster than this as that would result in ejection of the cartridge before the bullet had left the barrel, which would destroy accuracy, produce high pressure gas coming out of the breech and (hypothetically) give rise to the possibility of two bullets in the barrel at the same time – which is not healthy.

The operation of a machine gun relies heavily upon the ammunition firing reliably. Ammunition is mass produced, and occasionally manufacturing errors allow a dud to slip through, at which point a conventional machinegun will stop firing. Also, after a lot of firing, there is a risk that particles within the propellant will start to block some of the small holes in the recoil system, leading to the gun not reloading properly and stopping. (Inevitably, Murphy's Law dictates that this is likely to happen during a fire-fight, just at the time the gun was most needed). The solution is to use something other than propellant to drive the action of the bolt. This is what a chain gun does.

Chain Guns

In a chain gun the unloading mechanism is driven by an electric motor rather than by the gas from the propellant. The major advantage is that a dud round (i.e. one that does not fire when struck by the firing pin does not stop the process) does not stop the process. The gun is therefore highly reliable. It is also possible to vary the rate of fire, but running the motor faster or slower. This is of great benefit in applications such as aircraft and helicopters, where the supply of ammunition is strictly limited, and the rate of fire can thus be adjusted to match the target type. Chain guns are increasingly the preferred option for guns of 7.62m to 30 mm calibre mounted in armoured vehicles, such as the Warrior or Challenger 2 and on helicopters – the AH-64 Apache has a 30 mm chain gun.

Notwithstanding their substantially increased reliability, the need for an electric motor and power supply adds weight, and therefore chain guns are not used by Tommy when he is on his feet, or "dismounted."

GATLING GUNS

The maximum speed at which a machine gun can fire is determined by the length of time it takes one round to get down the barrel. This is because having two rounds in the barrel at once can only be achieved by opening the breech before the first round has left the barrel, which is pointless. If that rate of fire is not enough – or if you want a longer barrel for more accuracy – the final solution is to have more than one barrel. We have now journeyed back to the Gatling gun.

Gatling guns have several barrels, arranged on a central shaft. Each gun is loaded at the same point of rotation, fired at the same point and the empty cartridge case ejected at the same point. The barrels are rotated by an external electric motor. Clearly a 7 barrel Gatling gun has 7 times the rate of fire of a single barrel version. They are most common in aircraft – most famously the GAU-7 on the American A-10 Thunderbolt II which is capable of firing 30 mm armour piercing shells at the rate of 6,000 per minute. The Vulcan six barrel gun fitted to most American fighter aircraft, fires 20 mm rounds at a similar rate. There is a 7.62mm version, typically fitted to helicopter gunships.

Chapter 19 Appendix Two; Armoured Fighting Vehicles

Armoured vehicles are both complex and expensive. This Appendix is intended to give you a deeper insight into the world of both the tank crew man and the tank designer.

The fundamental feature of any fully armoured vehicle is that it is protected. A person inside is generally immune to the effects of small arms fire, blast and shrapnel. The vehicle itself will continue to function (possibly with some minor damage to things like sights and radio antennae) when under small arms or artillery fire (unless the artillery gets a luck direct hit). This near invulnerability is a huge advantage for the crew, who can go about their business unimpeded by the enemy. While the demise of armoured vehicles is often forecast by some commentators the huge tactical advantage of near invulnerability to most weapons is always attractive; which is why armoured vehicles (including tanks) remain in widespread service.

Of course, since the first tanks appeared in the First World War there has been substantial development in anti-armour weaponry. This in turn has driven further development of armour itself into a classic cycle of weapon and counter-weapon.

LIMITS OF WEIGHT AND SIZE

There are limits on how heavy a tank can be, and these are not always driven by the most obvious features. British tanks, designed for operations in Northwest Europe, have to be able to cross bridges there (even when being carried on a 20 ton tank transporter). When on their tracks they have to be able to operate on most of the terrain most of the year, which limits their ground pressure. The ground pressure is simply the tank weight divided by the area of track on the ground. Generally tracks can be no more than 1.5 times the vehicle width or turning becomes very difficult. The width of the tank is constrained by the size of German railways – as tanks are often moved by train. The upshot of all this is that the maximum weight for a tank is about 70 tonnes. The British Challenger and American M1 Abrams weigh about this. The German

Leopard 2 comes in a little lighter (it used to be a lot lighter, but protection levels have been raised). The French Leclerc and Russian T90 are significantly lighter, at about 45 tonnes, but they only have three man crews (about which more later). Some of this weight is required for guns, engine and transmission, combat supplies and crew. A fair amount of it is required for the structure itself, which means that the weight of pure armour that can be added to a tank is also limited.

The choice then is between putting a little armour plate everywhere, or most of it where the enemy is most likely to be (and thus whence the anti-tank rounds will come). This is an area known as the frontal arc, illustrated below.

Figure 19.1 Distribution of Armour Protection

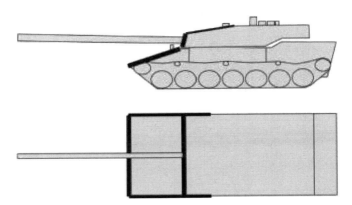

Armour Types

The most basic sort of armour is made from steel and is known as RHA, which stands for rolled homogenous armour. This has the advantages of being structurally strong, so that it can carry the weight of the tank, and steel working is a well-known process. The disadvantage is that steel represents the simplest target for anti-armour rounds. As we saw in Chapter 6, anti-armour rounds come in three flavours: kinetic energy rounds such as sabot and chemical energy rounds such as HEAT (shaped charges with copper jets) and HESH (explosive squash heads). All of these work best against RHA. However there are some tricks that the tank designer can perform with RHA to improve its performance with minimal increases to cost and weight. The first of these is to slope it.

Figure 19.2 The Benefit of Sloped Armour

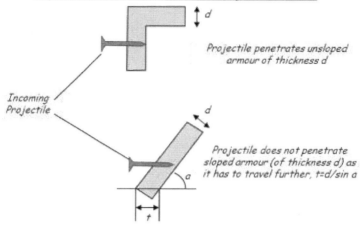

Projectile penetrates unsloped armour of thickness *d*

Incoming Projectile

Projectile does not penetrate sloped armour (of thickness *d*) as it has to travel further, *t=d/sin a*

Sloping armour has two benefits. It increases the chance of an incoming projectile bouncing off without penetrating and if the projectile does not bounce off it has a greater thickness of armour to penetrate. Sloped armour was first exploited by the Russians with their T-34. The Germans caught on in 1943 with their Mk V ("Panther") but not their Mk VI ("Tiger"). The British finally produced a tank with sloping armour in the 1960s with the Chieftain.

The second trick is to space the armour, as shown below:

Figure 19.3 The Benefit of Spaced Armour

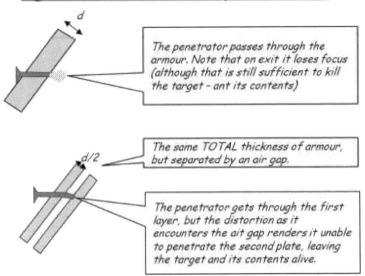

d

The penetrator passes through the armour. Note that on exit it loses focus (although that is still sufficient to kill the target - ant its contents)

d/2

The same TOTAL thickness of armour, but separated by an air gap.

The penetrator gets through the first layer, but the distortion as it encounters the ait gap renders it unable to penetrate the second plate, leaving the target and its contents alive.

This does not increase the weight of the armour, but it does increase the overall volume. However the benefits of spaced armour are significant. Both sabot and HEAT projectiles flow like a liquid when they are cutting through armour plate, and they are therefore affected by changes in the material. When they exit the first plate they lose focus which massively reduces their penetrative power when they hit the second plate. A HESH round, which relies on transmitting a shock wave through the armour, is in principle completely defeated by spaced armour[286].

CAGE ARMOUR

Cage armour is really a retrofit of spaced armour. It is designed solely to defeat HEAT rounds, typically those fired from small launchers such as the ubiquitous RPG7. By deflecting the (slow moving) projectile at the point of impact before it detonates cage armour undermines the entire HEAT principle. The advantage of cage armour is that it is light (relative to armour plate), easy to

---

[286] The armour should not send a scab off from the inside. Of course, detonating several kg of explosive on the outside still produces huge forces, and it the armour is insufficiently strong the vehicle will still be blown apart.

retrofit and cheap. But is has little effect, if any, against anything other than HEAT rounds.

LAMINATE ARMOUR

The logical extension from spaced armour is to have more than once space. It is not actually the space that causes the problem for the penetrator but the boundary between differing materials. It therefore becomes attractive to have multiple layers, some of which may be ceramics (which are highly heat resistant). The sketch below illustrates:

Figure 19.4 Laminated Armour

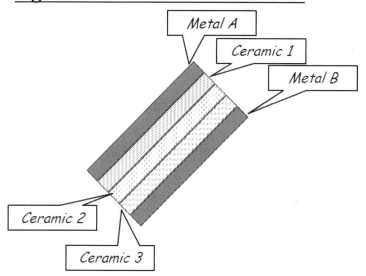

The ultimate form of this armour is the famous British Chobham. The two problems with laminate armour are that it is very hard to make (and thus expensive) and it is not structural, so it has to be added as a skin over structural steel. Any tank crewman will tell you that these are penalties worth paying.

REACTIVE ARMOUR

A slightly lateral thinking approach to armour is to consider it as food for the penetrating projectile – which will "eat" armour until either it is satisfied or there is no more. Reactive armour cunning feeds fresh armour to the projectile to eat outside the hull of the tank. Have a look at the diagram below:

Figure 19.5 – Explosive Reactive Armour

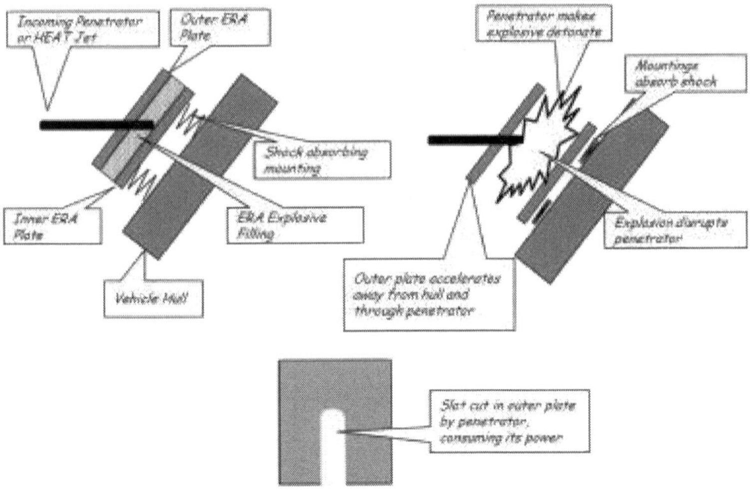

The incoming projectile detonates the explosive between the plates. The outer plate is forced away from the armour, in the process passing new metal into the projectile path all the time. As the drawing on the right shows, this means that the heat round expends its effort cutting a slot in the ERA plate rather than drilling a hole in the hull. The back plate bounces off the armour and then follows the top plate, offering more fresh metal to the jet, if required. Between dissipating its initial penetration on the first plate and meeting the second plate the jet is severely disrupted by the shock waves of the explosion.

ERA is brilliantly simple, effective and easy to retro-fit. However remember that the HEAT jet is travelling at around 10,000 metres per second so the detail design required to get ERA working is complex. Note also that the amount of explosive is substantial – were the ERA directly mounted onto the armour it could (at the least) crack it.

ACTIVE ARMOUR AND DEFENSIVE AID SUITES

In the Sinai in the 1973 Arab Israeli wars Israeli tanks faced Egyptian infantry equipped with early Russian anti-tank missiles[287]. These had a relatively low velocity, (about 120 metres per second) and consequently a long time of flight to targets over 1,500 metres away. The Israelis discovered that if they saw the launch (from the smoke and dust kicked up by the missile's booster rocket) and could point their tank gun or machine gun at it and fire the greater speed of the tank rounds (over 750 metres per second) meant that they could get close to the launcher before the missile completed its trip to the tank. A direct hit was not necessary, as near misses made the missile crew flinched and seek cover. While they were doing that they were not flying the missile or tracking the target[288] and therefore the missile missed.

Nowadays there are several systems that can produce a similar effect. Firstly laser detectors will tell the tank crew is someone is lasing them (which is part of the engagement sequence for almost all tank guns and is a guidance method for some ATGW[289]). Options range from simply warning the crew to automatically rotating the turret to face the threat. Secondly SACLOS missiles (which are nowadays the most common) have an ultra violet flare on the back, which is tracked by the missile launcher to compute the corrections to send to the missile's steering. If a launch is detected it is possible to jam the UV frequency with a simple emitter. Of course, all of this adds cost and complexity to the tank.

ELECTRIC ARMOUR

Imagine an ERA plate without any explosive in the middle but with a high voltage being maintained between the two plates. As penetrators are made of metal they conduct electricity. When a penetrator connects the two plates is will make the circuit. If a high

---

[287] They were the AT-2 SAGGER (as NATO called them).

[288] Early versions of SAGGER required manual corrections when they deviated from the line to the target ("MACLOS"). Later versions corrected automatically so the operator had only to track the target ("SACLOS").

[289] Such as the (Russian) AT-16 and some versions of the (American) HELLFIRE

enough voltage is applied a huge current will flow, generating sufficient heat in the penetrator to vaporise it. The system works in theory but the complexities of strong electric fields on the outside of a tank are significant, as is the near instantaneous provision of large electrical currents.

Of course warheads have developed as well to overcome the latest developments in armour.

TANDEM WARHEADS

The solution to single box ERA is to fire two warheads at it. The first, smaller warhead only has to penetrate the ERA to cause it to detonate. The second warhead, fired a few milliseconds later then has a straightforward armoured target to defeat. Arranging these warheads is not trivial as the slug from the first warhead must not get in the way of the (faster) jet from the second. Nor must the shockwaves from the first detonation or the ERA detonation be allowed to interfere with the jet formation from the second warhead.

All of this was accomplished, and is now standard in many missiles. Unfortunately for them the obvious upgrade for the armour designers was to make double ERA boxes, the first being detonated by the first warhead, leaving the second intact and ready for the second jet, which it will defeat. No doubt some laboratory somewhere is developing a triple HEAT warhead.

TOP ATTACK (AND DOUBLE TOP ATTACK)

As we have seen, the armour on a tank is much thinner on top (where the threat that if races is only shrapnel and fragments) than at the front. It is therefore much easier to penetrate, but the tricky bit is getting a projectile there. One approach is to use an ATGM, but programme it to fly above the line of sight, and to fire its warhead downwards when it passes over the target. This is relatively straightforward, and works.

Or rather, it worked until ERA was fitted to turret tops as well, although engines were left unprotected. The warhead boffins then designed tandem warheads firing down, which worked until double ERA was deployed on turret tops.

FOGM

The FOGM is a Fibre Optic Guided Missile. The front of the missile contains a camera that relays a picture of the missiles view to the operator (or the guidance computer). The missile is thus liberated from having to follow the line of sight and the command link is unjammable and undetectable. Within reason the missile can fly any path, and can therefore attach from the top with a powerful warhead, which can be multiple if required. Advanced versions can lock onto a target, and are thus fire and forget, provided the cable does not snap.

Explosively Formed Projectiles (EFP)

We have seen how a HEAT warhead uses explosive to produce a very high velocity jet of liquid copper to penetrate armour, with the limitation that the detonation must be very accurately timed to ensure that the jet is focussed. If the detonation is outside of the optimum distance the jet will not be as well formed and the penetration will be substantially reduced. We have also seen that the easiest place to penetrate an armoured target is from above.

While it is very hard to get a HEAT warhead in precisely the correct place above a target, getting a projectile there is not – artillery can deliver sub-munitions there. The challenge is to find a way of giving the relatively small, slow and light sub-munitions sufficient penetration. HEAT warheads won't work as they can't be delivered close enough or accurately enough. The answer is an explosively formed projectile. Rather than producing a narrow jet travelling at 10,000 metres per second, EFPs produce a solid projectile travelling at around 2,000 metres per second. This will remain stable and be able to travel a significant distance (tens of metres or more, depending on the actual device) and retain its penetrative power.

High tech applications of EFPs are as artillery sub-munitions. The artillery projectile bursts and delivers a number of sub munitions well above the target. These then descend under a parachute. They include a sensor capable of detecting a tank (usually through its heat signature). When the sensor detects a tank the charged detonates, simultaneously forming the EFP and sending it towards the tank, which it will hit within a few milliseconds.

The low tech solution, which was widely used in Iraq, is to set up the warhead at an ambush point. When a tank passes it detonates. As this warhead does not have to fit into an artillery shell it can be much larger and therefore more penetrative. These can penetrate the side (or underneath) of a tank.

MINES

If attacking the top of an armoured vehicle is complicated its underside is easy to attack, provided one knows where the armoured vehicle will be. As we saw in Chapter 9, anti-tank mines comprise a large charge of explosive that is intended to force the bottom of the armoured vehicle to mould itself to the top with catastrophic consequences for the occupants. The mine[290] is a weapon of choice for insurgents, and has caused devastation in Iraq and Afghanistan.

It is possible to design vehicles to be mine resistant, primarily by shaping the bottom of the vehicle to deflect blast. While this increases the vehicle height it is very effective against straightforward blast mines. Most armoured fighting vehicles do this to varying extents depending on how the overall design requirement rates the threats of mines versus more conventional anti-armour weapons (which are more effective against high targets than low ones).

The insurgent response was to replace straightforward blast mines with EFP. These are able to penetrate even "mine-resistant" hulls to devastating effect.

RAIL GUNS

In the constant battle between weapon and counter-weapon higher velocity projectiles are always sought. However the practicalities of gun design mean that for explosively propelled projectile (i.e. bullets) the maximum possible muzzle velocity is about 1,750

---

[290] In this context, mines are often referred to as "roadside bombs" or "IEDs" in the media. A general implication is that if the weapon is in manufacture it is a mine. If it is locally made it is an improvised explosive device (IED). If it goes bang by the side of the road it is a roadside bomb. As ever, linguistic precision is required to have a useful discussion.

metres per second. Clearly a projectile with a velocity higher than this is desirable, but achieving this requires some other form of propellant.

One avenue, which is under constant research, is an electromagnetic rail gun. Rather than using explosives, the projectile is accelerated using the same principles as are used in an electric motor. Static test guns have been built. Typically they can launch a projectile weighing 3Kg at over 2,250 m/s. Unfortunately doing this requires huge electrical currents, of the order of 5,000 amps. Delivering this even for the short time required is massively challenging and at the moment it is not possible to produce a system that could fit into a tank. This problem is broadly similar to the problem with electric armour. It remains to be seen whether it can be achieved; significant sums are being invested.

ENGINES

Moving an armoured vehicle requires a powerful engine. If the vehicle weighs around 40 tonnes then there are commercial HGV engines available that can do this. As the weight increases these engines have to be modified to deliver sufficient power – the 70 tonne Challenger 2 needs a 1,200 horsepower engine. More powerful engines burn more fuel, which in turn makes the vehicle larger and heavier.

One potential solution to the problem is to use a gas turbine rather than a conventional piston engine. The advantage is that gas turbines are much smaller and lighter than piston engines of similar power. They also have fewer moving parts and are thus more reliable. Unfortunately they also need much more air (which means bigger air cleaners) and clever gearboxes as they have a narrower power band. The American M1 Abrams has a gas turbine as does the Russian T-80 (although some versions of the T-80 have reverted to piston engines, as has the T-90).

SUMMARY

Combining firepower, protection and mobility is a continual game of trade-offs. The ultimate boundary of what is possible is set by bridges load carrying capability and what can fit on a rail track or train. The size of a man is also a significant limit. Within these broad criteria many solutions are possible, although the current crop of tanks, Abrams, Leopard 2 and Challenger are very similar. In the absence of The Cold War the urgency of armoured development has abated, and the current designs are likely to remain in service for many decades to come.

Unless there is a technical break thorough or a new military threat

Chapter 20 Appendix Three. Tommy Glows in the Dark; Nuclear, Biological and Chemical Weapons

In Chapter 2 we identified nuclear, biological and chemical weapons as a viable method of killing *Homo sapiens*. This Appendix considers Nuclear, Biological and Chemical warfare in a little more detail.

This book eschews the term "weapons of mass destruction," a phrase that was actually created by the Soviet Union and is now often on the lips of politicians as it is imprecise and overly emotive. It is also inaccurate.[291] The estimate of killed and wounded from the Hiroshima and Nagasaki are around 150,000 and 75,000 respectively. The bombing of Dresden in 13th/ 14th Feb 1945 caused 55,000 killed and wounded and the firebombing of Tokyo 9th/10th March 1945 is estimated to have killed 100,000, which looks like mass destruction to me achieved by nothing more than high explosive and incendiaries. Instead we shall call this NBC warfare. Let's take the components in order.

NUCLEAR WEAPONS

Tommy exists on the battlefield. While strategic nuclear exchanges[292] will affect him at some time, they are not relevant to this book, so we will restrict ourselves to tactical nuclear weapons. Nominally these have a yield of under about 20 Kilotons - one kiloton being the explosive power of one thousand tons of high explosive. The Hiroshima bomb yield was about 15 Kilotons. The Dresden air raid dropped about 4 thousand tons of explosive. A nuke is a very big bang.

---

[291] Of course, a nuclear bomb actually gets its terrible energy from the destruction of mass ($E=mc^2$ and all that) so it literally is a weapon of mass destruction. But a chemical weapon isn't....

[292] A strategic exchange involves firing lots of warheads at enemy cities. This was the theory behind the mutually assured destruction which, to the surprise of some and the delight of all, prevented The Cold War from becoming hot. Trident is a strategic system. Strategic warheads tend to be much larger than tactical warheads.

When a nuclear bomb is detonated, explosive charges compress radioactive material (usually Uranium or Plutonium) until they are dense enough for a nuclear chain reaction to start. Increasing numbers of neutrons collide with atomic nuclei, releasing energy and more neutrons. The energy comes from the destruction of small amounts of matter, which turns into large amounts of energy, as a result of Einstein's $e=mc^2$. This energy manifests itself as the bomb's immediate effects.

First comes heat. The centre of the bomb reaches temperatures in the millions of Centigrade. This vaporises anything close to it, ignites the next closest and scorches matter further away. Further heating effects are caused by the radiation.

Next is radiation. At the time of detonation massive amounts of energy are released as light waves, of all wavelengths. The most obvious is in the visible spectrum where it will appear as a bright flash ("instant sunshine"). At the same time as the flash is detected, a large radio pulse will arrive – often called the electromagnetic pulse, or EMP, this will cook and destroy all unprotected electronics. The pulse will also contain gamma radiation, which will cause a radioactive dose.

Finally comes blast; the near instant heating of the air causes it to expand rapidly, creating a large shock wave which travels out at the speed of sound. It inflicts damage in exactly the same way that any other blast would, although the scale is somewhat larger. As the air gets hot, it also becomes less dense, and starts to rise. As well as causing the characteristic mushroom cloud, this sucks air back to the epicentre, creating a second blast wave in the opposite direction to the first.

And that is about it. Radiation sickness does not kill instantly, so if Tommy has survived the two blast waves he's still combat effective. The best place to protect oneself from the immediate effects of a nuclear explosion is in the bottom of a deep trench with overhead cover, or inside an armoured vehicle. Not for nothing did West German building regulations during The Cold War require all houses to have a cellar.

The extent of the effects varies with the height of detonation, as do the secondary effects. Just like artillery shells, there are three types of burst. Subterranean bursts are ones where the entire nuclear fireball is contained within the earth. There are huge blast effects, but the heat and radiation are all contained. Other than atomic demolitions,[293] they are unlikely to occur on the battlefield. Ground bursts are where the fireball touches the ground. The significance of this is that when the hot air starts to rise it will take dust and debris with it. This dust will mix with the highly radioactive bomb residue (i.e. the matter that was not destroyed in the conversion of mass to energy, which is most of it). It will become radioactive, and when it falls back to earth in the final triumph of gravity it is known as fallout. Fallout kills by radiation. Air bursts are where the fireball does not touch ground and therefore there is minimum fall out.

Figure 20.1 below shows the extent of the effects of tactical nuclear weapons of 1KT and 20KT air bursting at optimum height. Note that a lethal radiation dose may not kill immediately. Conflagration means the spontaneous combustion of organic matter, such as Tommy. Outside this distance 3rd degree burns will occur to unprotected flesh, with burns of diminishing severity at greater distances. An overpressure of 5 psi causes widespread fatalities, and injures most people.

Figure 20.1 Tactical Nuclear Weapon Effects

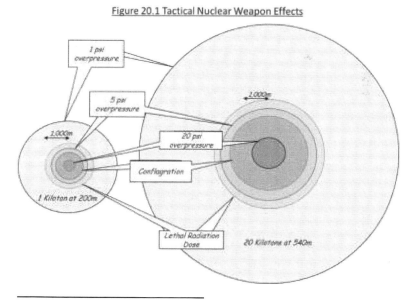

---

[293] An atomic demolition is using nukes to demolish stuff like mountains to fill in passes.

We can see that by far the furthest reaching immediate effect is blast. In fact, provided Rupert and Tommy are entrenched or in their vehicle they'll survive unless they are in the immediate vicinity of ground zero. We can also see that anyone who is not in a tank or a well-made trench with overhead cover is in desperate trouble. Bridges, headquarters, logistic areas, ports and airfields could all be devastated. A 1psi overpressure breaks glass. At 3psi most houses collapse and the associated wind speed is over 100 miles per hour so anything outside is going to be shaken up.

Also note that an MLRS battery firing HE sub-munitions deliver's about the same destructive effect as a one kiloton nuke without the hassle of nuclear weapons or the risk of stating a nuclear war.

DELIVERY

There are three ways to get a nuclear warhead to its target. The easiest and shortest ranged is to use artillery. A nuclear warhead can be made to fit into a 155mm round, and nuclear shells have been made for most calibres over that. Firing the weapon is exactly the same although there are some pretty complicated procedures associated with getting the warhead to the gun, armed and loaded. Nuclear warheads aren't the sort of thing that you leave lying about.

The next method is to use a missile, such as ATACMS or the Russian FROG. These too have conventional warheads, so firing is routine - it's the warhead handling procedures that are complex.

The final method is by aircraft. This is not the preferred option for tactical nukes, but it is straightforward. The main concern is what happens if Biggles gets himself shot down before he releases the weapon. Biggles of course has one other concern, which is what will happen to him after weapon release, as aircraft don't appreciate the severe turbulence that the detonation will to create. Still, that isn't Tommy's problem, and Biggles gets flight pay to deal with stuff like that.

So, Tommy and Rupert will probably survive the immediate effects of the nuclear strike. There are secondary effects, which are all radiation based. Obviously the area close to ground zero will be highly irradiated, and therefore very radioactive. As it's also a flattened, molten mess there is no benefit in going there, and the effects are local.

The second effect is fallout – radioactive particles dropping to the ground having been irradiated when they got sucked into the fireball. Surviving fall out, at the tactical level, is pretty much the same as surviving in a chemical environment.

CHEMICAL WEAPONS

Unlike nuclear weapons, which have so far only been used once and then in a strategic role, chemical weapons have been used frequently, and are inherently a tactical weapon. They are a little more complicated, but have two key features.

The first is their persistence. Some chemical weapons are non-persistent. Once they have been delivered onto a target and done their killing, they dissipate. This is really a function of their volatility (how quickly they evaporate) and their density. Broadly it would be surprising if a non-persistent chemical weapon remained in lethal concentrations at the target for more than a few hours. By contrast, some persistent agents last for weeks. While they all attack Tommy, persistent agents also deny the easy use of ground, and anything stored on it.

The other classification is how they attack the body:

> **Blood Agents** interfere with the circulation of oxygen. Hydrogen cyanide is an example. They present an inhalation hazard but not a contact hazard. They are fast acting but non-persistent

> **Blistering Agents**, such as Lewisite and Mustard gas, create blisters on skin and in the lungs. They are persistent, and an inhalation and contact hazard.

> **Choking Agents**, such as Phosgene, attack the lungs in much the same way as Blister agents. They are only an inhalation hazard

> **Nerve Agents**, such as Sarin, Tabun and VX, attack the nervous system. They are lethal; the casualty will eventually stop breathing. Antidotes exist and there are some pre-treatment drugs which improve resistance, but do not

confer immunity. Most nerve agents are non-persistent, although VX is persistent and some of the G types can be thickened. Non persistent nerve agents present primarily a vapour (i.e. inhalation) hazard, although a drop of liquid on unprotected skin would kill. Persistent nerve agents, such as VX poses a contact hazard as well.

Surviving a chemical attack is theoretically simple, don't breathe it in and don't touch it. Most sophisticated armies have chemical warfare suits (known to the British as "noddy kit") and respirators that enable this. Of course, the challenge for Tommy is to make sure he has his noddy kit on before the attack arrives. In practice this means wearing everything but the respirator, and putting that on fast on suspicion of an attack, under 9 seconds is the standard.

While wearing a respirator keeps Tommy alive, it does significantly restrict his vision, makes aiming a weapon more difficult and make breathing harder. It is reckoned to be equivalent to carrying an extra 7 Kg, so Tommy tires more quickly. As NBC suits are worn on top of everything else they make Tommy hotter and thirsty, although the most modern respirators have a drinking facility. Most armoured fighting vehicles have an NBC pack, which filters the air being blown into the vehicle and generates an overpressure so that any leaks are of cleaned safe air out, rather than toxic air in. Crews still get to wear their noddy suits and respirators though, and of course they are closed down.

The real impact of chemical weapons on Tommy is caused by the impact of having to wear the protective suits. The main ones increased fatigue, particularly on commanders, and reduced operating efficiency and a sense of isolation – the reduction in field of view plus the fact that everyone looks the same means individuals can't recognise each other and thus any team activity takes longer. Verbal communication is significantly impaired, although radios come with an adaptor for the mouthpiece – these work well.

There are three main uses for chemical weapons. The first is to degrade an enemy just before launching an assault using non persistent agents, the intention being that they will have dispersed just before the assault is launched. If the timing works perfectly the enemy will still be wearing his respirator while the attackers will not.

The second is to use persistent chemicals to deny an area. This is most effective on static installations such as airfields. Even if the aircraft are in shelters when the strike arrives, their tyres will carry chemical agent into the shelters when they return from their next sortie unless decontamination procedures are arranged. The final one is to contaminate stores and combat supply dumps, again with persistent agents. Again, this creates a requirement for decontamination and sophisticated procedures to prevent scenarios such as a contaminated piece of tank ammunition being loaded into the inside of a tank.

Decontamination is hard work. The process is simple; an inert powder like Fullers Earth is used to soak up drops of agent, and then brushed off. This works well for people and small items. For larger items liquid bleach is used, and is pumped under pressure to clean surfaces from top to bottom. When combined with vigorous brushing this should remove and destroy the agent. The Soviet Forces in The Cold War took this to an extreme, and had jet engines which strayed decontaminant onto vehicles at high velocity, temperature and pressure. This contrasted starkly with the bucket and stirrup pump issued to British vehicle crews.

Chemical weapons are best delivered as an aerosol, and this can be achieved in three ways. The simplest is for an aeroplane using spray tanks, which works brilliantly until the plane is shot down. The next is to use a tactical missile, with a clever warhead that vents a spray at the end of its trajectory. This is almost unstoppable. Both of these require a thickened (and therefore persistent) agent, as the chemical has to sink to the ground surface before it achieves any tactical benefit (if it wasn't thickened it would evaporate before it got to ground level and Tommy).

The final method is to use artillery with special shells. These comprise the liquid agent and a small bursting charge. The shell hits the ground, the bursting charge detonates, rupturing the shell case and spreading the liquid agent. One tricky bit is making sure that the bursting charge does not cause the agent to evaporate too quickly. Another tricky bit is getting enough shells onto the target quickly enough to build up lethal concentrations, as the persistency of the agent reduces the size of this problem increases. One of the best weapons available is a multiple rocket launcher such as the Russian BM21.

One other point the would-be chemical aggressor should consider is how he is going to store and load his chemical weapons. If he is using artillery system he needs to consider what would happen if the launchers, or their ammunition, were hit by counter battery fire. This would then effectively become a chemical strike at the launch point, some miles behind his leading troops.

The final hurdle for delivering a successful chemical attack is predicting the weather. Hot days increase evaporation rates, rain and snow reduce it. And of course, wind can play merry hell[294] as chemical weapons only work if they are in contact with humans, less than 7 feet above the surface.

Given the complexity of actually delivering a chemical attack and the relative ease with which its primary, lethal effects can be avoided one may ask "Why bother?" It's a good question, but even the threat of chemical weapons increases the workload on Tommy. For a start, an NBC sentry is required – just in case. He has to be upwind, surrounded by detector paper and in full noddy kit. He can't be the ground sentry and he can't be on radio watch, so this is a 50% increase in workload. Ammunition has to be produced in complex, multi layered packaging that enables clean rounds to be slid straight into clean vehicles, and everything has to be covered in tarpaulins to prevent droplets landing on them. A whole new class of combat supplies, NBC equipment, is created which increases the logistic burden. People have to be trained in mapping chemical strikes and their downwind hazards, commanders have to consider the contamination state of their vehicles (dirty outside – clean inside, dirty outside – dirty inside etc.) and of course a whole new branch of training is required. Chemical weapons are unlikely to kill Tommy, but the mere threat of their use makes his life much harder.

Of course, to a poorly trained or equipped soldier chemical weapons are devastating. The same is true for non-combatants, livestock and wildlife.

---

[294] When chemical weapons were used in the First World War many of the early attacks managed to gas their own men as well, or sometimes instead of, the enemy.

BIOLOGICAL WEAPONS

Imagine that you are a professional boxer, and you have a prize fight in two days' time. Postponement is not an option. If you heard that your opponent had influenza you would be delighted. If it's really bad he won't show, and you win by default. Even if he turns up, you know he won't be at his best, so the odds favour you. So if you were planning to start a war wouldn't it be great if the entire enemy had flu or something worse?

Well, most diseases are caused by either a virus or a bacterium. Isolating them is a straightforward medical process, as is growing them. And of course we don't have the chemical warfare problem of building up an attack concentration, as viruses and bacteria naturally multiply and spread. Have we in fact found the perfect weapon?

Well, maybe. There are some challenges, the first of which is infecting the target. We have to get the agent into the air he is about to breathe or the food and water that he is about to ingest. This can be done, but it is at the cloak and dagger end of the several pints of beer, Tommy will notice someone squirting an aerosol at his face. Assuming we can infect Tommy, we then need him to pass the disease onto his colleagues; if we pick a highly contagious disease this is possible, as we know from every year's flu epidemics.

We have to use a new disease, because if Tommy has been exposed to it before the antibodies in his immune system will kill the infection before spreading it to enough of his colleagues. This in turn leads to next problem. What will the army think if suddenly a significant proportion of its soldiers report sick, all with the same, new disease? Even if families and civilians are infected, someone will spot that the concentrations are in garrison towns. The only real solution to this problem is to infect everyone, and now we're straying close to genocide.

Of course, we also need to ensure that our own troops are inoculated, and someone will notice the inoculation programme. The combination of an inoculation programme in our army, followed by an outbreak of a hitherto unknown or rare disease with highest infection rates in garrisons is likely to compromise the surprise of our attack. Of course, if people start dying it could be construed as the start of the attack – and if biological weapons are indeed grouped with nuclear weapons this could trigger a devastating response.

Finally, somewhere in Tommy's army there will be a biological warfare research centre. They will be investigating militarily useful pathogens, devising inoculations and stockpiling doses. It may be that the agent has been anticipated and vaccines produced in which case there will be little military gain.

In summary then, for a well-equipped and well trained soldier like Tommy, NBC warfare is actually little more than yet another inconvenience. Modern weapons in the hands of properly trained soldiers can deliver at least the same military effect with less risk. The threat of use of NBC weapons now comes primarily from third rate armies, rogue states and terrorists. Their targets are more likely to be the civil population than Tommy's battlefield. However the complexities of acquiring these weapons and then delivering them effectively to the target are not trivial. Don't lose sleep worrying about it.